PRAYER, VICTORY, AND THE PROMISED LAND

A Handbook for the Spiritual Warrior and Anyone Who Wants to Grow in Jesus

DALE A. ROGERS

This book is a work of non-fiction. Unless otherwise noted, the author and the publisher make no explicit guarantees as to the accuracy of the information contained in this book and in some cases, names of people and places have been altered to protect their privacy.

LifeRich Publishing is a registered trademark of The Reader's Digest Association, Inc.

LifeRich Publishing books may be ordered through booksellers or by contacting:

LifeRich Publishing
1663 Liberty Drive
Bloomington, IN 47403
www.liferichpublishing.com
844-686-9607

Because of the dynamic nature of the Internet, any web addresses or links contained in this book may have changed since publication and may no longer be valid. The views expressed in this work are solely those of the author and do not necessarily reflect the views of the publisher, and the publisher hereby disclaims any responsibility for them.

Any people depicted in stock imagery provided by Getty Images are models, and such images are being used for illustrative purposes only. Certain stock imagery © Getty Images.

Scripture quotations taken from the New American Standard Bible®, Copyright © 1960, 1962, 1963, 1968, 1971, 1972, 1973, 1975, 1977, 1995 by The Lockman Foundation. Used by permission. (www.Lockman.org)

Scripture taken from the King James Version of the Bible.

Scripture taken from the *Amplified Bible*, copyright © 1954, 1958, 1962, 1964, 1965, 1987 by The Lockman Foundation. Used by permission.

Scripture quotations marked (TLV) are taken from the *Holy Bible, Tree of Life Version*, Messianic Jewish Bible Society, 2017. Used by permission. All rights reserved.

ISBN: 978-1-4897-3881-3 (sc)
ISBN: 978-1-4897-3880-6 (hc)
ISBN: 978-1-4897-3882-0 (e)

Library of Congress Control Number: 2021921236

Print information available on the last page.

LifeRich Publishing rev. date: 02/28/2022

CONTENTS

LIST OF FIGURES

ACKNOWLEDGMENT

I give all the praise, glory, and honor to my Lord Jesus Christ for all He has done. Without Him, nothing would be possible (John 15:5). Jesus has brought me to places in my life that I never considered possible. Jesus provided all the material for this book. I just typed it in my computer. I would like to thank my wonderful wife for her unceasing love, support, and encouragement in completing this book. Her encouragement and support have been immeasurable. Many thanks to my sister. Her efforts with editing were vitally important to the completion of this book. I would also like to offer many thanks to Rick Meyers, who wrote the <u>e-Sword</u> program. I used e-Sword extensively in the writing of this book. Good job Rick!

> [5]But I have trusted in Your lovingkindness; My heart shall rejoice in Your salvation. [6]I will sing to the LORD, Because He has dealt bountifully with me.
>
> —Psalms 13:5–6 (NASB)

PREFACE

In 1975 I was in the Air Force. In January of that year I asked Jesus to be my Lord and Savior. It was a pretty dramatic salvation experience. It all started when I had just stepped out of the shower after mulling over the troubles and problems in my life when God showed up in my bathroom. The presence of the Holy Spirit was powerful. This was the first time in my life that I had come face to face with the reality that God was alive and real. He lifted all my sins and problems off of me and showed me His forgiveness, love, mercy, holiness, and so on. What really shook me up was seeing His holiness compared to my feeble, sinful nature. No one else was around and no one walked me through the sinner's prayer. It was just Jesus and me. At this time, I had no idea what to do with such a profound experience. It wasn't until a few days or so later that He made it clear what I needed to do. Once I understood, I asked Jesus to be my Lord and Savior. Such a dramatic experience set the stage for what was yet to come. During that period, God also made it clear as to what He wanted me to do for a career, and that was to get a degree in engineering. After leaving the Air Force I went to college and received a Bachelor's degree in electrical engineering. I later earned a Master's degree in the same field.

The church I attended after getting saved was pretty good, and the pastor and I became friends for many years until he passed away in 2010. Not long after I became a Christian, I went to church on a Sunday morning and while standing in the foyer I found myself grieving over the cavalier and carnal attitude I saw among some of the people. It upset me quite a bit and I wanted no part with this attitude. I considered it dangerous given the sacrifice Jesus made for all of us. While I was still standing there in the church foyer, I told God I didn't want any part of such an attitude and that He could do whatever He wanted with me. Perhaps several weeks went by. Standing in the foyer again before services started, the Holy Spirit presented me with a decision. I could either choose a nominal Christian life and never go beyond the boundaries of church culture, or I could choose a different path. While on this path, I could expect trials and tribulations but it would lead me to a place that would be far greater in my relationship with Jesus. I chose the latter because I knew this is where He wanted me to go but it wasn't without fear of the unknown, and what those trials and tribulations would be. Jesus took me down a path that very few people have had the privilege to go. Since then I have had a lifetime of supernatural experiences, many quite dramatic. God would take me places, teach me spiritual warfare, and many other things about the various realms written about in the Bible. These experiences have continued throughout my life.

Not long after deciding to take the more difficult path, I had a dream that was clearly from God. This dream indicated what I would be doing in later years as a part of my ministry.

The dream started when I found myself being ushered into a spectacular mansion. The one ushering me took me down a grand hallway that was magnificent and looked like ones in some European castles with elaborate and valuable decorations. As I walked down this hall, I came to someone who I recognized was Jesus. At this point, the whole scene changed. I found myself in the back courtyard of a large house. It was constructed like the homes of centuries past in the Middle East. The outer walls were similar to adobe with flat roofs of several levels. In the courtyard area were a number of people that I recognized from church. The place was filthy as were the people. They were undisciplined, unruly, and had a cavalier attitude about their relationship with Jesus. The dirt represented sin. There was a canvas awning covering much of this area to provide a modest level of protection from the elements. The people could have been living in the house where they would be in a much more secure and clean environment but because of their sin and failure to live according to God's word, they weren't permitted to. The sad part of this scene is that no one was even aware of the decrepit conditions in which they lived.

I had the opportunity to observe this for a little while. At some point someone shouted, "The enemy is coming! The enemy is coming!" Everyone then scrambled up to the roof and positioned themselves around the perimeter. I looked over a hill nearby and saw enemy troops coming toward the house which they then surrounded. It was a frightful scene as I perceived the enemy soldiers were quite powerful, determined, and without mercy. Much to my shock, most of the people on the roof started socializing with the enemy. Some even grabbed hold of the enemy soldiers they were talking to and brought them up on the roof where they had a most lively conversation and were joking and laughing. I was incensed. Such behavior was completely unacceptable.

After this battle was over and the enemy gone, I decided the people needed to be trained in warfare. I had the entire group standing in a military formation where I started to teach. The dream then ended.

This dream indicated the spiritual gift God would give me and what I would do with it. Many years passed until I was ready for the task at hand, and it was only in recent years that the Holy Spirit gave me a more formal commission through Joshua 1:6. Not long after, I had my own radio show on a local Christian station where I taught about the need for revival and what people needed to do to realize it. Unfortunately, it was cut short because of the extensive business travel I got stuck on. This set the stage for writing this book. Portions of this book consist of lessons and sermons I had written over the years. I have also taught Sunday school lessons to the entire church as well as preached for the pastor when he was out of town.

CHAPTER 1

Introduction

Prayer, victory, and the promised land. These three terms encompass far more than most people realize. They comprise far more than simple prayers on Sunday morning, victory over death and sin, or enjoying the presence and fellowship of the Holy Spirit. Victory over death and sin is a fundamental truth about the plan of redemption realized through Jesus Christ but there is much, much more. The goal of this book is to shed light on this path, to renew the vision that so many have lost sight of, and to provide instruction on how to get there. True victory is that state of growth in your relationship with Jesus when you will be doing the things He did, and more (John 14:12). The promised land involves the exploration of His creation and things of a heavenly spiritual nature to a degree that no one can fathom unless they have lived it. In other words, the promised land encompasses both the spiritual and the physical. There are no limits to what can be realized! Any perceived boundaries are due to our human limitations and frailties, and not on anything God may appear to have placed in the way. Prayer is the primary means of building your relationship with Jesus to the point these goals are realized. The benefits of accomplishing these goals are immeasurable and none of it is out of reach.

> but just as it is written, "THINGS WHICH EYE HAS NOT SEEN AND EAR HAS NOT HEARD, AND which HAVE NOT ENTERED THE HEART OF MAN, ALL THAT GOD HAS PREPARED FOR THOSE WHO LOVE HIM."
>
> —1 Corinthians 2:9 (NASB)

The Lord Jesus Christ has provided His people with incredible resources. He has given us all the resources we need through the Bible and the Holy Spirit to live this victory and to enter into the promised land. The journey is simple but it takes work.

Throughout this book you will find that the Father, Jesus, and Holy Spirit are referred to interchangeably. The concept of the trinity may be difficult to grasp because of our limited understanding but the three are indeed one.

In order to understand what needs to be accomplished to realize the goals presented in this book, the problems we are all faced with today as Christians must first be identified and dealt with. Chapters 1 through 5 identify many of these problems and the dangers they present. The remaining chapters present the solution.

Few people in past generations have explored what it means to attain a lasting victory or to enter the promised land written about in the Old Testament. The journey into the promised land is provided as an analogy through the experiences Israel had when they entered the promised land written about primarily in the books of Exodus and Joshua.

Most have no idea what that state of victory means or what the promised land is, much less how to get there. People adhere to the idea that they need to follow Jesus here and there. Although being a follower has it merits, almost no one understands that we have not just the freedom, but the responsibility to take the initiative and push forward to gain this victory. There is nothing wrong taking initiative so long as one stays within the boundaries of the His Word and will. Those boundaries are defined in the Bible and by the Holy Spirit. Taking the initiative does not imply that one is not following Jesus. Rather, Jesus expects us to do so. To be clear, I am not saying we should get ahead of our Lord, but rather we are to take the initiative to fulfill the responsibilities laid out in His Word. The Apostle Paul wrote about this in Philippians 3. We should all do likewise.

The state of the church today is sad. We are clearly in the age of the apostasy written about in 2 Thessalonians 2:3. This does not mean you have to go along with the crowd. God never closes the door to victory to His people! All that remains is for each of us to make the decision and go after it.

Living a truly victorious life and entering into the promised land are based on one's relationship with Jesus. The primary tool at our disposal to realize this goal is prayer. It takes work, dedication, persistence, and surrender to the Holy Spirit. The results of this work are more valuable than anyone can possibly imagine.

The *effectiveness* of prayer is dependent upon a variety of factors, the greatest of which is faith based on one's relationship with Jesus. Prayer and building a relationship with Jesus are a continuous cycle stressed throughout this book as the primary goal for all Christians. Prayer and one's relationship with Jesus are inseparably linked.

> With all prayer and petition pray at all times in the Spirit,
>
> —Ephesians 6:18a (NASB)

Through relationship, and the prayer that helps to build it, we are able to fulfill the responsibilities we have as Christians. When reading the Bible, you will find that from cover to cover, the primary theme is all about the relationship between God and humanity.

The subject of sin must also be addressed. There is a great need for the church to face and deal with sin. A church culture with such a cavalier attitude toward sin is dangerous. Sin is an issue, however unpleasant, that we will all face and deal with sooner or later. Far better to deal with it now than wait until judgment day. The church in general is so compromised with the world that people don't even recognize the sins they commit. In order for people to repent of their sins they first need to know what they are.

> [3]For the time will come when they will not endure sound doctrine; but wanting to have their ears tickled, they will accumulate for themselves teachers in accordance to their own desires, [4]and will turn away their ears from the truth and will turn aside to myths.
>
> —2 Timothy 4:3–4 (NASB)

Unfortunately, in today's churches the trend is to only preach and teach feel good messages rather than to preach and teach the truth. They have entertainment that is often used as an emotional substitute for true worship. Only after true repentance comes will true worship will be realized.

The benefits of walking with Jesus in a holy and righteous manner are immeasurable. Maintaining a lifestyle of holiness and righteousness does take work but the results are so sweet and glorious it is more than worth the effort.

Churches, denominations, and ministries throughout the world today have mechanisms in place for people to submit prayer requests. This is not an ideal situation. People become conditioned to rely on others whom they view as being closer to God, more anointed, more faithful, etc., rather than relying on their own prayers and relationship with Jesus. The outcome is that people seldom mature to the point that their own faith grows and their own prayers are effective. They forever remain in their spiritual diapers. Of course, people do need help and prayer support from time to time regardless of their spiritual level, however that need will diminish as one becomes more mature. The saying, "If you give a man a fish you feed him for a day but if you teach a man to fish you feed him for a lifetime," is applicable for prayer too.

Learn how to rely on Jesus and to build faith by building your relationship with Him through prayer. Part of this growth process is learning to *surrender* to the Holy Spirit. It will take work and it isn't always easy. Each of us is stubborn in our own way (self dies hard) so surrendering to the Holy Spirit is a process that will put you in situations that are not always comfortable and easy. These lessons can be quite difficult at times.

> [2]Consider it all joy, my brethren, when you encounter various trials, [3]knowing that the testing of your faith produces endurance. [4]And let endurance have its perfect result, so that you may be perfect and complete, lacking in nothing.
>
> —James 1:2–4 (NASB)

Another analogy of growth is the process of going through basic training for the military. In basic training a prospective soldier learns the discipline and ways of warfare so they can fulfill the responsibilities their leaders give them. So too, we as Christians must be educated in our relationship with Jesus, the responsibilities we have, and how to do what it takes to grow. We must then put this education into practice. The primary source of education is the Bible and the Holy Spirit (John 14:26). We must discipline ourselves to accomplish our responsibilities.

The church today is much different than it was during the time the book of Acts writes about, or even 60 years ago. Today the church for the most part is apostate and sound asleep. Many people, even though realizing the apostate state of the church and what scripture has to say about it, choose to remain asleep thinking they are okay. Some just wait for others to stand up and take a leadership role. Neither approach will work.

Bible Reading: Luke 12:35–46

Today is the day of salvation. Now is the time to prepare to meet Jesus.

Churches often offer instruction on what we need to do without telling us how, or if so, give vague and weak terms that only scratch the surface. Not only are we told that we should accept the attacks of the devil (defeat) without complaining or doing anything about it, we are also instructed to treat defeat as a measure of spiritual maturity and wear it as a badge of honor. This teaching is heresy and is taught by cowards! You can have an overwhelming victory through Jesus, but you have to go after it.

> But in all these things we overwhelmingly conquer through Him who loved us.
>
> —Romans 8:37 (NASB)

> but thanks be to God, who gives us the victory through our Lord Jesus Christ.
>
> —1 Corinthians 15:57 (NASB)

One's relationship with Jesus transcends everything else in life and must be the top priority and focus. Virtually everything else is secondary.

The time has come for all of us to wake up and accept our God-ordained responsibilities and to make disciples of all the nations. The primary tool we as Christians have at our disposal to make this happen is prayer.

The church has a job description and it is summarized in Matthew and is known as The Great Commission.

> ¹⁹Go therefore and make disciples of all the nations, baptizing them in the name of the Father and the Son and the Holy Spirit, ²⁰teaching them to observe all that I commanded you; and lo, I am with you always, even to the end of the age.
>
> —Matthew 28:19–20 (NASB)

The above verses from Matthew provide a top-level description of our responsibilities. Underneath this heading, various jobs and functions within the church need to be accomplished to realize the goal. Similarly, a corporation will have a CEO with a high-level job description that may be as simple as, "lead this company and make it profitable." Underneath the CEO will be people working many different positions in order to realize that goal. Jesus is the head of the church. Through the Bible and the Holy Spirit He has provided the education and gifts to fulfill all the various positions in the church so the primary goal of Matthew 28:19–20 can be realized.

The Apostle Paul outlined the various positions and gifts provided by the Holy Spirit throughout his letters so the church will be able to fulfill its mission on earth.

Jesus started His ministry and expects us to follow in His footsteps, using Himself for our example, and by relying on the empowering and teaching of the Holy Spirit and the Bible. We are expected to do the things He did, and more.

> Truly, truly, I say to you, he who believes in Me, the works that I do, he will do also; and greater works than these he will do; because I go to the Father.
>
> —John 14:12 (NASB)

The details of how the duties and responsibilities are to be fulfilled are presented throughout the entire Bible. Important lessons from the book of Acts and Paul's other letters explain how the early church worked to fulfill the Great Commission. Remember at this time in the history of the church, the Bible as it is known today, did not exist. Early Christians only had the Old Testament (the Law and the Prophets, or the Tanakh). Given what the early church was able to accomplish should serve as sufficient evidence of the value of the Old Testament and building a solid relationship with the Holy Spirit.

In Acts, a hierarchical structure of the various offices and responsibilities emerge in the early church.

Bible Reading: Acts 6:2–4

The apostles were few in number and by definition of their position were expected to live at the highest spiritual level, and have the closest relationship with Jesus. Their position certainly didn't preclude others from have a close relationship, but it was a requirement for the office they held. At that level it was expected their faith would bring solid answers to prayers and provide a covering for the people under their watch. As apostles of the church, they led and facilitated the health and growth of the church.

For us today there are several things that need to happen first in order for the church to be prepared to a sufficient degree to fulfill its responsibilities. Repentance of sin is the most important followed by education of what these responsibilities are and how to fulfill them. The church must then put this education into action to fulfill the Great Commission.

People will argue they live a holy life and are not involved in the numerous vices of the world today. This is all good however, when you read God's Word you will find there are things that the church fails to do. Webster [1] defines *sin* as:

> The voluntary departure of a moral agent from a known rule of rectitude or duty, prescribed by God; any voluntary transgression of the divine law, or violation of a divine command; a wicked act; iniquity. Sin is either a positive act in which a known divine law is violated, or it is the voluntary neglect to obey a positive divine command, or a rule of duty clearly implied in such command. Sin comprehends not action only, but neglect of known duty, all evil thoughts purposes, words and desires, whatever is contrary to God's commands or law.

The omission of fulfilling our God-ordained responsibilities is just as much a sin as the commission of any number of evil acts. It is for the failure to do His will that we, both individually and collectively as a church, need to repent. We need to open our eyes to the vision and resources God has provided in His Word and through the Holy Spirit. Prayer is the most powerful and effective tool we have at our disposal to accomplish all of these goals. The church has largely lost sight of its vision and to an even greater degree, how to fulfill it.

> Where there is no vision, the people are unrestrained, But happy is he who keeps the law.

—Proverbs 29:18 (NASB)

The time has come for the current state of the church to change. Only through prayer and revelation will we be able to build our relationship with Jesus and fulfill our God-ordained responsibilities.

Prayer is man's communication with God

Revelation is God's communication with man.

A relationship with Jesus that is built on prayer will facilitate the manifestation and refinement of the spiritual gifts He has for each and every one of us. Prayer and relationship are parts of a cycle that should continue to build over time. One only needs to read the book of Acts to see the results of fervent prayer on part of the early Christians. Notice throughout the book of Acts that prayer was an important part of the lives of the apostles, church leadership, and the entire body of Christ. God worked many miracles through prayer and the church grew and prospered in spite of the obstacles they faced. Effectively learning the lessons from their examples and putting them into practice in our lives and churches today is imperative.

Prayer is the primary mechanism by which we communicate and build our relationship with the Holy Spirit, overcome obstacles, trials, and tribulations, and spread the Gospel throughout the world.

Again, the effectiveness of prayer is based on faith and faith is based on one's relationship with Jesus. In order to be effective in prayer, we first must know Jesus, know who we are in Him and understand what that relationship means, what our roles and responsibilities are and how to fulfill them. Building a relationship with Jesus must be the primary focus for virtually everything else is secondary to it. We must understand the power and authority that we possess and be willing and able to exercise it at any time, so long as it is within the bounds of God's Word and will. We are to be ready in season and out of season.

> ¹I solemnly charge you in the presence of God and of Christ Jesus, who is to judge the living and the dead, and by His appearing and His kingdom: ²preach the word; be ready in season and out of season; reprove, rebuke, exhort, with great patience and instruction.
>
> —2 Timothy 4:1–2 (NASB)

> Therefore, confess your sins to one another, and pray for one another so that you may be healed. The effective prayer of a righteous man can accomplish much.
>
> —James 5:16 (NASB)

The key words in James 5:16 are *effective* and *righteous*. In order for one's prayers to be effective and accomplish much, the individual must be righteous and understand what it takes to be effective.

In the book of Acts and throughout Paul's letters we read about the many miracles, signs, and wonders worked through the Christians of the day. James 1:17 makes it clear that God doesn't change. Therefore, there is no reason or excuse for these miracles, and more, to not be worked today. The only difference between the church then and now is the dismal state we are in today. The time has come to repent and get to work for our Lord Jesus Christ.

In 2 Chronicles we read:

> ¹³If I shut up the heavens so that there is no rain, or if I command the locust to devour the land, or if I send pestilence among My people, ¹⁴and My people who are called by My name humble themselves and pray and seek My face and turn from their wicked ways, then I will hear from heaven, will forgive their sin and will heal their land.
>
> —2 Chronicles 7:13–14 (NASB)

Notice that this is a promise with a condition. If and only if the repentance is real and sincere will God hear from heaven, forgive our sins, and heal our land. Revival must begin with the church.

The spiritual health of any nation is the responsibility of the church. And it is the responsibility of the church, individually and collectively to repent of their sins, to maintain a high moral standard, refuse to conform to the world, and to be a priestly nation. There are many examples throughout history and the Bible concerning what happens when a nation or fails to repent.

Intercession is a priestly responsibility that cannot be given to anyone who is not a Christian. We are witnessing an epic failure of the church to fulfill its responsibilities. There is no excuse. Fifty plus years ago this nation was much different and spiritually better than it is today. The church was the focal point of the community and a significant force in maintaining the moral character of the nation. When I look around, listen to testimonies in church, listen to prayers, etc., there is one common factor throughout—a selfish attitude. These testimonies almost always have something to do with what God did for them rather than how God worked through them to advance the church. Many are trying to get what they want from God rather than focusing on what they can do for Him. Selfishness is an unacceptable attitude indicating a lack of maturity and frequently is founded on humanism, which is of the devil.

> "My people are destroyed for lack of knowledge. Because you have rejected knowledge, I also will reject you from being My priest. Since you have forgotten the law of your God, I also will forget your children".
>
> —Hosea 4:6 (NASB)

The word *Torah* refers to the first five books of the Bible. It is Hebrew for "law" and is sometimes referred to as the "law of Moses." The Torah is the foundation for the rest of the Bible and is just as valid and applicable to our lives today as it was when it was written. The Torah is also a covenant as God said in Exodus and Deuteronomy.

Then the LORD said to Moses, "Write down these words, for in accordance with these words I have made a covenant with you and with Israel."

—Exodus 34:27 (NASB)

These are the words of the covenant which the LORD commanded Moses to make with the sons of Israel in the land of Moab, besides the covenant which He had made with them at Horeb.

—Deuteronomy 29:1 (NASB)

A covenant has legal obligations for both parties. God initiated the covenant and so He is legally bound to keep His Word. We, as recipients of the covenant are likewise bound to obey its terms.

The importance of the Old Testament cannot be overstated. God has provided all the resources necessary to accomplish all He has destined His people to do throughout the entire Bible, and through the Holy Spirit. Knowledge of the Bible is sorely lacking today. Many of the teachings, boundaries of conduct, festivals and holidays, etc., particularly in the Old Testament (or Tanakh) have been dismissed as being archaic, dated, and no longer applicable. Teachings of this nature are based on church or denominational doctrines, evil influences of the world, and the desire to compromise with the world.

When churches advertise themselves as "New Testament" churches it doesn't make any sense. You can't have the New Testament without the Old Testament for the New Testament is founded upon the Old Testament. A good book that discusses the validity of the Torah is *Torah Rediscovered* by Ariel and D'vorah Berkowitz [2].

1.1   Religion and Relationship

There are a variety of definitions for religion and most involve the practice of a set activities and rituals so the practitioner is accepted by whomever they view as deity.

Christianity is not a religion. The overarching theme of the Bible, from cover to cover, is about relationship between God and humanity. You can't have a relationship with a philosophy, a fantasy, or an inanimate object. For a relationship to exist, the parties involved must be alive and must engage in communication and interaction. With Christianity, God has already accepted everyone insomuch as there is no religious practice that will gain one acceptance. Everyone, without exception, has sinned and failed to live up to God's standards. God has provided the way of salvation through Jesus. There is no other way. Everyone that has ever lived or will live faces a choice which is to accept Jesus as Lord and Savior or to reject Him.

CHAPTER 2

Repentance and Revival

A great need exists for the church to repent of it sins. We are in the end times and the apostasy of the church is clearly evident. Being in the apostasy does not mean you must adhere to this deplorable state. Nor can it be used as an excuse for failure.

Revivalists generally address only personal sin. Only true repentance can bring about a true revival. That repentance must include all levels, from leadership on down. Repentance is not an option. Repentance is a responsibility for all Christians. Revival must start with the church before it spreads throughout the land.

> for all have sinned and fall short of the glory of God,
>
> —Romans 3:23 (NASB)

For church leadership to have a "holier than thou" attitude founded on pride, is sin. Addressing the corporate sins of the church will also implicate church leadership which can present a sticky situation for the revivalist who is invited to speak. Speaking the truth without fear, even if the it offends someone, needs to become the norm. Pride must be repented of. There is simply too much at stake for the church to take a cavalier attitude towards sin.

The word *repent* is defined [1] as:

> To sorrow or be pained for sin, as a violation of God's holy law, a dishonor to his character and government, and the foulest ingratitude to a Being of infinite benevolence.

The compromise with worldly philosophies and allowing sinful behavior and doctrines of demons to infiltrate and become established as church doctrine is sin. The subjects of sin, repentance, and holiness are seldom heard from the pulpit. The church has descended into such a state of mediocrity that it is hardly recognizable compared to what it should be. Most are now little more than religious social clubs. Some churches are even teaching that Jesus is but one of many ways to heaven. This is a lie of the devil.

Bible Reading: Deuteronomy 4:2; John 14:6; Acts 4:12; 1 Timothy 2:5; Revelation 22:18–19

Some seminaries today have become so watered down that they teach students how to write a sermon that doesn't include the name "Jesus" because they don't want anyone to become offended. Some embrace Islam. Bowing down to worldly views and other religions is an act of cowardice by those who are ashamed of the Gospel.

Bible Reading: Mark 8:38; James 4:4

When churches feel they have to adapt to the world around them so the world will find something attractive and come to church, compromise is manifest. Compromise with the world is sin. The church should never adapt, or try to conform to the world. Rather, it should be the opposite! The church should be the driving force for the world! The world should conform to the church! If the miracles that Jesus did were happening in the church and through Christians in the world around them, rest assured, the churches would be filled to overflowing. Jesus was our example. So why are these miracles, and more, that Jesus did such a rarity today? The reason is sin.

> But your iniquities have made a separation between you and your God, And your sins have hidden His face from you so that He does not hear.

> —Isaiah 59:2 (NASB)

That sin is the failure to grow spiritually to the extent that the Holy Spirit is able to work miracles through His people and fulfill the Great Commission we are commanded to do. Fulfilling the Great Commission is more than just preaching to the lost. Remember, the Holy Spirit performs these miracles, not people. Most people, including church leadership, are either too immature or have embraced or supported the corporate sins so it is rare to experience and work miracles. People are simply unaware of the sin that is present in their lives and churches. Corporate sins are often rationalized away, or excused through church or denominational doctrine.

The little box so many Christians live in and attempt to stuff God into may be labeled *Ignorance is Bliss*. Ignorance is simply an excuse for failing to grow. The blame for failure lies primarily with church leadership. There are a variety of reasons for this, with ignorance and fear being the greatest. Failure often involves ignorance, the denial of the power of the Word, and fear of "offending" even one person in the congregation (see Matthew 15:12–14). Some pastors are in fear of losing their position or congregants if they preach with truth and power. Don't forget that Jesus never minced words. Plenty of people were offended at what He said. Those who were offended were those who hated the truth.

> ¹Then the LORD spoke to Moses, saying: ²Speak to all the congregation of the sons of Israel and say to them, `You shall be holy, for I the LORD your God am holy.'
>
> —Leviticus 19:1–2 (NASB)

Notice that what God said to His people is not just a decree. It is a command. As a command it means the people have a responsibility to accomplish certain things in order to be holy. God provided us with all the necessary instruction in His Word to become holy.

Because of the flesh, and the fact all of us must deal with sin, fulfilling the instructions from our Lord to be holy takes work. In order to be holy, one must be free from sin so much as it is possible. Taking a passive attitude toward scripture thinking it is just a decree from God that doesn't require any effort on our part is inconsistent with all of scripture. An attitude or teaching of this nature is yet another example of the doctrines of demons found in the church today. We are provided with instructions throughout the entire Bible as to what we must do to be holy and righteous.

In view of these issues it is therefore critical to examine God's Word to see what and where our failures are, and to be diligent to repent and move forward. Indeed, the greatest failure is the failure to develop your relationship with the Holy Spirit to the point that your life will be as Jesus described in the Gospel of John,

> Truly, truly, I say to you, he who believes in Me, the works that I do, he will do also; and greater works than these he will do; because I go to the Father.

> —John 14:12 (NASB)

and what Paul described in 1 Corinthians,

> ⁴and my message and my preaching were not in persuasive words of wisdom, but in demonstration of the Spirit and of power, ⁵so that your faith would not rest on the wisdom of men, but on the power of God.

> —1 Corinthians 2:4–5 (NASB)

> If you love Me, you will keep My commandments.

> —John 14:15 (NASB)

Are the traditions of man more important to you than being obedient to your Lord Jesus Christ who is your creator and savior?

God destined His people, the church, to be a priestly nation. Christians have the responsibilities of a priest. Priests must provide intercession, guidance to salvation, and spiritual leadership in the community and nation in which they live. The church should be the moral foundation for the nation. This is a civic responsibility. Therefore, the church should have a majority vote in public policy and ensure the nation maintains a moral foundation, and any laws that are instituted have a Biblical foundation.

The failure of the church to fulfill its civic responsibilities has resulted in the horrific spiritual decay within the church and nation we see today.

2.1   The Gravity of Sin

Prior to Jesus fulfilling the plan of redemption, animal sacrifices were done for an atonement of sins. Animal sacrifices are only a limited picture of the price Jesus paid on the cross. I don't suggest performing animal sacrifices as doing so is not necessary. Nevertheless, there is merit to just picture it in your mind. Take a lamb that you have raised from birth. This lamb is more than a pet. It is part of your family. Picture yourself slicing this lamb's throat and watching it bleed to death right in front of you and your family with the full understanding of what this represents. I know a messianic rabbi who sacrifices a lamb for every Passover and it is never a pleasant experience. Such a graphic and painful picture of the gravity and cost of sin is something we would certainly benefit from. How much more diligent to avoid sin should we be then, knowing that Jesus the Son of God paid such a horrible price in full for us.

The movie *The Passion of the Christ* [3] provides perhaps the most vivid and accurate depiction of Jesus' last hours and crucifixion produced by the entertainment industry. Crucifixion is a horrible and torturous way to die and yet He willingly did so for each and every one of us. We should *never* have a cavalier attitude toward sin.

2.2   Salvation and Judgment

> "But for the cowardly and unbelieving and abominable and murderers and immoral persons and sorcerers and idolaters and all liars, their part will be in the lake that burns with fire and brimstone, which is the second death."
>
> —Revelation 21:8 (NASB)

The true Christian is expected to live according to God's word and not adhere to a cowardly attitude. Cowardice is often an indication of an infantile level of spiritual growth. The fact that so many have never advanced beyond this point is shameful. Jesus' words refer to people who have been Christians for some time and have had the opportunity to grow and learn, and not those who are new Christians or may be inherently weak in this area. To stay at a lower level and never grow is a precipitous state. Scriptures throughout the Bible point to the dangers of failing to grow, and address it repeatedly for good reason. It is interesting to note that sins listed in Revelation 21:8 appear to be the most prevalent in the end times, which we are currently in today.

From Revelation 21:8, the terms *cowardly* (NASB) or *fearful* (KJV) and *unbelieving* generally go together. The words *cowardly* or *fearful* are translated from the Greek term, deilos (deilos). The root stems from the Greek term deos (deos) and translates as dread, timid, and by implication, faithless or fearful. If one truly believed in the power of the Gospel and had faith in Jesus, cowardice would not be present. Rather, there would be faith, boldness, and confidence.

Several commentaries [4] [5] [6] on Revelation 21:8 provide clarification on the scope of its meaning. Let's look at what they have to say:

John Gill:

> **But the fearful,...** Not the timorous sheep and lambs of Christ, the dear children of God, who are sometimes of a fearful heart, on account of sin, temptation, and unbelief; but such who are of cowardly spirits, and are not valiant for the truth, but who, through fear of men, either make no profession of Christ and his Gospel, or having made it, drop it, lest they should be exposed to tribulation these are they that are afraid of the beast, and live in servile bondage to him.

> **And unbelieving;** meaning not merely atheists, who do not believe there is a God, or deists only, that do not believe in Christ; but such who profess his name, and are called by it, and yet do not truly believe in him, nor embrace his Gospel and the truths of it, but believe a lie; these are condemned already, and on them the wrath of God abides, and they will be damned at last; though it may have a regard to such also who are infidels as to the second coming of Christ to judgment, and who are scoffers and mockers at it:

Adam Clarke:

But the fearful – Deilois; Those who, for fear of losing life or their property, either refused to receive the Christian religion, though convinced of its truth and importance; or, having received it, in times of persecution fell away, not being willing to risk their lives.

Albert Barnes:

But the fearful – Having stated, in general terms, who they were who would be admitted into that blessed world, he now states explicitly who would not. The "fearful" denote those who had not firmness boldly to maintain their professed principles, or who were afraid to avow themselves as the friends of God in a wicked world. They stand in contrast with those who "overcome," Revelation 21:7.

The key lesson of Revelation 21:8 and others, within the context of what the *entire* Bible says, points to the danger of not taking your relationship with Jesus seriously. Stagnancy is not an option. Remaining in an infantile state of growth is not an option. We would all do well to steer as far away from this precipice as possible.

Bible Reading: Matthew 7:21–27

From Matthew 7:21, John Gill [6] has some good commentary:

John Gill:

Not everyone that saith unto me Lord, Lord,... Not every one that calls Christ his Lord and Master, professes subjection to him, or that calls upon his name, or is called by his name; or makes use of it in his public ministrations. There are many who desire to be called, and accounted Christians, and who make mention of the name of Christ in their sermons, only to take away their reproach, to cover themselves, and gain credit with, and get into the affections and goodwill of the people; but have no hearty love to Christ, nor true faith in him: nor is it their concern to preach his Gospel, advance his glory, and promote his kingdom and interest; their chief view is to please men, aggrandize themselves, and set up the power of human nature in opposition to the grace of God, and the righteousness of Christ. Now not everyone of these, no, not any of them,

shall enter into the kingdom of heaven. This is to be understood not of the outward dispensation of the Gospel, or the Gospel church state, or the visible church of Christ on earth, in which sense this phrase is sometimes used; because such persons may, and often do, enter here; but of eternal glory, into which none shall enter,

but he that doeth the will of my Father which is in heaven. This, as it may regard private Christians, intends not merely outward obedience to the will of God, declared in his law, nor barely subjection to the ordinances of the Gospel; but more especially faith in Christ for life and salvation; which is the source of all true evangelical obedience, and without which nothing is acceptable to God. He that seeth the Son, looks unto him, ventures on him, commits himself to him, trusts in him, relies on him, and believes on him for righteousness, salvation, and eternal life, he it is that does the will of the Father, and he only; and such an one, as he is desirous of doing the will of God in all acts of cheerful obedience to it, without dependence thereon; so he shall certainly enter the kingdom of heaven, and have everlasting life; see John 6:40 but as these words chiefly respect preachers, the sense of them is this, that only such who are faithful dispensers of the word shall enter into the joy of their Lord. Such do the will of Christ's Father, and so his own, which are the same, who fully and faithfully preach the Gospel of the grace of God; who declare the whole counsel of God, and keep back nothing that is profitable to the souls of men; who are neither ashamed of the testimony of Christ, nor afraid of the faces of men; but as they are put in trust with the Gospel, so they speak it boldly, with all sincerity, not as pleasing men, but God, and commend themselves to every man's conscience in the sight of God: such as these shall have an abundant entrance into the kingdom and glory of God. The Vulgate Latin adds this clause, "he shall enter into the kingdom of heaven", and so does Munster's Hebrew edition of the Gospel according to Matthew.

Nothing here is intended to imply any Christian can "lose" their salvation. However, God never takes away our free will to choose. If someone knowingly and willingly decides of their own free will to "go back to Egypt," then that is their decision. I once knew man who started down this path. God took him home before he went too far. It is a real tragedy that someone would even consider such a thing.

> for it is not the hearers of the Law who are just before God, but the doers of the Law will be justified.
>
> —Romans 2:13 (NASB)

> But prove yourselves doers of the word, and not merely hearers who delude themselves.
>
> —James 1:22 (NASB)

Plenty of scriptures throughout the Bible warn about the consequences of neglecting and having a cavalier attitude toward salvation, sin, holiness, and judgment. There is no clear line drawn in the sand that defines the point of no return. God did this deliberately. If He had clearly defined the boundary the wicked would do only what is minimally necessary to avoid hell, and do so without any love for God or appreciation for what Jesus accomplished on the cross. They would only be interested in saving their own skins.

The scriptures and discussions concerning this subject are intended to encourage people to evaluate their own relationships with Jesus. As far away as it may seem, judgment day is coming for each of us without question or exception. The Apostle Paul made it clear that we will be judged for the good and the bad (2 Corinthians 5:10). The importance that we all run the race and be diligent in doing so cannot be stressed enough. Life is very short—nothing when compared to eternity. During this short "probationary period" of life, we will each determine by our own decisions where we stand for all eternity.

> For I consider [*from the standpoint of faith*] that the sufferings of
> the present life are not worthy to be compared with the glory that
> is about to be revealed to us *and* in us!

> —Romans 8:18 (AMP)

God gave Paul a taste of what is to come and he wrote about his attitude and goals with eternity in view. We would all do well to learn from his writings and apply the same determination as he did to run the race set before us.

Bible Reading: 1 Corinthians 3:12–15

2.3 The Separation of Church and State

This section addresses the civic responsibilities the church as in view of a legal doctrine the wicked have attempted to force upon the church.

The so-called "separation of church and state" is a legal doctrine [7] based in part on a private letter Thomas Jefferson sent to the Danbury Baptists in 1832. The phrase was taken grossly out of context. Thomas Jefferson was writing about the importance of Christians being involved in the civil affairs of this nation. In addition, this statement is not found in any of the founding documents or the Constitution of The United States of America.

America began as a number of British colonies which were naturally dominated by the British social and civil customs. One was a legal requirement to belong to the established Anglican church. People were taxed in order to support the church. Those who were part of another denomination, such as Baptists and others, and refused to be party to these taxes were persecuted and some thrown into prison. Eventually the First Amendment to the United States Constitution which was enacted in 1791 dealt with the situation:

> Congress shall make no law respecting an establishment of
> religion, or prohibiting the free exercise thereof; or abridging
> the freedom of speech, or of the press; or the right of the people

peaceably to assemble, and to petition the government for a redress of grievances.

The government is restricted from either instituting, giving favor to, or prohibiting the free exercise of one's religion. Nothing whatsoever is stated that prevents or discourages Christians from being involved in civil affairs.

Historical documents clearly indicate it was important and even required by several state constitutions that a political office be held by a true (in word and in deed) Christian. In the writings of the founding fathers as well as other prominent people of the day they considered it very important that Christians be involved in the civil and governing affairs of the nation.

Many so called "documentaries" on TV today profess to present an accurate picture of the lives of our founding fathers. However, they conveniently ignore much of the cultural issues and the Christian nature of the lives they led. Such documentaries are one piece of a larger picture that is designed to eradicate Christianity from today's society.

Charles Finney (1792–1875) started his professional life with the desire to be an attorney. He became a Christian and was a leader and revivalist in what is known as the Second Great Awakening which occurred during 1825–1835. One of his famous quotes is:

> The time has come that Christians must vote for honest men and take consistent ground in politics, or the Lord will curse them... God cannot sustain this free and blessed country, which we love and pray for, unless the Church will take right ground. Politics are part of religion in such a country as this, and Christians must do their duty to the country as part of their duty to God.
>
> —Charles Finney (circa 1832)

Many Christians have accepted the interpretation of the "separation of church and state" as fact and have withdrawn from their civil responsibilities. Worse yet, few have put forth any effort to maintain their God given and lawful rights.

As a result of this and other issues, the church in general has withdrawn from society and now represents an epic failure as a nation of priests.

> Our constitution was made only for a moral and religious people.
> It is wholly inadequate to the government of any other.

> —John Adams to the Officers of the First Brigade of the Third
> Division of the Militia of Massachusetts, October 11, 1798

The church must take its right stand in society otherwise the nation will eventually collapse. Unfortunately, we see this happening right before our eyes today.

> *Apathy on part of the people breeds*
> *tyranny and corruption on part of the government.*

If Christians fail to be involved in the civil affairs of this nation, the resulting power vacuum will by definition be filled by the wicked.

Sadly, for a great number of people, their Christianity is displayed only within the walls of a church.

> They profess to know God, but by their deeds they deny Him,
> being detestable and disobedient and worthless for any good deed.

> —Titus 1:16 (NASB)

In light of the so-called separation of church and state and the First Amendment, the subject of Islam needs to be addressed. It is not just a religion but an oligarchic theocracy, where a few religious elitists rule, often with a heavy hand. Evidence of such rule is seen throughout the Muslim countries in the Middle East, and throughout history. A theocracy is not protected by the Constitution of the United States. With Islam, religion, Sharia law, and the state are all one. The First Amendment is specific about protecting the rights of the people from the government. It addresses the practice of religion, not a theocracy. Christianity was by far the predominant religion when the Constitution was written so it is reasonable to assume the First Amendment equates religion with Christianity. Numerous statements by the founding fathers of this nation support this assertion.

As evidenced by the writings of many of the founders and others, the

United States of America was established by Christians with a government founded upon Biblical principles. The inspiration and guidance by the Holy Spirit throughout the foundation process are often ignored. In addition, this nation is a republic, and not a democracy or a theocracy.

The most fundamental differences between a Republic and a Democracy include [8]:

> **Democracy** In any democracy—either a direct or a representative type—as a form of government, there can be no legal system which protects the individual or the minority (any or all minorities) against unlimited tyranny by the majority. The undependable sense of self-restraint of the persons making up the majority at any particular time offers, of course, no protection whatever. Such a form of government is characterized by the majority omnipotent and unlimited. This is true, for example, of the representative democracy of Great Britain; because unlimited government power is possessed by the House of Lords, under an Act of Parliament of 1949—indeed, it has power to abolish anything and everything governmental in Great Britain.

> **Republic** A republic, on the other hand, has a very different purpose and an entirely different form, or system, of government. Its purpose is to control the majority strictly, as well as all others among the people, primarily to protect the individual's God-given, unalienable rights and therefore for the protection of the rights of the minority, of all minorities, and the liberties of people in general. The definition of a republic is: a constitutionally limited government of the representative type, created by a written constitution—adopted by the people and changeable (from its original meaning) by them only by its amendment—with its powers divided between three separate branches: executive, legislative and judicial. Here the term "the people" means, of course, the electorate.

The social benefits of a republic are innumerable and have been well documented for hundreds of years. Because of the wisdom of the founders, we have the freedoms we exercise today. Unfortunately, many of those freedoms are being stolen, due in large part to our neglect.

Bible Reading: 2 Chronicles 7:13–14

2 Chronicles 7:13–14 is a promise with a condition. God will forgive our sin and heal our nation **if and only if** we, His people, fulfill our part.

2.4   Obedience and Disobedience

Bible Reading: Deuteronomy 28

> *Revival starts with the church.*
> *Repentance is an act of obedience*
> *and it starts with you.*

We must build our relationship with our Lord Jesus Christ so He will fulfill His part of scripture and bring revival first to the Church, then to the rest of the nation and world. It must be emphasized that we as Christians will be held accountable before our Lord Jesus on judgment day for what we do, both the good <u>and the bad</u>.

> For we must all appear before the judgment seat of Christ, so that each one may be recompensed for his deeds in the body, according to what he has done, whether good or bad.
>
> —2 Corinthians 5:10 (NASB)

With the compromising behavior of such a large percentage of the churches, it is no surprise that God's blessings and anointing are so rare today.

Bible Reading: Matthew 12:29–30

Because of compromise with the world we, as Christians, allow the devil to plunder our churches and our nation.

> *Surely, we will be judged for our failures, especially when those failures result in the downfall of an entire nation and the multitude of souls who die without Christ in the process.*

An epic failure if this magnitude is inexcusable especially when we have the Holy Spirit, the Bible, and such easy access to resources such as the Internet to a far greater capacity than at any time in the history of the human race.

Bible Reading: Hebrews 2:1–4

In Deuteronomy 28 God tells how He will bless obedience and curse disobedience. Verses 1–14 outline the blessings for being obedient. That's 14 verses. Verses 16–68 outline the curses for disobedience. That's 53 verses. Clearly, much more is said concerning the consequences of disobedience than for obedience. It shouldn't be hard to understand why. We are far more inclined to sin than we are to be righteous. And this is true, even for many Christians.

Since God doesn't change, Deuteronomy 28 is still just as valid today as when it was written. The following statement has its foundation in Matthew 12:30 and Luke 11:23:

> *By rejecting the truth, you embrace a lie. In the end, truth will become an offense and object of hatred to you.*

This fact is abundantly clear in our society today. We are witnessing what Paul wrote in Romans and in 2 Thessalonians:

Bible Reading: Romans 1:28–32; 2 Thessalonians 2:8–12

These scriptures point to the dire need for prayer on behalf of the church. First for repentance and receiving forgiveness for sins, and second for intercession on behalf of our communities, our nation, and the rest of the world.

> Be diligent to present yourself approved to God as a workman who does not need to be ashamed, accurately handling the word of truth.
>
> —2 Timothy 2:15 (NASB)

Some people will attempt to absolve themselves of any responsibilities by stating that God is in control so there are no worries, and that they are in right standing with God because they pray and ask forgiveness regularly. Asking forgiveness and true repentance are not the same thing. True repentance will come when sin is revealed by the light of the knowledge of God's word in view of His holiness, and what He expects of us.

God has a plan but it is presumptuous to think you know all about it and have everything figured out. A presumptuous mindset such as this is often based on pride rather than humility. It is not God's will that this nation fails and falls from its place of blessing and prosperity in the world. Scripture makes it clear that we as Christians have a duty to ourselves and to our nation to be priests. As priests the church should be doing the things (preaching, miracles, etc.) that Jesus, the early apostles, and church did. Clearly this is not happening today to anywhere near the degree that it should.

An amazing observation is how Christians

- are so willing to expend energy and resources rationalizing away their responsibilities,
- criticize and judge others who speak outside their small box of understanding, and
- analyze how to cope with the present state of the world through social programs and psychological means such as counseling

rather than doing the very thing that will bring the greatest and best solution—and that is to **repent**!

This phenomenon is clear evidence that people love their sins more than they love God, and would rather adhere to man's traditions and methods of solving problems rather than God's. God's way is simple.

> *Humility is not an emotion.*
> *It is a choice and state of mind.*

Bible Reading: Romans 12:2; 1 Corinthians 2:12; 1 John 2:15; James 4:4

No church will become successful in God's eyes if it compromises with the world. Often, pastors view church membership and finances as measures of success. Such a worldly view of success will not pass on judgment day. Fulfilling the Great Commission according to God's plan as laid out in His Word is the only way to bring true success. If a church will follow God's plan and not compromise with the world, then and only then will the membership and financial prosperity increase as God has promised and in the way He has promised.

The measure of success for any church should be in the fulfillment of the Great Commission in Matthew 28:19–20 and Ephesians 4:11–12. The preparation spoken of in Ephesians involves education and that education involves practical application, for faith without works is dead.

The blessings of obedience cannot be overstated.

Bible Reading: Leviticus 26

When people are healed, delivered, raised from the dead, and so on, then multitudes will flock to the church. Evidence of this is clear throughout Jesus' ministry, the rest of the New Testament, and the Book of Acts in particular. It is important to note that miracles such as was mentioned do indeed occur around the world. Rather than rare occurrences, they should be commonplace.

Bible Reading: Isaiah 1:18–20

CHAPTER 3

Precursors to Repentance

Humility and brokenness are the primary precursors to repentance. As mentioned earlier, repentance is the first step to a successful prayer life and relationship with the Holy Spirit. In order for true repentance to take place, we must first humble ourselves before our Lord and experience the brokenness that leads to repentance. Humility and brokenness are decisions but may also come as a result of the revelation of one's sins and how horrible and insane sin is.

> *The nature of pride is to hide and deny sin.*
> *The nature of humility is to reveal and acknowledge sin.*

Various scriptures speak of the dangers of pride. As Christians, it is essential for us to maintain a humble state of mind throughout our lives.

3.1 Brokenness

The modern definition for *broken* means to be being fragmented, ruptured, torn, etc. Brokenness is viewed as a state more often brought about by an act or situation external to the individual in such a manner that the person is utterly devastated.

The sacrifices of God are a broken spirit; A broken and a contrite heart, O God, You will not despise.

—Psalms 51:17 (NASB)

Years ago, brokenness had a different meaning. Charles H. Spurgeon (1834–1892) said it well in his commentary on Psalms 51:17 [9]:

"The sacrifices of God are a broken spirit." All sacrifices are presented to thee in one, by the man whose broken heart presents the Saviour's merit to thee. When the heart mourns for sin, thou art better pleased than when the bullock bleeds beneath the axe. "A broken heart" is an expression implying deep sorrow, embittering the very life; it carries in it the idea of all but killing anguish in that region which is so vital as to be the very source of life. So excellent is a spirit humbled and mourning for sin, that it is not only a sacrifice, but it has a plurality of excellencies, and is pre-eminently God's "sacrifices." "A broken and a contrite heart, O God, thou wilt not despise." A heart crushed is a fragrant heart. Men condemn those who are contemptible in their own eyes, but the Lord seeth not as man seeth. He despises what men esteem, and values that which they despise. Never yet has God spurned a lowly, weeping penitent, and never will he while God is love, and while Jesus is called the man who receiveth sinners. Bullocks and rams he desires not, but contrite hearts he seeks after; yea, but one of them is better to him than all the varied offerings of the old Jewish sanctuary.

Brokenness has lost much of its original meaning. The original meaning would likely be revived again if spiritual revivals of the magnitude that occurred in previous centuries would come to us. The most unfortunate fact is that most Christians don't take sin as seriously as they should. Such a cavalier attitude is not only unacceptable, it is sinful and dangerous. As long as this cavalier attitude persists, revival will not come.

Experiencing the state of brokenness described above is not pleasant. Neither was dying on the cross. Repentance is not something the flesh will easily submit to. Repentance is an act and experience we all have the responsibility to go through repeatedly and willingly. When you experience this, you will be amazed at the subtleties of sin. The Holy Spirit will reveal things to you that you never noticed before.

We all sin and we all need to maintain a lifestyle of humility. Doing so makes the process of repentance much easier. If Jesus as 100% man and 100% God willingly endured the suffering of the cross, how much more so should we whom He redeemed be willing to allow the Holy Spirit to bring us to a state of brokenness and repentance?

> *Without brokenness, there can be no repentance.*

By allowing the Holy Spirit to bring about brokenness and repentance, and by experiencing these on a regular basis it will become much easier and more natural to seek His righteousness and holiness, and rid ourselves of a sinful lifestyle. The flesh must be put in subjection to our spirit and to the will of our Father in heaven. Dealing with this subject requires a conscious effort, and is all part of the "pressing forward" Paul spoke of in Philippians 3:12.

Some important points to keep in mind are:

1. Repentance and the surrender of oneself to God must be done consciously and constantly. We must resist the devil and persevere in trials and tribulations. Through surrender we will grow closer to God and become more Christ-like. The flesh does not surrender easily.

   Bible Reading: James 4:7–10

2. Living in the Holy Spirit and allowing Him to work through you are evidence of a humble life.
3. To live a broken life, one must avoid the ways of the world, counsel of the ungodly, and hate the way of sinners. Churches that have compromised with the world think they will gain the acceptance of the world. It doesn't work this way. We must delight in the law of God and meditate on it always and obey it (Joshua 1:8, Psalm 1:1–2). The world would be more willing to accept and respect the church if the church would learn the power of God and exercise it

throughout their communities. Revival will come and the Gospel will spread like wild fire.

4. The love of this world must die in the life of a broken Christian. The mad rush for wealth, position, fame, and power is not the will of God. Willful disobedience to the Word of God is also very dangerous for the believer.

    Bible Reading: 1 John 2:15–17

In verse 16, John identifies the three root sins—the lust of the flesh, the lust of the eyes, and the boastful pride of life. It is from these three root sins that all other sins are categorized [10]. Let's look at this more closely:

a. The "lust of the flesh" is the motivation for sensual self-gratification. It could be called moral impurity, sexual lust, or in the broadest term, sensuality.
b. The "lust of the eyes" is the materialistic motivation in human nature. This lust could be called temporal values or idolatry. It is evidenced by a greater emphasis on material things than spiritual things and an ungodly concern for temporal or worldly possessions.
c. The "boastful pride of life" is simply stated as pride. It is an ungodly evaluation of one's importance or merit.

5. Whether Jesus comes back in our lifetimes or not, we must prepare ourselves to meet Him. This includes purifying ourselves from all unrighteousness and doing His work so we are ready to go with Him when He comes (1 John 3:2–3).

3.2 Humility

Humility is a state of mind required for those who desire to have a relationship with the Holy Spirit. One who does not maintain a humble state of mind is living in the flesh, and the flesh is at enmity with God. In other words, if you are not humble, you are living in the flesh and that is sin. The subject of humility should be taught as part of the basic introduction to the Christian life. Maintaining humility provides a degree of insulation between you and sin (pride in particular) and allows the Holy Spirit to reveal sins that would otherwise go unnoticed.

> *Humility comes before exaltation.*
> *Pride comes before destruction.*
> (see Proverbs 18:12)

- Humility is a decision and not a feeling that just happens to come on you. In James 4:10 we are instructed to humble ourselves before God and He will lift us up.
- Humility before God is to know His righteousness, His holiness, His justice, His grace, His judgments, and indeed, His whole nature in view of our sinful nature. This knowledge and experience will not be realized without humility.
- Humility is the foundation upon which our relationship with the Holy Spirit is constructed.
- Humility should be taught as part of the most fundamental traits of our relationship with Him.
- An important fact is that humility does *not* translate into being a doormat!

The nature of humility is to surrender one's will to the Holy Spirit. Doing so will make the lessons to be learned in life much easier. People often resist and complain about the trials and tribulations they go through. Resisting and complaining about trials and tribulations have roots in a life not completely surrendered to God. That life is founded on pride, and pride will always resist the will of God. For these reasons, our Lord needs to put people through the same lesson over and over. Being humble and surrendered to Him so that a trial would only need to be endured and learned once is a better state to be in. Not only is humility a necessary ingredient in life, but learning and applying the Word of God in every situation is also necessary.

When people cry out and pray for wealth they often do so with an attitude of selfishness. An attitude of selfishness within this context may be founded on the prosperity doctrines found in many churches, and not for the desire to have needs met. Seeking these things before seeking God is idolatry (Psalms 37:4, Matthew 6:33). To see God as a means rather than an end is to make Him your servant, which is to elevate yourself above God, and that is sin. Such selfishness is founded on the spirit of humanism and it has no place in the life of a Christian. People can operate in selfishness without realizing what they are doing.

A truly humble person will come to understand what Paul wrote in Philippians 3:8–11.

There is nothing wrong with wealth and enjoying the good things the world has to offer as scriptures attest. It becomes a problem when material things or the desires for them become an idol. Jesus comes first. When we grow to the point that our greatest delight is in our Lord, He will give us the desires of our heart (Psalm 37:4; Matthew 6:33). This doesn't necessarily mean it will all come at once. He will give us our desires in accordance to our ability to receive, and in accordance with His will. Remember, all things may be lawful but not all things are expedient (1 Corinthians 6:12). We must not lose focus of what we are on earth to accomplish. Once at a level of maturity, the surpassing value of knowing Jesus will overshadow everything the world may have to offer. Although, at this point we may enjoy prosperity, it will never take precedence over our relationship with Jesus and become an idol.

Humility is the avenue through which all the blessings of God flow. It is the avenue by which the Holy Spirit is able to operate through His people and do the things Jesus did.

If only we would all endeavor to humble ourselves and let Jesus reign in our lives. If we would do this then we would experience what Paul wrote in Philippians 4:13, "I can do **all** things through Him who strengthens me" (NASB). This is not just a statement concerning the endurance of trials and tribulations, but that of an overwhelming conqueror (Romans 8:37).

Throughout scripture God gives favor to the humble of heart. Jesus proclaimed that we are holy because He is holy (Deuteronomy 7:6, 14:2, 28:9; Isaiah 62:12). In order to receive the holiness He has proclaimed for us we must open the door of brokenness and obedience. Pride and holiness cannot coexist. Humility is the foundation upon which holiness is built. We need to see our sins as our heavenly Father sees them. We need to experience repentance. What is repentance?

From *Easton's Bible Dictionary* [11] on the word *repentance* we read:

There are three Greek words used in the New Testament to denote repentance.

1. The verb *metamelomai* is used of a change of mind, such as to produce regret or even remorse on account of sin, but not necessarily a change of heart. This word is used with reference to the repentance of Judas (Matt. 27:3).
2. *Metanoeo*, meaning to change one's mind and purpose, as the result of after knowledge.
3. This verb, with the cognate noun *metanoia*, is used of true repentance, a change of mind and purpose and life, to which remission of sin is promised.

Evangelical repentance consists of

1. A true sense of one's own guilt and sinfulness.
2. The apprehension of God's mercy through Christ.
3. A hatred of sin (Psalms 119:128; Job 42:5–6; 2 Corinthians 7:10) and turning from it to God.
4. A persistent endeavor to live a holy life and to walk with God and keep His commandments.

The true penitent is conscious of

- Guilt (Psalms 51:4, 51:9).
- The pollution of sin (Psalms 51:5, 7, 10).
- Helplessness without Christ (Psalms 51:11, 109:21–22).

Thus he apprehends himself to be just what God has always seen him to be and declares him to be. But repentance comprehends not only such a sense of sin, but also an apprehension of mercy, without which there can be no true repentance (Psalms 51:1, 130:4).

When people see themselves in the light of God's holiness and their sinful nature, it becomes apparent how hopeless they are, how much they need God's grace, and how dependent upon Him they truly are.

Bible Reading: Psalms 51:1; Psalms 130:4; Hebrews 10:29

Perhaps the most important factor in repentance is that you need to be willing to face sin for what it is. You must be willing to:

- Allow the Holy Spirit to reveal your sins to you.
- Experience that killing anguish Spurgeon wrote about, and remorse that comes with the realization and revelation of the true nature of sin.
- See the cost of sin and the unfathomable price that Jesus paid for us.
- See the insanity that sin is, and how God's mercy toward us keeps us from experiencing the immediate effects of it (Matthew 7:7).

3.3   Maintaining Humility

Once we allow the Holy Spirit to bring us to a genuine state of brokenness, what must be done to maintain it? How do you remain humble? We will find that the things we do to maintain a humble and broken state of mind are applicable to every aspect of our Christian life.

Maintaining a state of humility and brokenness is not the nature of the flesh. How easy it is to allow self back on the throne! This conflict is something we all deal with.

In a nutshell, use focus and discipline to maintain a humble mindset. Of course, the key ingredient here is prayer. Living in a state of brokenness and humility does not equate to feeling miserable as some attempt to portray. Rather, this mindset is the door through which the Holy Spirit will operate so His people will experience the fruit of the Spirit in its fullness.

> [22]But the fruit of the Spirit is love, joy, peace, patience, kindness, goodness, faithfulness, [23]gentleness, self-control; against such things there is no law.
>
> —Galatians 5:22–23 (NASB)

Jesus was our perfect example and is our perfect help.

> These things I have spoken to you, so that in Me you may have peace. In the world you have tribulation, but take courage; I have overcome the world.
>
> —John 16:33 (NASB)

Some denominations and movies that depict the life of Jesus overemphasize His humility to the point that it is nauseating. He is unfortunately portrayed to be humble to the point of defeat, humble to the point of being a door mat. He was not. There is also the tendency to equate humility with passivity. Jesus was certainly not passive, and so neither should we.

Humility and a warrior mindset go hand in hand. This fact is clear, even among those who don't know Jesus. Observe the characteristics of the professional warriors, such as the Navy SEALs, the Army Rangers, and various other Special Forces teams. Most of these people remain remarkably humble in spite of the fact that they are the most highly trained and capable warriors in the world.

> *The goal of pride is to make a hero out of a fool.*

Pride and arrogance will get you killed in battle. Look at the men who were given the Congressional Medal of Honor. Most of these medals were given posthumously. Those who survived will tell you they were just doing their jobs; that they were not heroes and were not deserving of such a great honor.

The warrior mindset, mental training, and discipline that people go through in the military are directly applicable to the Christian life. You don't need to go into the military to accomplish this though. All of what we need is written in the Bible and provided by the Holy Spirit. Nevertheless, we can also learn a great deal from the experiences of those around us who have served in the military and law enforcement. More is discussed on the warrior mindset in Chapter 9.

> Have I not commanded you? Be strong and courageous! Do not
> tremble or be dismayed, for the LORD your God is with you
> wherever you go.

> —Joshua 1:9 (NASB)

In the above verse, God proclaims courage and strength to Joshua so he would be able to lead Israel into the promised land, and to defeat the inhabitants. We recognize today that the experiences and difficulties Israel went through are an example to us in our Christian walk. Likewise, God proclaims strength and courage so we might enter into the promised land that flows with milk and honey. Christians must appropriate His strength and courage through obedience to Him.

> The LORD is the one who goes ahead of you; He will be with you.
> He will not fail you or forsake you. Do not fear or be dismayed.

> —Deuteronomy 31:8 (NASB)

Maintaining a balanced mindset of humility may seem like a daunting task. Start with the basics the Holy Spirit will guide and provide. A tree doesn't come down with one swing of the ax. Reading about what needs to be done is the easy part. The doing of it often seems beyond human capabilities. Man's way is to derive complex solutions for complex problems. God's way is to provide a simple solution for complex problems. Do what He says and He will take care of the complexities.

God made our job simple.
The devil deceives people into thinking our job is
so complex and difficult that it is unattainable.

Remember, the Holy Spirit is your helper and teacher!

> I am the vine, you are the branches; he who abides in Me and I in
> him, he bears much fruit, for apart from Me you can do nothing.

> —John 15:5 (NASB)

The teachings and sermons so often encountered today instruct people as to *what* they need to do without teaching the *how*. This unfortunate fact is what keeps so many in bondage (Hosea 4:6). The solution is education.

The most basic but important step of *how* is summed up in 2 Corinthians 10:5 which says,

> We are destroying speculations and every lofty thing raised up against the knowledge of God, and we are taking every thought captive to the obedience of Christ.

> —2 Corinthians 10:5 (NASB)

Take every thought captive to the obedience of Christ. In order to do so you need to judge every thought, word, image, feeling, and emotion— that is, everything received through your senses as well as everything that goes on in your mind. How you judge any given situation must be based on the Word of God and the Holy Spirit, and the knowledge they provide. Learn to listen to the Holy Spirit and to read and study the Bible, learn it from cover to cover, and learn it well.

Everything that is not of God must be rejected. The entertainment of evil things will eventually get you into trouble. Practice and discipline are critical for spiritual warfare since the mind is what the devil attacks. Success can take a lot of work and willpower, especially when dealing with emotions. The devil uses external spiritual and physical attacks to bring you down as well. In reality, those external attacks are meant to degrade your mind.

> *Defeat is in the mind.*
> *Victory is in Jesus.*

Gaining victory over the devil begins with the mind. Prayer is the primary tool available to realize victory. In the chapters that follow there are many warfare prayers to use for this purpose.

As you reject the bad, you must also dwell on the good.

Bible Reading: Philippians 4:8–9

Although the task is simple, it takes mental discipline and effort to accomplish on a moment by moment and day by day basis.

In the course of growing in Jesus, always keep His Word in mind. Paul makes this clear in the letter to the Colossians,

God instructed Joshua as he was about to lead Israel into the promised land.

Bible Reading: Joshua 1:7–8

So too, put His Word into practice in your life so you may enter into the victory that He has promised. Don't deviate to the left or to the right so you may have success wherever you go in life.

In all that has been said on the subject of brokenness, the most important aspect is the renewing of the mind. Indeed, the renewing of the mind is essential for us to experience and live a normal Christian life. Romans 12:2 says,

> And do not be conformed to this world, but be transformed by the renewing of your mind, that you may prove what the will of God is, that which is good and acceptable and perfect.
>
> —Romans 12:2 (NASB)

The renewing of the mind comes through mental discipline and prayer with the result that the Holy Spirit will help bring about changes. The result is holiness and righteousness and a closer relationship with Jesus. The process of mental discipline also means making changes in how you do things. Priorities are likely going to need changing. There are things that you do now that may need to be placed lower on your priority list. Righteousness and holiness must become a higher priority.

CHAPTER 4

Hindrances

Sin is the hindrance to prayer and growth and manifests in many forms. It hinders your relationship with the Holy Spirit and is a hindrance to a holy life. Dealing with sin is never a pleasant issue. We must all face sin sooner or later. Confronting it now and working to live a holy and righteous life is far better than waiting until judgment day. By then, it will be too late to do anything about it. Those who say it is okay to sin because, "it is all covered by the blood of Jesus" or, "it is all paid for on the cross" adhere to a philosophy that is clearly heresy.

Bible Reading: Romans 6:12–16

Remember Paul is writing this to Christians. From these and many other passages throughout the Bible, it is clear sin is an issue that must be dealt with and not treated with a cavalier attitude.

> *Recovering from sin is invariably more difficult and takes more work than it would to resist temptation in the first place.*

Hindrances may be external or internal. Some of the more common hindrances are wrong motives (James 4:3), pride, lack of faith, worldly cares, laziness, and so on. This chapter will address some of those that have been the most damaging to the church as a whole in recent years.

Again, one only needs to look at the recent history of this nation, particularly since World War II. Back then, the church was a significant force at all levels of society. Today it is little more than a religious social club. Over the years the church has withdrawn from its moral and civic duties as a nation of priests. The result is a power vacuum that the devil most eagerly fills. Compromise with the world, and hence the devil, have allowed a myriad of evil influences to gain a foothold in the church.

Seldom are holiness, repentance, and the fear of God preached or taught any more. Even if these subjects are taught, they are likely watered down to the point of having no effect, or with the assumption that the congregation is already well informed on the subject. In reality people are not adequately educated because if they were the church would be a much different place.

God's judgment on sin appears frequently throughout the Bible. For example, the entire chapters of Deuteronomy 28 and Leviticus 26 are devoted to the consequences of sin and righteousness. Scriptures that deal with these issues are too numerous to list, but they make it clear that Christians will also be judged.

Bible Reading: 2 Corinthians 5:10; Matthew 16:27; Romans 14:12

If only people would grasp the importance of these verses and be diligent about walking with Jesus!

The omission of good works, failure to fulfill the great commission as Jesus intended; these are every bit a sin as committing a myriad of other crimes and sins. Where is your heart? Do you go to church to experience the presence of the Holy Spirit thinking this is enough? Do you rely on the anointing that is on the pastor thinking this is enough? Do you just go to church to get your spiritual batteries recharged so you can get through the week only to repeat the process next week, and the week after? Do you go to church, put some pocket change in the plate when it goes by thinking you are in good standing because you have paid your fire insurance premiums? These attitudes are irresponsible and unacceptable. Church is not a social club or a place to get an emotional high. It is a place of prayer (Matthew 21:13), where people can grow, learn the Word of God, live it, and put it into practice.

Bible Reading: Ephesians 4:11–13

The focus in this passage in Ephesians is the "equipping of the saints for the work of service." Church leadership is responsible for making this happen, and it is the congregation's responsibility to put it into action to build up the body of Christ, which also means to fulfill the Great Commission. Jesus expects us to reproduce. That is, a church will produce pastors and teachers who will start new churches. This process is to be repeated throughout generations.

Bible Reading: Matthew 13:23

Scripture is clear that we are in for a struggle if we choose to grow in Jesus. That struggle will be minimized *if* we are obedient to His Word. Building faith takes work which also means building your relationship with Jesus takes work.

Bible Reading: John 6:28–29

The Gospel Hymn *Trust And Obey* [12] says it well.

Trust and Obey

The LORD will give grace and glory: no good thing will he withhold from them that walk uprightly.
*O LORD of hosts, blessed is the man that trusteth in thee.*Psa. 84:11-12; Isa. 50:10

1. When we walk with the Lord in the light of His Word,
2. Not a shad - ow can rise, not a cloud in the skies,
3. Not a bur - den we bear, not a sor - row we share,
4. But we nev - er can prove the de - lights of His love
5. Then in fel - low - ship sweet we will sit at His feet,

What a glo - ry He sheds on our way! While we do His good will,
But His smile quick - ly drives it a - way; Not a doubt or a fear,
But our toil He doth rich - ly re - pay; Not a grief or a loss,
Un - til all on the al - tar we lay; For the fa - vor He shows,
Or we'll walk by His side in the way; What He says we will do,

He a - bides with us still, And with all who will trust and o - bey.
not a sigh or a tear, Can a - bide while we trust and o - bey.
not a frown or a cross, But is blessed if we trust and o - bey.
for the joy He be - stows, Are for them who will trust and o - bey.
where He sends we will go; Nev - er fear, on - ly trust and o - bey.

Refrain

Trust and o - bey, for there's no oth - er way

To be hap - py in Je - sus, but to trust and o - bey.

WORDS: John H. Sammis, 1887. MUSIC: Daniel B. Towner, 1887.
43

4.1   Church Leadership

The vast majority of Christians, both leadership and congregations, are not aware of the nature of the cultural traps and lies of the devil to which everyone is subjected. It would not be fair to single out any individual or denomination since the problem is so pervasive throughout church culture. The church has been lulled into a false sense of security. Once enlightened, the leadership has the responsibility to change this errant culture in order to get in line with Biblical teaching.

All Christians have the responsibility to be obedient to His Word. Pastors and teachers have a higher level of responsibility and as so will incur a stricter judgment for what is taught or not taught (James 3:1). The health of the church is the responsibility of its leaders. If the leadership fails then the church fails, and if the church fails, then families, communities, and the nation will fail. This tragedy is clearly happening before our eyes.

All Christians, regardless of their position in the church, have the responsibility to investigate scripture, learn on their own by relying on the Holy Spirit, and putting His Word into practice.

A majority of the pastors I have met have been resistant to any influence that falls outside the small box of their church culture, regardless of its benefit. They prefer to be masters and lords of their fiefdoms. Although the goal of protecting "their" flock (or their jobs) has its benefits, being resistant to change that is in line with scripture is not. Being closed to anyone who may have knowledge or spiritual insights that exceed their own is not the correct attitude. Rather, further investigation and verification with scripture (*not* church or denominational doctrine) should be accomplished, then used for the benefit of the congregation.

Preaching the Gospel and demonstration of the power of God go together as Jesus, the Apostle Paul, and many others, both taught and did (1 Timothy 1:7). Jesus demonstrated what we, as His people, are to accomplish to fulfill the Great Commission. None of the miracles that Jesus, the Apostle Paul, and others did are unreachable for us today. They are a responsibility that can only be fulfilled through building a relationship with Him to the point that the Holy Spirit is able to do these works (John 15:5). It is this simple.

In Matthew 10:8 Jesus commanded the twelve apostles to heal the sick, raise the dead, and cleanse the lepers. In Luke 10:9, Jesus commanded the seventy to heal the sick and preach the Gospel. Jesus' words still stand and are just as applicable to Christians now as they were then.

Bible Reading: Matthew 24:35; Mark 8:38, 13:31; Luke 9:26

From the above verses (and others that relate to this subject), the same message is repeated. Repetition is significant since it leaves no question as to the validity and importance of the message. No room is left to excuse failure.

Pastors and leaders must understand some of the traps they have fallen in, as well as how to get out.

- If the Holy Spirit is not able to do the miracles through people that Jesus did (and more) as a normal mode of operation, your church is nothing more than a religious social club. If you are obedient to His Word this will change (John 14:15).
- Never try to become acceptable to the world. This approach will never work so give up trying it. Learn to be acceptable to God by doing His will and you will realize success beyond your wildest dreams.
- Be honest and transparent. Stop presenting yourself as a bastion of knowledge and righteousness. You are a human being with a sinful nature just like everyone else (Romans 3:23). Own it! People will respond better to honesty and transparency in a more positive manner than you may realize. Teach people to not focus on you but on Jesus and all that He has to offer His people. When you do this, you will be surprised at the blessings that will follow.
- Stress humility and repentance of sins—both personal and corporate for leadership and the congregation. This must start with the leadership. Anything less leads to pride and more sin.
- Obedience to God is more important than maintaining a position in church. Don't worry about those who are resistant to change.

Pray for them and explain, through scripture, why change is necessary.

- Pray! Pray! Pray! The style of prayer presented in this book has proven to be remarkably effective. Use it and teach others. Without effective prayer you will never accomplish much. The importance of effective prayer cannot be overstated (James 5:16).

> *Repentance and prayer are the most important actions needed by the church to bring about revival.*

When the church grows to the point that miracles are a normal occurrence, the world will flock to the church. The church then will become the driving force of society it is supposed to be.

God has strong words to say concerning the lack of leadership within the church. The following passage from Isaiah fits the state of church leadership today.

Bible Reading: Isaiah 56:9–12

Verse nine indicates how the wicked see the church as something to be devoured. We see persecution against the church growing daily. Persecution is not a measure of spirituality but evidence of failure. Verses 10 and 11 outline the current state church leadership. They have no concept of their sad spiritual state (Revelation 3:14–22) and the effect it has on their congregations, communities, and nation. Verse twelve speaks of the corporate sins such as the spirit of entertainment and others, some of which are discussed in this chapter.

Bible Reading: Ezekiel 34:1–10

The above passage from Ezekiel speaks for itself.

You can't change the past but you can change the future, and the course of your life and ministry through the decisions you make today. Now is the time to pursue your relationship with Jesus with all of your being! Now is the time to repent!

Bible Reading: Ezekiel 37:1–14

4.2 The Spirit of Entertainment

The spirit of entertainment has had a detrimental effect on the church. The origins can be traced primarily to television and to a lesser extent, movies. Entertainment has the effect of providing information with no effort on part of the recipient. It breeds spiritual laziness. Many churches today have expended considerable resources to develop the best drama club, the best choir, the best worship team, and so on. Worship is essential however it must be secondary to prayer. If the focus were on prayer and growth, the worship will come much more naturally and not be done with a spirit of entertainment.

How often do people sit in church, listen to a sermon, and forget a majority of what was spoken even before they get out the door? Lessons and sermons seldom get written down and put into practice.

Bible Reading: Matthew 21:12–13

Although culture is different today, human nature has not changed. How have we made the church into a robbers' den? By catering to the spirit of entertainment we succumb to an emotional feeling we call worship rather than making our relationship with the Holy Spirit the top priority. We are robbing our Lord (and ourselves) of the relationship He desires to have with us, and paid for on the cross, and replacing it with an emotional high. Many will no doubt argue this point but all one needs to do is to observe any of the majority of church services. Where is repentance and serious prayer found in the church? Where is the weeping and remorse for sins? Only *after* true repentance and fervent prayer will praise and worship be experienced in its fullness as intended by our Lord Jesus. If the church had its priorities straight, true worship will be sweet and come from the depths of our souls. It will be an experience with far more depth and meaning than the emotional high entertainment provides.

There is a time and a place for everything. The church should first and foremost be a place of prayer. Entertainment, however necessary and pleasing it may seem should never take precedence over your relationship with the Holy Spirit and the mission the church has to fulfill. Entertainment has unfortunately become an idol in the churches. This sin is polluting the church and quenching the Holy Spirit (1 Thessalonians 5:19). God will never be able to work in His people as He desires until these sins are dealt with. Although the motive for providing entertainment (concerts and such) in the church may be to attract people for the purpose of evangelizing, it is seldom backed up with enough prayer to make this effort effective to the degree it should be. In reality, people have greater concerns than being entertained. There are many health problems, family problems, financial problems, and so on that need to be dealt with. Entertainment is often used as an escape from the realities of life. Our nation is sick and dying. The church needs to provide the solution, which is to use the power of God to give substance to the words (1Corinthians 4:20).

4.3   Spiritual Laziness

The spirit of entertainment is perhaps the greatest, but not the only, contribution to spiritual laziness. The spirit of laziness has had a significant negative effect on the church. How easy it has become to think it is okay to ride on the pastor's coat tails (after all, that's what we pay him for).

How easy it has become to become complacent about spiritual matters in our own lives and push so many responsibilities on the pastor!

One example of the consequences of spiritual laziness within the church is the exceptionally high suicide rate. The solutions offered by society for this problem can never make up for the vacuum left by the absence of the Holy Spirit. One of the primary results of this vacuum is hopelessness. The churches' responsibility as a nation of priests is to make sure this problem is minimized. This takes prayer as well as accepting our personal, spiritual, and civic responsibilities. Many Christians absolve themselves of their God-ordained responsibilities by saying something to the effect of, "I don't need to do anything because God is in control...," or, "It was all nailed to the cross so there are no worries." This is evidence of spiritual laziness.

> *Don't fall into the trap of wanting all the benefits of salvation and none of the responsibilities.*

People inevitably attempt to solve the near unfathomable complexities of the problems of society with complex solutions. Those solutions are either minimally effective or doomed to failure. As was said earlier, God's solution is remarkably simple and successful.

Bible Reading: 2 Chronicles 7:13–14

In verse 13, we see that God causes the weather and environment to change in order to get His peoples' attention. Many Christians see what is happening, know what the Bible has to say about it, but do nothing. This is a failure of epic proportions and is founded on spiritual laziness. In verse 14, the solution is remarkably simple—humble one's self, seek God (that is, to work on your relationship with Jesus), pray, and REPENT! Once the church does this, God will do the rest.

Bible Reading: Hebrews 10:26–31

We would all do well to take God's Word seriously. No one has the luxury to be lazy, especially when such decisions have dire consequences that will be felt for all eternity. Look at the parable of the talents from Matthew chapter 25. In particular, we need to examine the demise of the third and lazy slave that failed to multiply the talents given him.

Bible Reading: Matthew 25:26–30

Although the ills of society will never be completely eliminated, the church has the responsibility to minimize these problems as much as possible. The consequences of spiritual laziness are grave. We will all be judged for what we have done and failed to do in this life.

Bible Reading: Proverbs 18:9, 24:30–34, 26:13–16; Ecclesiastes 10:18

Spiritual laziness is a wasting and destructive spirit. Others can see one who is lazy and become lazy themselves. The result is that lives are wasted in a multitude of ways. This waste is the cause of destruction for many.

God will not use someone who is lazy. Note that all the great men of God written about in scripture were busy doing something when God called them. They weren't sitting around waiting for some great anointing or revival to fall out of heaven. Daniel, Joshua, Gideon, and David are among many who were busy and diligent when God called them.

Laziness is the greatest hindrance to spiritual growth in the church today. If nothing is done to reverse this trend, persecution and death will become the norm. Persecution and the murder of Christians is already happening throughout the nation today, and more so in other countries. There are many people who are not inherently lazy but have been taught that this behavior is acceptable in the church. Such teaching is most often based on church culture and doctrines that foster this behavior, often without anyone realizing what is happening. Laziness is a tool and deception of the devil used to render the church ineffective so he can go about his evil deeds with as few hindrances as possible.

Many Christians may be diligent, successful, and prosperous people in their careers but that good mental attitude they employ every day is left at the door when they walk in the church. It is a horrible tragedy that church culture fosters this attitude.

> So then, my beloved, just as you have always obeyed, not as in my presence only, but now much more in my absence, work out your salvation with fear and trembling;
>
> —Philippians 2:12 (NASB)

Some characteristics of one who is spiritually lazy are:

1. One who is lazy will always be the servant of others. The Christians of this nation are more and more becoming the servants of the wicked. Laws are being passed and others, including the Constitution, are ignored with the result that Christians become servants and slaves to the wicked.
2. One who is lazy lacks discipline. Only through discipline can one apply the Word to their lives and grow spiritually.
3. One who is lazy brings others into laziness. How easy this is!
4. One who is lazy will be defeated by the enemy or is already living in a state of defeat. One who is stagnant in their growth is in a state of defeat.

5. One who is lazy will live in spiritual poverty. Spiritual poverty can also bring about physical poverty.

6. One who is lazy turns on their bed but doesn't get out of it (Proverbs 26:14). This is to say they are full of words but lack action.

7. One who is lazy is afraid to take any risk. Spiritual growth requires taking risk and stepping out in faith.

8. One who is lazy is wise in their own eyes without realizing just how foolish they really are (Proverbs 26:16).

9. One who is lazy will resist work. Building a relationship with Jesus takes work so one who is lazy will never grow out of their spiritual diapers.

10. One who is lazy will resist growing because this requires sacrificing self on the cross, and that takes work.

11. One who is lazy is a procrastinator. They will fail to do what needs to be done when it needs to be done. Why do today what you can put off until tomorrow? And tomorrow never comes.

12. One who is lazy prides himself in it.

13. One who is lazy thinks they are entitled to every spiritual blessing without having to do any work to earn them. This problem is compounded by the entitlement mentality so prevalent in society today.

14. One who is lazy doesn't want (or perhaps even believe or care) to be held accountable for their sins, after all, "it was all nailed to the cross."

15. One who is lazy has a distaste for the things of God. They do not want or see a need to move out of their comfort zone. This is to say that the things of God are not worth pursuing because they think they are okay in their present state. This is especially true for those who see themselves as a contributor and educator in the church when they have no idea they are living proof of Revelation 3:17.

16. One who is lazy is full of excuses (Luke 14:16–24).

17. One who is lazy is unteachable as they think they know everything or that they know enough (Proverbs 26:14). This is also the spirit of pride.

18. One who is lazy will cry out to others for help if tragedy strikes hoping others will do all the prayer and work necessary to change their situation.

19. One who is lazy is a spiritual parasite instead of a contributor to the edification of the church. Such a person is always being fed the Word but never puts it into action.

20. One who is lazy will fail to do anything about a problem until after it is too late.

Christians often desire to advance spiritually but are unwilling to go through the work to get there. You can't climb a mountain[1] by looking at it. It takes effort and work. The way has its costs, risks, and dangers but Jesus will always be there. In the end there is great reward. Running the race that Paul discussed throughout his letters requires discipline and work.

Scripture is filled with wonderful promises. Many are conditional, that is if we fulfill our condition, then Jesus will bring blessings beyond our imagination (1 Corinthians 2:9).

Bible Reading: Revelation 3:14–22

Spiritual laziness is the most likely cause of their dismal state. This message comes with a stern warning to those who refuse to repent. They will be utterly rejected by Jesus (verse 16). The only destination for those who have been rejected by Jesus is hell, and after this, the lake of fire. The spiritual condition of the present-day church fits the description of the church in Laodicea surprisingly well.

Bible Reading: John 10:27–30; Revelation 3:5; Romans 8:38–39

The verses above make it clear that Jesus and Jesus alone has the authority to erase or not to erase someone's name from the book of life, or to take them out of the Father's hand. The verses listed after this make it clear that no *created being or thing* can separate us from God.

This is a fearful state with consequences that are eternal! None of us

---

[1] The book *Hinds Feet on High Places* by Hannah Hurnard [24] is a beautiful allegory dramatizing the spiritual walk with Jesus we all need to pursue.

can take this lightly. Don't forget that everything we do in this life will determine our condition for all eternity!

Of all the seven churches addressed in Revelation, the church of Laodicea is the only one that did not receive a commendation from Jesus.

When I was a new Christian, I attended a church that taught the eternal security of the believer. A number of scriptures were presented to support this doctrine. When I read these and others throughout the Bible, I found many more scriptures that warned of the dire consequences of failing to take salvation seriously and grow in Jesus. Taking scriptures out of context is dangerous, especially if they encourage and attempt to justify spiritual laziness.

If you try to rationalize away the Word of God in an effort to avoid this accountability, you are lazy and you love your sins more than you love God. It is far, far better to repent of your sins and build your relationship with the Holy Spirit than to risk the alternative. The choice is up to you.

Laziness is combated with vision, focus, aggression, and discipline. This requires you to work on it now. Procrastination is not an option. Time is short.

A good start is to get up early enough in the morning to spend time in prayer and Bible reading before taking on other daily responsibilities. If this doesn't work then plan another part of the day. Stay away from activities that contribute to laziness. Watching TV is one of the greatest contributors to laziness. Although in moderation watching TV is okay, it should not be allowed to interfere with one's spiritual growth.

4.4 The Traditions of Man

There is a significant amount of culture and doctrine embedded in the church that has worldly and demonic origins. This is true of virtually all denominations. If the church is to succeed in its God-ordained responsibilities, worldly culture must be replaced with God's culture as defined in God's word and realized through a relationship with Him. Present day culture can be called the "traditions of man."

The traditions of man are some of the most subtle and damaging sins in the church. The traditions of man have the effect of invalidating the simplicity, power, and meaning of God's word. The result is that many other sins are tolerated and allowed into the church.

Bible Reading: Mark 7:5–13

Although the circumstances and culture have changed since Jesus spoke these words, human nature has not. If you look around at the church there is far more tradition ingrained in the church culture than most realize. Jesus' words are still just as valid now as they were when He spoke them!

The traditions of man have become so intertwined with denominational and church doctrines that it can be difficult to discern between the two. How easy it is to adhere to these doctrines rather than the Word of God and at the same time thinking it is all Biblical. We are no different than the Pharisees of Jesus' day. In reality we are worse off today since we have the Holy Spirit and the Pharisees did not. We are more guilty of this sin than the Pharisees!

Churches and denominations simply rationalize away miracles and the various spiritual gifts in general. This heretical rationale is completely inconsistent with scripture, invalidates God's word, and excuses sin and the lack of faith. Adhering to such doctrines is to call God a liar and His Word, the Bible, a lie. Because these people have refused to believe the Bible, God has largely withdrawn His presence from these churches. As a result, their teachings are hollow and without power and anointing.

In another example, there are many churches that advertise themselves as "New Testament" churches. To adhere only to the teachings of the New Testament and ignore the Old Testament is heresy. You can't have the New without the Old because the New is founded upon and builds upon the Old. The New cannot be understood without the knowledge, wisdom, and instruction the Old provides.

A simple case in point is the early church we read about primarily in the book of Acts. At this point in history, what we know as the New Testament today didn't exist. Early Christians only had the Old Testament—the Law and the Prophets, or Tanakh. The early church culture was founded upon Judaism because it was a natural progression since Jesus fulfilled the redemption plan. Several hundred years later, a cultural divide occurred that resulted in the present-day church culture. Look at the early church and you will see how God moved in His people to heal the sick, deliver those in bondage, work myriads of miracles, and advance the church. There is nothing but our sins to prevent the church from making this happening today.

When discussing God's 'law' it must be understood that this does not just include the New Testament. All scripture in the New Testament is written with the understanding that the reader has a solid understanding of the Old Testament. Those churches who proclaim they are 'New Testament' churches are only deceiving themselves into thinking they are more righteous and attractive to the world than those who don't adhere to this false doctrine.

The view that the teachings of the Torah are burdensome laws is a stand born out of ignorance and the spirit of rebellion. Virtually all of the Torah points to Jesus and is for our benefit. It defines the boundaries of behavior we should keep. Many will argue that, as Christians, we have the Holy Spirit and don't need to follow the teachings of the Torah. If this were not so, then God would not have ordained the Torah to be part of the Bible today. Others will quote Matthew:

Bible Reading: Matthew 5:17–19

Jesus <u>fulfilled</u> the Law and the Prophets (Old Testament, or Tanakh), and that is the plan of redemption that was initiated in Genesis 3:15. He <u>did not</u> abolish the Law and the Prophets. Therefore, the Law and the Prophets still stand just as much as they did thousands of years ago. In this passage, Jesus said nothing concerning what it meant by fulfilling the Law and the Prophets. Rather, He focused on the fact that nothing in the Law and the Prophets has been abolished. He also provides a stern warning to those who would teach otherwise. Sadly, there are many today that teach doctrines that are quite contrary to Scripture.

Much could be written concerning the extent of what we should practice today. This has been debated for generations and the subject is beyond the scope of this book. Suffice it to say, there is a lot more we should be doing when it pertains to keeping His commandments. The God-ordained holidays and festivals written of in the Torah are not just empty religious practices, but serve as continual reminders of who Jesus is and of His plan of redemption. Hence, when it comes to keeping His commandments, we would do well to celebrate His holidays and festivals. Not only does applying this head knowledge to physical action help solidify God's statutes in our hearts and minds, it also builds faith (Romans 10:17). This physical association is the same principle introduced in this book for effective prayer. Keeping His commandments should be a joy to the believer and not considered burdensome. God's Word, in its entirety, is the best source for learning about our Lord and Savior.

The Christian church started as a natural progression of Judaism. It was early in this era that pagan doctrines were allowed to take hold resulting in a cultural divide that we have with us today. Constantine (272–337) and others during this era are the primary cause of this rift. The church must take note of, and return to its roots.

The danger in the false interpretation of Matthew 5:17–19 is this: Many say that in fulfilling the plan of redemption, Jesus did everything so all we need to do is sit back and enjoy the ride to heaven. They contend that the Old Testament "laws" have little relevance today. In one sentence of misinterpretation, the Old Testament and the Torah in particular are abolished from church vocabulary. This interpretation is one of the most dangerous and there are many scriptures that warn against this. There are many passages that warn against altering scripture.

Bible Reading: Deuteronomy 4:2, 12:1, 28, 32; Revelation 22:18–19

Some people refuse to accept their responsibilities because they expect Jesus to return at any moment. They do little more than sit back and wait for His return thinking there is no sense in wasting effort to accomplish anything. This lazy attitude is indicative of the worthless slave Jesus spoke of in the parable of the talents (See Section 5.2).

Doctrines and teachings that fail to teach the substance of faith, or that excuse the lack of faith, ignore priestly responsibilities and many other things of this nature, are heresy. Those who teach these doctrines come under the judgment described in the scriptures above. We must all be careful to take God at His Word and obey it with all diligence. Christianity is not a hobby.

Bible Reading: Matthew 24:44–46

Biblical prophecies are being fulfilled around the world at an unprecedented rate, but we simply do not know when He will return. There is a clear benefit in knowing the signs of the times but our primary focus should be on being ready. Until that hour, we need to be busy fulfilling our mission.

Bible Reading: 2 Timothy 2:15

2 Timothy 2:15 indicates this work takes education and application. Other scriptures indicate that we as Christians have responsibilities to fulfill. The church is asleep and the world is going to hell but few seem to notice or care enough to take their God-given responsibilities seriously enough to do something about it.

Bible Reading: 2 Timothy 3:16–17

Scripture must be studied *in its entirety*, not just portions taken out of context to suit someone's or some church's doctrine (tradition).

People by nature enjoy traditions. Traditions are a familiar pattern of behavior that are generally enjoyable and perhaps offer a sense of security. Traditions eventually become an integral part of a culture. It makes much more sense to enjoy the traditions and practices God has provided in His Word because they have a distinct purpose, and are by definition, of Godly origin. They not only edify but educate. They are designed to keep one focused on their relationship with Him. Man's traditions will inevitably have the effect of invalidating Scripture and denying the knowledge, education, and experience it was intended to accomplish.

> *Layers of analogy, symbolism, ritual, and metaphor serve only to obfuscate the simplicity and power of the Gospel.*

Religious practices should be limited to what is defined in Scripture. Anything outside this will only distract from what really needs to be focused on, and that is relationship with Jesus.

The importance of the following points cannot be emphasized enough.

In a nutshell, they describe the process of how to get to the level where all of us need to be so God's will is fulfilled in the church. These steps are not a one-time process. They need to be repeated as often as necessary because of our sinful nature.

1. Repentance removes the wall between you and God (Isaiah 59:2).
2. Humility opens the door to the Holy Spirit and to answered prayer.
3. Prayer builds your relationship with Jesus.
4. Building your relationship with Jesus builds faith.
5. Faith comes by hearing and hearing by the word of God (Romans 10:17; Galatians 3:5). Faith comes through education and practice of His Word.
6. Again, faith is built with prayer, prayer, prayer, and practice, practice, practice (James 2:17).
7. Faith brings the anointing and empowerment from the Holy Spirit to go out and make disciples of all the nations (Matthew 28:18–20). Miracles will be worked through you wherever you go. The glory of God will rest on you to a degree beyond your comprehension.

Bible Reading: Jeremiah 29:11–13

4.4.1 The Blood of Jesus

Many Christians traditionally use the phrase 'blood of Jesus' to spiritually cleanse this or that, to heal, to protect, to signify the forgiveness of sins, etc. Since the Holy Spirit is who actually accomplishes the task, just ask Him to do it. The phrase 'blood of Jesus' has been used since around the second century AD but this longevity doesn't make its usage correct. In the New Testament, the 'blood of Jesus' invariably refers to Jesus' perfect sacrifice for sins, and the completion and perfection of the Father's redemption plan accomplished through Him. When people use the 'blood of Jesus', they are invoking the terms of the covenant that was fulfilled through Jesus' sacrifice on the cross. There is nothing in Scripture that refers to the 'blood of Jesus' as a distinct power or energy that can be used as a tool.

The closest the phrase 'blood of Jesus' appears to indicate something other than the fulfillment of the redemption plan is found in Revelation 7:14 and 12:11. It is possible the use of this phrase originated from these two verses. Nevertheless, it is still indicative of the fulfillment of the redemption plan. The perspective is a little different, and perhaps confusing, in Revelation than elsewhere in scripture because it is the only book of the Bible that is written about spiritual matters from a spiritual point of view. The rest of the Bible is written about both physical and spiritual matters from a mostly physical point of view.

Jesus made it clear that He would provide us with the Holy Spirit as a helper and He never said anything about giving us His blood to be used as a tool. Because of this misunderstanding on part of the church, many people have viewed Christianity as a bloody religion and have rejected it.

The use of 'the blood of Jesus' is a distraction from what we are to focus on, and that is relationship with the Jesus. A thing doesn't protect, heal, or cleanse—Jesus does.

Although people have been using this phrase for generations, often to great effect, the usage is incorrect. It is effective because Jesus understands what His people are requesting to be done and He answers. What sense does it make then to request a thing to do something when you can easily go directly to Jesus and ask Him? Focusing on or placing faith in the blood of Jesus rather than Jesus Himself is a form of idolatry.

Sadly, there are many more rituals, metaphors, analogies, "mysteries", and such used by some denominations rather than going directly to Jesus. As was said earlier, such doctrines serve only to obfuscate the power and simplicity of the Gospel, and hence your relationship with Jesus.

4.5   The Deceptive Nature of Wealth

Once people discover the wonderful blessings God has for them, there is a tendency to use prayer for selfish gain, and consequently lose sight of their mission. This is a trap. The "prosperity doctrine" preached in a number of churches is clear evidence that many have fallen into this trap. The lure and deception of wealth can lead us to take our eyes off Jesus.

There is nothing wrong with wealth and possessions. The love of wealth and possessions is what gets people in trouble. God's desire is to bless His people and He often does so in miraculous ways. However, there is so much more He wants to give us. I have personally known people whom God blessed with wealth but unfortunately, they were not able to deal with it properly and eventually fell into great ruin. On the other hand, those who were prepared to receive wealth did well and continued to prosper once it came their way. This also points to the need for wisdom.

We all need to have an income to provide for our families and to meet the obligations we have. Scripture is clear that our Lord will take care of us. Perhaps the most notable passage is found in the Sermon on The Mount in Matthew.

Bible Reading: Matthew 6:24–34; Psalms 37:3–11

In Matthew 6:33 we see that seeking Him first and foremost is imperative. One is truly in a position to receive wealth and prosperity when their relationship with Jesus transcends the desire for worldly things. When someone reaches this point, only then will they see worldly things in their proper perspective (Philippians 3:8). The surpassing value of knowing Jesus makes the things of this world as nothing but filth in comparison. Many may agree with this because the head knowledge is simple. Self dies hard so getting it into the heart can be much more difficult. It must be experienced, and often through trials and tribulations.

Bible Reading: James 4:3–4

If priorities and motives are not correct, scripture is clear that this is adulterous. No one is perfect and we all fail (Romans 3:23). Don't forget that He created us all. He understands us better than we understand ourselves. Very few, if any, people have these priorities in perfect order. Our Lord Jesus has promised to take care of us. This is without question. Of course, if someone does something foolish, they should expect to experience the consequences for what they did. In all these things we should press toward that upward call (Philippians 3:14). In so doing, remember what the Apostle Paul wrote in 2 Timothy 2:13:

If we are faithless, He remains faithful, for He cannot deny Himself.

—2 Timothy 2:13 (NASB)

Our Lord will make a way where there seems to be no way! Praise God!

CHAPTER 5

God's Warnings

We must all keep in mind that our Lord is righteous, just, reasonable, loving, merciful, holy, and so on. He is perfect in all His ways. Because He is perfect, the boundaries between all of His characteristics do not change as they do with people. God's mercy and love are beyond human comprehension. The fact that Jesus paid the price for sin once and for all should not be perceived as a license to sin. Taking His grace and forgiveness for granted is dangerous.

2 Corinthians 5:10 makes it clear that this is an individual judgment and that Christians will be judged for both the good and the bad. We are each individually responsible for our actions in this life.

Bible Reading: Hebrews 10:26–31

Knowing these things, how much more diligent should you be in your relationship with Him? How much more should you pray to overcome the sins that so easily beset you?

Bible Reading: Hebrews 12:1–2

Although there are many places throughout the Bible that discuss the blessings of obedience and the curses of disobedience (the most notable is Deuteronomy 28), the focus here is on Matthew 25.

Matthew 25:1–30[2] presents two parables. The first in verses 1–13 is the

---

[2] All verses cited in this chapter are from the NASB unless otherwise noted.

parable of the ten virgins. The second in verses 14–30 is the parable of the talents. Both parables are linked even though they present different stories. The first describes the nature of the judgment and the second describes the conditions that bring about judgment.

In the first parable, Jesus used the term *virgin* to indicate the church. This is because the wedding supper of the Lamb has not taken place yet. Virgin is also used to indicate His bride is clean and spotless, and sins have been forgiven and washed away. Regardless of this wonderful outcome, each and every one of us must be careful to work out our salvation (Philippians 2:12).

Both parables present the expectation of a fearful judgment upon those who fail to attend to their relationship with Jesus. Christians often don't take their relationship with Him or the possibility of such a judgment seriously. Indeed, many churches and denominational doctrines fail to adequately address this issue. Whether you agree with the theology or not is not the issue. Your relationship with Jesus and where it is going is the issue. If your choice is to keep one foot in the world and one foot in the church then you are treading on thin ice. Are you simply seeking fire insurance or do you want to build your relationship with Him and fulfill His commandments?

Bible Reading: Joshua 24:14–15

5.1 The Parable of the Ten Virgins

Bible Reading: Matthew 25:1–13

Verse 1: *Then the kingdom of heaven will be comparable to ten virgins, who took their lamps and went out to meet the bridegroom.*

Verse one establishes who our Lord is speaking about: the kingdom of heaven. He is not talking about the kingdom of darkness, the kingdom of this world, those who are not saved, or the domain of the devil. The kingdom of heaven may be considered the subjects of God's kingdom taken collectively. The kingdom of heaven is the church.

The ten virgins represent Christians. They do not represent any other group of people. In Greek, the word *parthenos* (παρΘένος) for "virgin" is from the root for "separated". As evidenced by many scriptures, we are to be separate from the world.

An important note is that Jesus stated <u>twice</u> who He is speaking about. He is speaking about the church both collectively and to each of us as individuals. The fact that a subject is addressed multiple times in scripture like this is cause for us to take due notice of it and to treat it with the highest level of importance.

Each of the virgins had a lamp. The lamp itself represents the physical body, and the oil represents the Holy Spirit who resides within.

Each of these virgins went out to meet the bridegroom. Clearly, they knew Him and were expecting Him to arrive, otherwise there would be no reason to go out to meet Him.

Verse 2: *Five of them were foolish, and five were prudent.*

This verse tells us that five of these ten virgins were wise and five were foolish—that's 50% wise and 50% foolish. This 50% factor is found elsewhere in scripture in Matthew 24:30–41 and in Luke 17:34–36. **This means only 50% of the people who call themselves Christians will be ready and hence only 50% will be taken!** Oh, that we would pay attention to His Word and be ready for His return! Again, understand that God is not arbitrary about anything He says or does.

Verses 3 and 4: *For when the foolish took their lamps, they took no oil with them, but the prudent took oil in flasks along with their lamps.*

The foolish represent those Christians that, spiritually speaking, live payday to payday. They are not new Christians but are still in their spiritual diapers, and should be more advanced in their relationship with Jesus than they are. These are people that go to church to just get their "spiritual batteries recharged," and think of church more in terms of social opportunities than in opportunities for growth. They are mediocre Christians who are still living on the milk of the word (Hebrews 5:12–14).

The wise are those who actively pursue the things of God. They are filled with the Holy Spirit and are actively building their relationship with Jesus, and fulfilling their God-ordained responsibilities. They are doing their part in fulfilling the Great Commission.

Verse 5: *Now while the bridegroom was delaying, they all got drowsy and began to sleep.*

We see here the bridegroom was delayed. The church became drowsy and went to sleep. Letters to the seven churches in Revelation chapter 3 indicate that we live in the age of the church of Laodicea, which was neither hot nor cold. Today's church to a great extent, is either lukewarm or sound asleep. It is not awake and alert to the world events that are fulfilling Biblical prophecy right in front of their eyes. Tragically, it is not the moving force in society that it once was, and is not ready to meet Jesus. Although some Christians recognize the signs of the times, they do nothing to be ready. Churches don't notice the moving of the Holy Spirit to repent of their sins and prepare for His return to take His bride. They hear words spoken that God wants to bring revival but they do nothing except sit around and wait for something to happen. Those who hear the words from God that He wants to bring revival do little, if anything, to make it happen. This is the apostasy.

> But prove yourselves doers of the word, and not merely hearers who delude themselves.
>
> —James 1:22 (NASB)

Verse 6: *But at midnight there was a shout, 'Behold, the bridegroom! Come out to meet him.'*

There is an announcement that the bridegroom, Jesus, is coming and the Church should go out to meet Him. This verse indicates:

1. Some form of announcement from heaven will be made. Attentiveness is important since the mechanism by which this announcement will be made is not discussed.

2. It will come at a time few expect so being prepared for this to happen at any moment is important.

3. There will only be a very short period of time between the announcement and the arrival of the bridegroom.

This event presents the final opportunity for the church to be ready.

Verse 7: *Then all those virgins rose and trimmed their lamps.*

The entire church arises and trims their lamps. The act of trimming is done so a lamp will burn its brightest. From a spiritual standpoint, the act of trimming is an act of repentance and prayer for forgiveness of any remaining sins and for the infilling of the Holy Spirit. Those who are already filled with the Spirit will be ready. Those who are not filled with the Spirit will not be able to complete this task. Again, there will only be a very short period of time to complete this.

Verses 8 and 9: *The foolish said to the prudent, 'Give us some of your oil, for our lamps are going out.' But the prudent answered, 'No, there will not be enough for us and you too; go instead to the dealers and buy some for yourselves.'*

The foolish have run out of oil. The reason the wise cannot provide any of their oil is because it will take time. It will take work to minister to the foolish. It will drain them spiritually at a time when they can least afford it. The wise tell the foolish to go out to the dealers to buy some. The dealers are pastors and teachers. Purchasing is an act that requires them to make payment for something. That payment is their self, will, and lives. We must die to self and allow Jesus to sit on the throne of our lives. Through this daily surrender, prayer, repentance, asking forgiveness, ministering to others, we become filled with the

Holy Spirit. Through these activities one's relationship with Jesus is built. All of this takes time and effort and the foolish are out of time.

Verse 10: *And while they were going away to make the purchase, the bridegroom came, and those who were ready went in with him to the wedding feast; and the door was shut.*

While the foolish were out working on the process of being filled with the Holy Spirit, the bridegroom arrived. Those who were ready went with him. In the words John Gill [6],

> "and they that were ready; not by a mere profession of religion, or submission to Gospel ordinances, or by an external righteousness, or negative holiness, and abstinence from the grosser sins of life, or an outward humiliation for them, or by a dependence on the absolute mercy of God; but through being clothed with the wedding garment, washed in the blood of Christ, being regenerated and sanctified, and having the oil of grace in their hearts, a spiritual knowledge of Christ, faith in him, and interest in him: such are ready for every good work, and to give a reason of their faith and hope, to confess Christ, and suffer for his sake; and are ready for death and eternity, and to meet the bridegroom, and for the marriage of the Lamb, to enter into the new Jerusalem."

The foolish were not there. These are the ones who hold to a form of righteousness but deny its power. They were left behind. The door to heaven and the wedding feast of the Lamb is shut.

Verses 11 through 13: *[11]Later the other virgins also came, saying, "Lord, lord, open up for us." [12]But he answered, "Truly I say to you, I do not know you." [13]Be on the alert then, for you do not know the day nor the hour.*

When the foolish arrived, they knocked on the doors of heaven asking to be let in. In verse 12, Jesus issues a most alarming statement. He says, "Truly I say to you, I do not know you." Whether we think Jesus will return for us now or in a thousand years, we do not know. We are therefore instructed to be ready at all times. Knowing the surpassing value of knowing Jesus, why wouldn't any born again Christian want to know Him even better? Those Christians who don't know the love of Christ that surpasses all knowledge, who are not filled up to all the fullness of God, or know the fellowship of His sufferings being conformed to His death, simply don't know Him. Jesus wants this intimate relationship with us that surpasses any human description. Through this relationship the things of this world will be viewed as filth in comparison (Philippians 3:8–11).

The importance of these three verses cannot be overstated. Since it is evident this parable is speaking of the church, what kind of life should you be living? For those who hear the words, "Truly I say to you, I do not know you," what is to become of them? They will pay a terrible price for their mediocrity.

Only God knows the dividing line between the foolish and the wise. Those who are wise will make sure they are actively working on their relationship with Jesus.

Revelation 20:4 speaks of a multitude of martyrs who were beheaded for their faith in Christ. For some time now, there have been rumors floating around about the manufacture and distribution of guillotines in the United States. The Canadian government's official acquisition website requested bids for the manufacture of hydraulic guillotines in May 2020[3]. Based on this information, one could reasonably expect these types of activities to be taking place in other parts of the world.

Christians must repent of their sins now and pray for revival now!! Living a mediocre life is unacceptable. Jesus died on the cross for you. He paid a terrible price for your sins. All eternity is before you and in view of this, what is hindering you from pushing forward? How can you neglect so great a salvation? How can you take salvation with such a cavalier attitude? Indeed, to do so is to spit on the cross on which Jesus died.

Only 50% of the church will be considered acceptable to our Lord and make it to the wedding supper of the Lamb. What priority should

---

[3] See the Canadian government acquisition website https://buyandsell.gc.ca/procurement-data/tender-notice/PW-PD-005-78707. The Canadian government solicitation number is 45045-190091/A. See also https://www.naturalnews.com/2020-11-15-canadian-government-publishes-bid-request-for-programmable-hydraulic-guillotines-covid-19.html for more information.

you place on your relationship with Him? Are the worldly things you deal with every day more important to you than your salvation? Your actions speak louder than words!

In Philippians 3 Paul stresses we are to press forward. The word *press* is extremely important here. From Webster [1] it means:

1. To urge with force or weight; a word of extensive use, denoting the application of any power, physical or moral, to something that is to be moved or affected. We press the ground with the feet when we walk; we press the couch on which we repose; we press substances with the hands, fingers or arms; the smith presses iron with his vise; we are pressed with the weight of arguments or of cares, troubles and business.
2. To drive with violence; to hurry; as, to press a horse in motion, or in a race.

And then again in Philippians 2:12,

> So then, my beloved, just as you have always obeyed, not as in my presence only, but now much more in my absence, work out your salvation with fear and trembling;

> —Philippians 2:12 (NASB)

There is no excuse. God has provided an incredible store of resources today, starting with the Bible. The internet is tremendously valuable and can provide resources that only a few years ago were not available or only available at significant cost, and likely only found in a pastor's library. The church is without excuse. Today is the day of salvation. Everyone must repent of their sins now. Get your eyes off the things of the world and focus on your Lord Jesus Christ. The things of this world, wealth, houses, whatever, are nothing compared to knowing Jesus. Build your relationship with Him. When you do this and experience Him, nothing else will matter in comparison. You will enter into that state of Victory which is beautiful beyond description. When you accomplish these things:

- Miracles, healing, signs, and wonders will be manifest through you.
- The world will take notice and seek you to be blessed and get what you have.
- You will store up treasures in heaven that cannot rust or be stolen.
- Your joy will be full.

The spiritual warfare that we go through now is not an end in itself, it is a means to an end.

There are those who will say, "I don't agree with your theology and this is why, blah, blah, blah... ." My response is, "Oh, so it's easier for you to argue theology than repent of your sins? Truly you love your sins more than you love God."

There are those who will say, "I get up at four every morning and spend two hours praying and reading the Bible, and I spend three days a week fasting. I do this and that and so on... ." My response to this is, "Oh, so you would rather justify yourself than repent of your sins? Truly you love your sins more than you love God."

Some will cite John 10:27–29 which says,

> [27]"My sheep hear My voice, and I know them, and they follow Me; [28]and I give eternal life to them, and they will never perish; and no one will snatch them out of My hand. [29]"My Father, who has given them to Me, is greater than all; and no one is able to snatch them out of the Father's hand.
>
> —John 10:27–29 (NASB)

This is often used as justification for the doctrine of the eternal security of the believer. Without looking any further than just this verse, Jesus stated that no one is able to snatch them out of the Father's hand.

> He who overcomes will thus be clothed in white garments; and I will not erase his name from the book of life, and I will confess his name before My Father and before His angels.
>
> —Revelation 3:5 (NASB)

These verses from John and Revelation make it clear that Jesus has the authority to erase or to not erase someone's name from the book of life. No created being or thing has this authority or ability to do this. Don't forget what Revelation 3:16 says.

> So because you are lukewarm, and neither hot nor cold, I will spit you out of My mouth.

—Revelation 3:16 (NASB)

Those who are lukewarm will be rejected by Jesus. Let me say this again. *Those who are lukewarm will be rejected by Jesus.* Remember, God created us and gave us a free will. Your free will never goes away and you still have the right to choose whom you will follow. Scripture is clear that there are people who have turned away and "gone back to Egypt."

Bible Reading: Matthew 13:20–21; Mark 4:5–6; Luke 8:14; Acts 7:39

Why is it easier for you to make an excuse of some form rather than repent of your sins? It is because you love your sins more than you love God.

> If you love Me, you will keep My commandments.

—John 14:15 (NASB)

All of us have the flesh and the world to deal with so be diligent with repentance and seeking forgiveness from our Father in heaven through Jesus Christ our Savior. Be diligent about pressing forward in your walk with Jesus. God proclaimed that we are to be a holy people. This is not an option for the Christian, but a requirement.

Every Christian has a narrow path to walk and cannot afford to be distracted to the left or the right. Stay focused on Jesus Christ. If you veer either way you will be snagged by the things of the world, and these things will do nothing but cause injury and hinder your progress. Run the race in order to win the prize. We are not in competition with each other, but with the flesh and the things of the world—the lust of the flesh, the lust of the eyes, and the boastful pride of life. The purpose of the race is to overcome the world and to be righteous and holy so Jesus will be pleased with you. Those who are running this race, regardless of their present spiritual level, will cross the finish line and win. Those who are asleep will fail.

Where do you stand? What are you going to do about it? What is your choice in view of all eternity set before you?

Will you be like those Jesus spoke of in Luke 14:16–24 who made all sorts of excuses and thus failed to enter in?

5.2 The Parable of the Talents

Bible Reading: Matthew 25:14–30

In this parable, there are three categories of people.

1. A servant who was given five talents and earned five more.
2. A servant who was given two talents and earned two more.
3. A servant who was given one talent and buried it out of fear of his master.

All these servants have the same master and were given talents according to their abilities. Each had equal opportunities to bring increase. The third servant recognized some important and deep, but partial, understanding of the nature of God. The devil does not have this understanding nor can he imitate it. This parable is not talking about the unsaved, it is about Christians.

The demise of the third and unfaithful slave is fearful. It is so horrible it may seem that he never knew Jesus as Lord and Savior. But in order to be consistent with other scriptures, he apparently did. Some of the perceived characteristics the slave had are contrary to Jesus' true character. If this slave had a true understanding of what it means to reap where he didn't sow, he would have fallen on his face before God in praise and worship. The state of this third slave points to ignorance and lack of relationship with Jesus. We would all do well to steer clear of this situation and be as productive as possible with the gifts God has given us!

Interestingly, the phrase, "weeping and gnashing of teeth" occurs several times in the Gospels and is associated with people being sent to the furnace of fire or the outer darkness. The "weeping and gnashing of teeth" indicates two distinct groups of people. Those who are weeping are those who thought they would make heaven and didn't. Those who are gnashing their teeth are those who are wicked and full of hatred and anger toward God. They blame Him for their predicament.

This parable in Matthew uses money to illustrate the principles that are presented. Not everyone has money or other material possessions from which to apply these principles. The one thing that everyone does have is a level of relationship with Jesus and gifts from the Holy Spirit. It is the building of this relationship and the various things that outflow from it that bring reward (Matthew 6:19–20). Relationship with Jesus is the primary thing that will bring reward but certainly not the only. Each of us is given certain gifts and resources and how we use these will also determine our reward.

God's warnings to us don't stop here. Let's look at the letter to the church in Laodicea from Revelation again.

Bible Reading: Revelation 3:14–22

The focus here is the lukewarm state of the church. The thought of being spewed out the mouth of our Lord and Savior because of the failure to grow is horrible and fearful. To be completely and utterly rejected by our Lord is fearful indeed. The end result is to be sent to hell and eventually the lake of fire. People fail is because they love their sins more than they love God.

Sin is the worst form of insanity as outlined in Hebrews 10:26–31 cited at the beginning of this chapter.

Unfortunately, all have sinned willfully and will suffer loss on judgment day. Nevertheless, we must press forward and not back (Philippians 3:12–14). The Bible must be taken seriously. The Word of God must become your life-blood. The Bible holds the keys to life and death so it is critically important that it be put into practice in our daily lives. Don't lose heart but endure to the end.

As Paul says in the book of Philippians:

> [13]Brethren, I do not regard myself as having laid hold of it yet; but one thing I do: forgetting what lies behind and reaching forward

to what lies ahead, [14]I press on toward the goal for the prize of the upward call of God in Christ Jesus.

—Philippians 3:13–14 (NASB)

Throughout scripture it is clear that our Lord has given us all the resources necessary to excel and be victorious. In the letter to the church of Laodicea Jesus gives us the way out.

Jesus advises us to buy gold refined by fire from Him. What is this gold refined by fire written about in Revelation 3:18? Gold represents the substance of one's relationship with Jesus and its value to Him. The evidence of this is the fruit of the Spirit as described in Galatians 5:22–23.

[22]But the fruit of the Spirit is love, joy, peace, patience, kindness, goodness, faithfulness, [23]gentleness, self-control; against such things there is no law.

—Galatians 5:22–23 (NASB)

The refining by fire represents the efforts, trails, and tribulations we go through to facilitate our growth discussed in James 1:2–4.

[2]Consider it all joy, my brethren, when you encounter various trials, [3]knowing that the testing of your faith produces endurance. [3]And let endurance have its perfect result, so that you may be perfect and complete, lacking in nothing.

—James 1:2–4 (NASB)

Where you are is important but it is not as important as where you are going! Push toward the upward call of God in Christ Jesus!

Bible Reading: Ephesians 3:14–21

The door to victory is open wide. There is nothing but your own decisions keeping you from entering in.

Bible Reading: Hebrews 12:1–2

CHAPTER 6

The Importance of Relationship

Your relationship with the Holy Spirit is the most important part of your life. From this relationship you are able to fulfill your God-ordained responsibilities, and you are blessed in a multitude of ways, including many that are unseen. People often focus on all the benefits of salvation rather than the responsibilities that come with it. This is humanism, and humanism is sin. Everyone must take their relationship with Him seriously. The mindset of sitting in a pew to bask in the Son to get a Son tan while waiting for His return is completely unacceptable.

Getting where you need to be in your relationship with the Holy Spirit is impossible without the repentance of sins and obedience to God. Likewise, it is impossible to enter into the victory and promised land that Jesus has for you unless you are obedient to His Word and build your relationship with Him. Church and denominational doctrines (the traditions of man) have so clouded the understanding of the role the church is supposed to have in society that few have recognized where the sins are, and have lost the vision we are all supposed to pursue. The failure to repent and be obedient to God's Word will result in persecution, death, and slavery. These things are already on the increase around us today. This problem can only be solved by using *God's way* and not man's way.

Apart from a move by the Holy Spirit, many simply will not wake up until it's too late. Circumstances will get to the point of persecution, death, and slavery, and people will see it coming and still do nothing. All Christians must take their responsibilities seriously. Remember the saying, "An ounce of prevention is worth a pound of cure."

You can't build your relationship with Jesus by warming a pew, sitting in front of the TV, or by being passive about it. You must go forward and not look back as Lot's wife did. Living in a comfort zone is living in defeat. If you think you are okay where you are, you are not and are deceived by the devil. You are right where he wants you. Don't forget you are here on this earth for only a very short time. What are you doing with the time God has given you?

For example, many people invest considerable resources (money, time, effort, etc.) to learn and develop a career so they can be productive and provide financial security for themselves and their families. Although this is needed and has an obvious benefit, it is temporal. The importance of investing resources to your relationship with Jesus knowing the consequences are eternal can't be overstated.

Church is not a place for religious entertainment. First and foremost, church is a house of prayer.

Bible Reading: Isaiah 56:7

Secondly, church is a place of education.

Bible Reading: Ephesians 4:11–13; James 3:1

Pastors and teachers have the God-ordained responsibility to equip (educate and anoint) the saints for the work of service and to the building up of the body of Christ. The saints have the responsibility to apply their teachings. These verses in Ephesians are a high-level description that covers a wide range of responsibilities on the part of the congregation. Responsibilities include doing the things that Jesus did such as laying hands on the sick so they are healed, delivering those in bondage (deliverance from demons), and proclaiming the Gospel, to name a few. An important point to make is that pastors and teachers are responsible for the education and anointing of people for the purpose of becoming pastors and teachers. They are to go out to start new churches and repeat the whole process again and again.

In order for people to be adequately prepared, they must also be taught to learn from the Holy Spirit, and to not rely fully on the teachings of others (John 14:26). The teachings of others can only go so far.

> [4]And my speech and my preaching was not with enticing words of man's wisdom, but in **demonstration of the Spirit and of power**: [5]That your faith should not stand in the wisdom of men, but in the power of God.
>
> —1 Corinthians 2:4–5 (NASB)

The above verses from 1 Corinthians are very important. Without the power of God being demonstrated through people, faith will fall primarily on the wisdom of men. Such a situation is doomed to fail because it is incorrectly founded. Christians must grow to the point that the power of God is worked through them so that faith will manifest and grow. Without the fulfillment of these verses the church is a laughingstock and an epic failure.

The church is a place for many other things as well. It is a place of worship, a focal point of the community and all the ministries that proceed from it. The two key tasks (prayer and education) discussed above are often easily ignored, and are the most important. Without prayer and education, the other ministries will never succeed to any significant degree.

In 1 Corinthians 2:4–5, Paul makes it clear that he used "demonstration of the Spirit and of power" to build up the body of Christ, and as a means to educate the people in the way they should be living.

A point that needs to be made clear is that the demonstration of the power of God, which includes performing various miracles, signs, and wonders, and proclaiming the Gospel, all go together with all other aspects, offices, and capacities of who we are as Christians. To go out and proclaim the Gospel without the power of God to back up the words appears weak, foolish, and empty. Many of the people who don't know Jesus have an instinctual understanding of this and laugh at the church.

> *Words alone become the subject of debate but words with actions are irrefutable.*

The importance of growing in Jesus to the point that the Holy Spirit is able to manifest power through His people goes beyond anything that can be comprehended.

Bible Reading: 2 Timothy 1:7; 1 Corinthians 4:20; 2 Corinthians 12:9

From a worldly viewpoint, the realization of a lifestyle of demonstration of the Spirit and power appears daunting. People need to get their eyes off the limitations of the world and get their eyes on the greatness of God. After all, the Holy Spirit is our helper and He alone can perform these miracles, not people. No amount of piety on part of the Christian will ever bring about even the smallest miracle. It is all about Jesus and your relationship with him. Prayer is the moving force for growing in Christ to the point that these things become a lifestyle and common occurrence.

Getting where you need to be in your relationship with Jesus so that all these things will come to pass is **simple**. There is nothing complicated about this but it does take work.

Growing in Jesus has its risks. There are dangers, trials, tribulations, spiritual warfare, and so on, but more importantly, immeasurable rewards. The last thing the devil wants is a Christian that knows who they are in Christ and exercises power and authority. This is a power and authority that he has no means to conquer. Are you willing to take that step of faith on a daily basis and develop your relationship with the Lord of Lords and King of Kings? You will never get there by living in a comfort zone. Indeed, there are plenty of dire warnings in scripture concerning a lax and cavalier attitude. Remember, everything you say and do in this life has eternal consequences.

6.1 The Holy Spirit

The Holy Spirit is the most misunderstood, neglected, and ignored person of the Trinity. Often, people treat Him like a thing rather than a person. This attitude not only grieves Him but it is insulting and sinful. It also points to a lack of understanding about this relationship.

- Jesus is the Holy Spirit is the Father.
- The key to an anointed life is intimacy with the Holy Spirit.
- The key to realizing the points of spiritual growth presented in Chapter 10 is intimacy with the Holy Spirit.
- The key to accomplishing the things Jesus did, and more, as a normal lifestyle, is intimacy with the Holy Spirit.
- The key to fulfilling the Great Commission *in the way Jesus intended* is intimacy with the Holy Spirit.

This intimate relationship with the Holy Spirit must be closer than with anyone else, regardless of who they may be.

Bible Reading: Psalms 139:17; James 4:8; 1 Thessalonians 5:16–19

In James 4:8, we are instructed to draw near to God. Only then will He draw near to us. The Holy Spirit is more passionate about having an intimate relationship with His people than anyone can possibly understand. This intimacy will only come about if His people take the initiative to build it. The Holy Spirit is a perfect gentleman and will not force Himself on anyone so it is up to you to initiate the relationship.

Bible Reading: James 4:4–5

In 1 Thessalonians 5:17 we are instructed to pray without ceasing. This is a two-way communication and not a monologue. In verse 19 we are instructed to not quench the Spirit. How do people quench the Holy Spirit? Although the lack of prayer plays a significant role, refusing to die to self is the greater reason for quenching the Spirit. Quenching the Spirit can also be the result of adhering to the traditions of man. Rather, people need to learn to rely on the teaching of the Holy Spirit which is pure and uncorrupted.

Going back to James 4:8, drawing near is accomplished through communication.

Bible Reading: Acts 1:4–5

Jesus commanded His disciples to not do anything until they were empowered by the Holy Spirit. Of the 500 who witnessed Jesus ascending into heaven and the many more who were by now His disciples, only 120 were obedient. Those 120 were the ones that were filled with and empowered by the Holy Spirit. It should be clear that our Lord takes obedience very seriously.

Bible Reading: Acts 5:32; John 14:15–16

In verse 16, Jesus tells His disciples they will be given the Holy Spirit. Obedience and the receiving of the Holy Spirit are clearly linked. Loving Him and keeping His commandments are requirements for receiving the Holy Spirit. This happens at the point of salvation but it must continue to realize the benefits of a relationship with Him.

How many people today attempt to fulfill the Great Commission without the power of the Holy Spirit operating in their lives? The Holy Spirit should have the freedom to operate through you as He did through Jesus, the disciples, and the early church.

You will never experience the power and intimacy of the Holy Spirit to any appreciable degree as long as you maintain control of your life. You must die to self and put self on the cross. The only life you can live is a surrendered life. There is no other way.

> For whoever wishes to save his life will lose it, but whoever loses his life for My sake and the gospel's will save it.
>
> —Mark 8:35 (NASB)

You must surrender yourself and all that you are and hope to be to your Lord Jesus Christ. Surrendering of self is the top level of obedience written about in Acts 5:32. Surrender does not mean your life will become an empty vacuum. Rather, you will realize the fullness and fruit of the Holy Spirit to a degree never imagined, and understand how much better life really is with Him. The act of continual surrender is a process of growth that will allow the Holy Spirit to have the freedom to provide the anointing He so desires to give you. As you grow, you will experience an intimacy with the Holy Spirit that is precious beyond description. Self dies hard so you must go through trials and tribulations in order to build this state of surrender. Remember, even Jesus as a man learned obedience through the things He suffered (Hebrews 5:8). How much more so should we expect to be subject to trials and tribulations?

> ²Consider it all joy, my brethren, when you encounter various trials, ³knowing that the testing of your faith produces endurance. ⁴And let endurance have its perfect result, so that you may be perfect and complete, lacking in nothing.
>
> —James 1:2–4 (NASB)

Trials and tribulations are a natural process of growth. Rather than fighting against trials and tribulations, work through them with James 1:2–4 in mind.

> The grace of the Lord Jesus Christ, and the love of God, and the **fellowship of the Holy Spirit**, be with you all.
>
> —2 Corinthians 13:14 (NASB)

6.2 The Fear of the Lord

The fear of the Lord is a subject that is largely misunderstood today. There are two primary types of fear. The fear of the Lord and a worldly fear. The word *fear* occurs 400 times in the King James version of the Bible and 313 times in the New American Standard. With this high a number, it is well worth the effort to investigate and study the subject.

> The fear of the LORD is clean, enduring forever; The judgments of the LORD are true; they are righteous altogether.
>
> —Psalms 19:9 (NASB)

The fear of the LORD is the beginning of wisdom; A good understanding have all those who do His commandments; His praise endures forever.

—Psalms 111:10 (NASB)

A worldly fear leads one into rebellion against God (Numbers 14:9, 1 Samuel 12:14). Worldly fear is also an indicator of the lack of faith and hence a lack of relationship with the Holy Spirit.

Webster [1] defines the worldly and Godly fears as:

Worldly fear A painful emotion or passion excited by an expectation of evil, or the apprehension of impending danger. Fear expresses less apprehension than dread, and dread less than terror and fright. The force of this passion, beginning with the most moderate degree, may be thus expressed, fear, dread, terror, fright. Fear is accompanied with a desire to avoid or ward off the expected evil. Fear is an uneasiness of mind, upon the thought of future evil likely to befall us.

Godly fear In scripture, fear is used to express a filial or a slavish passion. In good men, the fear of God is a holy awe or reverence of God and his laws, which springs from a just view and real love of the divine character, leading the subjects of it to hate and shun everything that can offend such a holy being, and inclining them to aim at perfect obedience. This is filial fear.

Rewording this a bit, a holy awe and reverence are the *products* of a Godly fear. Fear is fear, but the distinguishing characteristic is the motivating factor behind it. One way to further understand this better is to review the characteristics of Godly fear.

A Godly fear:

1. Recognizes one's humble and sinful state in comparison to a holy and righteous God.
2. Recognizes that God's impartial and righteous judgment will come upon everyone.
3. Does not take His forgiveness, grace, and mercies for granted.

4. Realizes one's total dependence upon God for His provision, forgiveness, and mercies.
5. Is clean and endures forever.
6. Brings humility.
7. Brings a holy awe and reverence of God to the believer.
8. Hopes for His lovingkindness.
9. Is the beginning of wisdom.
10. Brings the comfort of the Holy Spirit.
11. Provides motivation to live a righteous and holy life.
12. Provides motivation to be obedient to God's commandments.
13. Coexists with a Godly love. From 1 John 4:18, we see that the worldly fear cannot coexist with love.

A Godly fear comes from the realization of these characteristics, especially the first four. Based on this, we are to work out our salvation with fear and trembling as Paul stated in Philippians 2:12.

Godly fear is sorely lacking today. When Godly fear is lacking, the desire and motivation to live a holy and righteous life is also lacking. This opens the door for sin to enter the church and sets the stage for the church to go to sleep and be rendered ineffective by the devil and his lies.

CHAPTER 7

Spiritual Gifts

There are a number of spiritual gifts and offices that are given by the Holy Spirit. All are important to the healthy functioning of a church.

Miracles, signs, and wonders are the signature of the church. Just preaching the Gospel is not enough. They go together. The words of the Gospel need to be backed up with power and demonstration of the Spirit (1 Corinthians 2:4). The unsaved have an almost instinctive knowledge of this so it is understandable why they laugh and mock Christians for their lack of power. Mocking is now turning into persecution since there is no power in the church, and the persecutors operate with impunity because there is no fear of God in them.

Bible Reading: 1 Corinthians 12:27–31

Some clarification concerning the various gifts is necessary. Not everyone has a gift for public service. Just because you may not have a gift in a certain area doesn't mean you don't have the power and authority through Jesus Christ to accomplish whatever the Holy Spirit wants to do through you. Someone who is not in the public service (evangelism, preaching, etc.) also has a critical role in the church. Those in public service need support. Such support encompasses both the physical and the spiritual. The physical support may include financing and logistics. The spiritual support may include prayer for protection and success in their position.

As sons and daughters of God, all Christians have power and authority to accomplish the responsibilities given to them by God. Each is given a spiritual gift that is appropriate for the individual. The Apostle Paul makes it clear that everyone and every gift is important for fulfilling the goal of the Great Commission.

Bible Reading: 1 Peter 4:10; 2 Corinthians 1:20

For example, my gift is to teach. Teaching is an anointing the Holy Spirit has given me and so it is easy and natural to flow in it, and to stand in front of a church or even one person and teach. I don't have the same kind of anointing for healing and so I don't feel as comfortable exercising this. Nevertheless, I still possess the power and authority through Jesus Christ to command healing. I have seen this happen. I just spoke the words and God did the rest. I've had similar experiences with prophecy and words of knowledge.

You don't need to be a spiritual giant for the Holy Spirit to work through you. It's just a matter of a little faith and trust in Him—a childlike faith. As you grow in your relationship with the Holy Spirit you can expect these things to become more commonplace. Trust Him! It's that simple. The devil is the one who deceives people into thinking this is complicated or that you need to be at some spiritual level that is well beyond your reach. We should all work toward the upward call of God and work to live in the promised land.

Another example concerns a friend I worked with some years ago. He wanted the gift of healing. He would take advantage of the ministries in his church as well as any opportunity that arose to pray for someone to be healed. He also kept a log of all the successes and failures so he could monitor his progress. In a very typical scenario, my wife and I were in a restaurant with him and his family after church. He told the waiter that he liked to pray for people and asked if he had any medical problems he would like to be prayed for. The waiter said he had a bad elbow so my friend prayed a simple prayer of healing and asked if anything had changed. Nothing happened. He prayed two more times before the waiter's elbow was healed. In the course of a year of praying for people his success rate increased. Today, he has some absolutely incredible testimonies.

My friend was willing to step out of his comfort zone to pray for people. He never made a big scene out of it either. When we were in the restaurant, the conversation and prayer were all done quietly and without fanfare. It was all tastefully and diplomatically done. No one was put on the spot, embarrassed, or made to feel uncomfortable. I doubt anyone in the adjacent tables was even aware of what was going on. God was glorified that day.

Another principle that is easy to miss is that my friend never pursued his gift of healing to glorify himself. He always made it clear to those who were healed that it was Jesus who healed them. Healing is a powerful witnessing point and opens the door to spreading the Gospel in a way that gets peoples' attention like no other. It is very personal, experiential, and irrefutable.

An important issue to deal with is the fear of failure. Healing is a matter that affects people deeply so learning to deal with fear is important. As my friend did, he simply stated that he liked to pray for people. He never made any promises. This had the effect of minimizing negative reactions on part of the people he prayed for if they didn't get healed. Even though he grieved over the failures where people he prayed for were not healed, he persisted and his persistence paid off. With my case of teaching, there was a time I couldn't stand in front of two people to speak. My pastor pushed me until I stood in front of the whole church to teach a lesson. The more I taught, the easier it became. Now I find it hard to sit in the congregation. I would rather be preaching. On one occasion I conducted a Bible study during lunch at work.

Manifestations of spiritual gifts incorporate an important Biblical principle: "Faith without works is dead." (James 2:20, 26) is the foremost. Just like exercising your muscles to build physical strength takes work, building faith for a particular spiritual gift also takes work. If you want something go after it (Matthew 7:7–8). God is true to His Word. I don't know what my friend's primary spiritual gift is but he wanted the gift of healing so he went after it and God honored his efforts.

Some people and denominations say that some or all of spiritual gifts (healing is the most notable) are not for today or they have passed away. They call God a liar and His Word a lie. These are people who quench the Holy Spirit and refuse to be obedient to His Word.

Bible Reading: Titus 1:6; James 1:16–17

God does not change. People, culture, and societies change but God does not. All that needs to be done on part of the church is to repent and endeavor to grow in Jesus. Failure to do so has dire consequences.

7.1 Finding Your Spiritual Gifts4

Many people struggle with what spiritual gifts they have. Learning your primary spiritual gift will greatly assist you in growing in Jesus and becoming effective in fulfilling your calling. The best way to determine your spiritual gifts is to go to Holy Spirit and the Bible.

No one can fulfill their ministry (at any level or capacity) by their own means. It all comes by way of the Holy Spirit, and He is not arbitrary about the gifts He gives to His people.

> And He has said to me, "My grace is sufficient for you, for power is perfected in weakness." Most gladly, therefore, I will rather boast about my weaknesses, so that the power of Christ may dwell in me.

> —2 Corinthians 12:9 (NASB)

In other words, God's grace and power operate through our weaknesses, leaving no room for boasting on our part, so God gets all the glory.

The three books which give the content for the study of spiritual gifts are 1 Corinthians, Romans, and Ephesians. 1 Corinthians was written from Ephesus in 54 or 55 A.D. Romans was written from Corinth in 56 A.D., and Ephesians was written from Rome in 64 A.D.

Bible Reading: 1 Corinthians 12:4–10, 28; Romans 12:3–6; Ephesians 4:11–12

---

4 This section contains excerpts from the paper *Revelational Ministry* written by George W. Seevers [10]. All cited scripture is from the NASB unless otherwise noted.

When Paul wrote 1 Corinthians from Ephesus, he no doubt shared with the Ephesians as he wrote. It is also highly probable that he shared with the Corinthians what he was writing to the Romans. And also, when Paul wrote the Ephesians from Rome, he must have shared with the Romans as he wrote.

Each of the books outlines different aspects of the spiritual gifts. These include <u>gifts</u>, <u>ministries</u>, and <u>effects</u>. To understand the spiritual gifts as the original recipients of these letters did, we must be aware of what all three of these letters say. The information on spiritual gifts can be brought together as follows:

Gifts 1 Corinthians 12:4, "Now there are a variety of gifts (*charismata*), but the same Spirit." (NASB)

1. ...if **prophesy**, according to the proportion of his faith
2. if **service** in his serving
3. or he who **teaches**, in his teaching
4. or he who **exhorts**, in his exhortation
5. he who **gives**, with liberality
6. he who **leads**, with diligence
7. he who shows **mercy**, with cheerfulness. (Romans 12:6–8)

Ministries 1 Corinthians 12:5, "And there are a variety of ministries (*diakonia*), and the same Lord." (NASB)

1. And He gave some as **apostles**,
2. And some as **prophets**,
3. And some as **evangelists**,
4. And some as **pastors** and **teachers** (Ephesians 4:11),
5. And God has appointed in the church, first **apostles**,
6. Second **prophets**,
7. Third **teachers**,
8. Then **miracles**,
9. Then gifts of **healings**,
10. **Helps**,
11. **Administrations**,
12. Various kinds of **tongues**. (1 Corinthians 12:28)

Effects 1 Corinthians 12:6, "And there are a variety of effects (*energema*), but the same God who works all things in all persons. But to each one is given the manifestation of the Spirit for the common good." (NASB)

1. For to one is given the **word of wisdom** through the Spirit,
2. And to another the **word of knowledge** according to the same Spirit,
3. To another **faith** by the same Spirit,
4. And to another gifts of **healings** by the one Spirit,
5. And to another the effecting of **miracles**,
6. And to another **prophecy**,
7. And to another the **distinguishing of spirits**,
8. To another **various kinds of tongues**,
9. And to another **the interpretation of tongues**.

The main teaching of Romans 12:3–8 is that our spiritual activity ought to correspond to the gifts which we each have received from Jesus. This means that although an individual does have one primary spiritual gift, that gift will be increasingly difficult for an observer to detect as the individual's relationship with Jesus is developed. Nevertheless, an individual will find that his primary spiritual gift is generally descriptive of his new nature, or spiritual nature.

Prophecy Romans 12 verses 6 and 9 present the gift of prophecy.

6. ...if prophecy, according to the proportion of his faith
9. Let love be without hypocrisy. Abhor what is evil, cling to what is good.

Service Romans 12 verses 7a and 10 present the gift of service.

7a. if service, in his serving;
10. Be devoted to one another in brotherly love; give preference to one another in honor;

Teaching Romans 12 verses 7b and 11 present the gift of teaching.

> 7b.   or he who teaches in his teaching;
>
> 11.   no lagging behind in diligence, fervent in spirit, serving the Lord;

Exhortation Romans 12 verses 8a and 12 present the gift of exhortation.

> 8a.   or he who exhorts, in his exhortation;
>
> 12.   rejoicing in hope, persevering in tribulation, devoted to prayer,

Giving Romans 12 verses 8b and 13 present the gift of giving.

> 8b.   he who gives, with liberality;
>
> 13.   contributing to the needs of the saints, practicing hospitality.

Leadership Romans 12 verses 8c and 14 present the gift of leadership.

> 8c.   he who leads, with diligence;
>
> 14.   Bless those who persecute you; bless and curse not.

Mercy Romans 12 verses 8c and 15 present the gift of mercy.

> 8d.   he who shows mercy, with cheerfulness.
>
> 15.   Rejoice with those who rejoice, and weep with those who weep.

The gifts outlined above include encouragements that can also allude to problems or weaknesses faced while exercising these gifts. By working through the problems and weaknesses we all face, God's strength is manifest so He gets all the glory.

7.2 Miracles

Miracles and healing in particular have an important place in the church. They help build the church, save the lost, edify everyone involved, and give all the glory to God. The lack of miracles being manifest cannot be excused or rationalized away. Those who attempt to rationalize miracles away display their lack of faith and relationship with Him.

Healing is a powerful witness because it is very personal and undeniable. However accomplished modern medicine is, there is a great deal it can't do. God can and does heal. Consider the millions of people who have died from various health related causes that would have lived long and healthy lives if the church had been proactive with its relationship and responsibilities with Jesus. Of course, there are many other miracles of great variety that meet a need for the betterment of the individual, society, and advancement of the church. Remember that regardless of the magnitude of the miracle, the Holy Spirit is who accomplishes it, not people.

Some chase after miracles and will even travel around the country following a particular ministry. This is idolatry. Miracles are the signature of the church; a signature of the Holy Spirit working through His people. If you seek Him and grow in Him then those miracles, signs and wonders will be a natural outflow of that relationship. Although the working of miracles through people is a measure of growth, it should not be viewed as the only defining factor. God decides what is worked through whom and when, where, and how. The Apostle Paul made his position on his relationship with Jesus clear in Philippians,

Bible Reading: Philippians 3:7–14

Paul's position on his relationship with Jesus is clear. He clearly understood the priority of knowing Him and that miracles are an outflow of that relationship. Anything this world has to offer, or any number or magnitude of miracles are nothing compared to knowing Him and the power of His resurrection.

There is no way to truly know the consequences of what God does through you. A person you lead to Jesus, a good deed, or any other thing the Holy Spirit may lead you to do may have positive consequences for years or generations to come. Miracles are certainly a key component in bringing about blessings, otherwise Jesus would never have done them or commanded us to follow in His footsteps. Miracles not only demonstrate the power of God but also meet a need. That need met can have a wide influence today and for many years.

Jesus provided Himself as an example of some of what can be done when you are in right standing with God, and empowered through the Holy Spirit. Therefore, following the instruction given in Hebrews 12:1–2 is imperative. The fact that Jesus commanded us to do these things makes them a responsibility, and not some unattainable goal.

CHAPTER 8

Who You Are In Jesus Christ

Gaining knowledge of who you are through Jesus Christ has the potential of greatly improving your prayer life. People usually have some basic knowledge, but we will discover that this is insufficient. The devil deceives Christians into believing they are powerless and without authority. The reality is each and every Christian has more power and authority through Jesus than anyone realizes. Educational resources inside or outside the church, such as seminaries, provide only a limited degree of understanding. We must therefore rely on the Holy Spirit, the Bible, and the lessons and experiences He provides. You will find the latter resources are by far the best when compared to the education one can get through others. Jesus is very eager to teach and work through His people. All that is necessary is to put forth a little effort and be open to learning and exercising those lessons. An important point to keep in mind is that every Christian not only has power and authority over Satan and all of his demons, but over all of God's creation (1 Corinthians 2:9).

Prayer is the key. Through prayer you gain in relationship with Him, gain in knowledge and understanding of His Word, and grow in the realization of who you are through Him. This is a continual cycle that results in growth.

> But the Helper, the Holy Spirit, whom the Father will send in My name, **He will teach you all things**, and bring to your remembrance all that I said to you.
>
> —John 14:26 (NASB)

People have the tendency to look to others for knowledge before looking to the Holy Spirit. Learning how to listen to the Holy Spirit is accomplished by building a relationship with the Him through prayer. Learning from others is easier than doing what it takes to learn from the Holy Spirit. Putting forth the effort to learn from the Holy Spirit is vastly more rewarding.

> As for you, the anointing which you received from Him abides in you, and you have no need for anyone to teach you; but as His anointing teaches you about all things, and is true and is not a lie, and just as it has taught you, you abide in Him.
>
> —1 John 2:27 (NASB)

During this growth process there are some things that need to be understood and put into practice. Be aware that *any* revelation you may think you receive must be filtered through the Bible (2 Corinthians 10:5) and the Holy Spirit. The devil is very crafty and makes every attempt to deceive God's people. Learning the voice of the Holy Spirit comes with building your relationship with Him. This is a process that goes forward a step at a time. Be diligent to press forward and at the same time allow the Holy Spirit to be your guide, for if you try to get ahead too fast you will likely make many more mistakes. Patience is a valuable virtue. In the same way that the growth of a child into adulthood is a process, growing spiritually is also a process. As 1 John 2:27 says, it is imperative that we abide in Him. Backsliding is not an option. In time, spiritual growth will become easier as you learn to recognize the voice of the Holy Spirit and the lies of the devil.

An example of the learning process occurred when I attended a seminar on prophecy some years ago. It was open to anyone who wanted to attend and there were perhaps 50 people in the audience. Those who taught the seminar consisted of several ministers who traveled around the country teaching in churches. After completing the lesson on prophecy, the speaker had each of us pick someone we didn't know and prophecy to them. We were then to trade places and repeat it. I wasn't expecting this so it caught me off guard. My mind was blank and it was uncomfortable to be in such a situation. Being put on the spot and having only the Holy Spirit to trust to provide a word proved to be an amazing experience. Some very positive and profound prophecies came out of the exercise for the whole group. There wasn't anything special about the teachers or the people attending the seminar. We were all just average people seeking to grow in Jesus and God honored our intentions. It was an experience I will never forget.

Although the seminar focused on prophecy, a similar approach may be done for any of the other gifts and manifestations of the Spirit written about in the Bible. The real key is learning to rely upon and trust the Holy Spirit. One of the most important points of this lesson is realizing that the Holy Spirit was there as an <u>active participant</u> to teach His people how to listen to and trust Him. He is a part of us in ways we haven't even fathomed and He is eager to be involved in every detail of our lives.

8.1   A Nation of Priests

Who you are in Jesus Christ includes a job description and that is we are to be a nation of priests. Priests have a responsibility before God to be righteous and holy so they can faithfully execute the duties of their office. Priestly duties also include civic responsibilities which are clearly evidenced throughout the Bible.

Bible Reading: Exodus 19:5–6; 1 Peter 2:5

The office of the priest carries with it some requirements.

- The priest must have a solid knowledge of God's word, which defines all the duties and responsibilities of the priest.
- The priest must also have a relationship with and be anointed by God.
- The priest has a honored position in society. This position of honor must be earned and maintained.
- The priest has the position of being an intercessor between the general populace and God. That is, we as priests are intercessors between God and those who do not know Jesus as Lord and

Savior. As intercessors, we are to spread the Gospel and pray for their salvation, and do as Paul did in 1 Corinthians 2:4–5.

- The priest is also to act as a moral compass for society, the community, and their nation. Involvement in civic activities including the governing of the nation, is required.

Some clarification on the last point is necessary. The established church in Europe became a political force that gained so much power that people found it burdensome and ungodly in its actions. This historical fact is one of the most pronounced reasons people came to the new world with the eventual foundation of the United States of America. There must be a careful distinction because the primary problem with the established church was its lust for power and control over the populace, which is obviously a sinful position.

The Founding Fathers and authors of the U.S. Constitution designed it in a manner to avoid these problems. They were clearly in favor of and stressed the importance of Christians being involved in the governing of the nation, but wanted to prevent the domination of any one religious organization. The goal of the church is not to have power and control over the populace in a burdensome manner, but to provide a moral foundation and maintain boundaries of acceptable behavior that assists in maintaining godliness and the salvation of as many as possible.

Each individual is called to fulfill a task according their God-given capacity. The church is to be the focal point of society and is to occupy its power base. Failure of the church to be in the power base enables the wicked to fill it, and they do so with a great deal of aggression and a militant attitude. The wicked strive to fill the power base because they think they have a birthright to it which, of course, is a lie of the devil. This phenomenon is evident at all levels of society.

The book of Leviticus lays out the duties and responsibilities of the priest. The many physical activities of the Levitical priest can be translated into spiritual activities we should be practicing, some of which we do by nature without realizing it. How all this translates to us Christians is a considerable study in and of itself. There is a dire need for knowledge. Since the church is so lacking in knowledge, it suffers the consequences presented in Isaiah 5:13 and Hosea 4:6.

Some of the lack of knowledge can be traced back to the cultural divide that occurred in early days of the church. The cultural divide between the Christian church and its Jewish roots needs to be repaired.

The church today must be a repairer of the breach; a restorer of the streets in which to dwell.

Bible Reading: Isaiah 58:11–14

The above passage from Isaiah is a promise with a condition. If we keep the Sabbath and honor it as a holy day, and delight in Him, then He will bless us (see also Mark 2:27). A natural extension of stating the Sabbath is that since this is God's commandment, His other commandments should also be kept. The Sabbath is mentioned since it is often the easiest to forget.

Do you love Him or do you view the Sabbath, the festivals and holidays and other teachings of the Old Testament as outdated, cumbersome, and not applicable today?

> If you love Me, you will keep My commandments.

> —John 14:15 (NASB)

8.2   Children of the King

In the beginning and before Adam and Eve sinned, God gave mankind dominion over the entire planet.

Bible Reading: Genesis 1:26–28

God gave Adam and Eve, and hence all humanity, dominion over the earth and all living things on the earth. After sin entered the scene, that dominion was passed on to the devil. He retained this until Jesus died on the cross. That dominion has now been passed back to its rightful owners—the children of the King. The problem is, the devil doesn't want to relinquish what he thinks is his. Dominion must be taken from him by force. Herein is the battle, and it manifests in both the spiritual and physical worlds.

Bible Reading: Ephesians 6:12; Job 38:12–13

When you asked Jesus to be Lord and Savior, you became a new creature. This is a spiritual statement. Your spirit was created anew and is now sinless. We all still deal with the flesh and the sin that is in it. As a Christian we are much more than a new creation.

Bible Reading: Romans 8:14–17

Let's briefly examine a few of the attributes of what it means to be one of His people. An earthly kingdom, such as the system present in Europe centuries ago, provides one of the best analogies. A king was considered the absolute ruler of his domain. All others were subservient to him. The king's children, his princes and princesses, commanded the same level of authority, power, respect, and honor as their father. Any violation or offense against them had the potential of experiencing the wrath of the king. The children of the king also had responsibilities by virtue of their position. They were to carry out the wishes of the king in the governing of his domain. In so doing these princes and princesses were expected to uphold their status as royalty through their behavior.

Since true Christians have been transformed into new creatures and born of the Spirit, we are now in that incredible and glorious position of being His sons and daughters—princes and princesses of God Almighty. Although through the analogy of a human kingdom we can understand the worldly benefits of a position of royalty, it hardly compares to the magnitude of what we have through Jesus Christ. We may never truly understand the depth and breadth of what it means to have a position of royalty with Jesus Christ in this life. The fact that this isn't defined in explicit terms in the Bible is important. The knowledge and understanding (revelation) of our position through Jesus is gained through our relationship with Him, and this is what we are to focus on. The more someone grows in Jesus, the easier it will be to comprehend and accept the roles and responsibilities given them.

> "I will give you the keys of the kingdom of heaven; and whatever you bind on earth shall have been bound in heaven, and whatever you loose on earth shall have been loosed in heaven."
>
> —Matthew 16:19 (NASB)

The sheer scope of the above verse in Matthew will never be truly understood in this life. Along with many other scriptures, some light can be shed on what this relationship means, and the incredible things He has for us. In view of the level of power and authority all Christians have, Satan and all his demons are nothing more than bugs to be squashed under their feet. Christians have not only a right to exercise power and authority, but also a responsibility to use it to advance the church.

> Behold, I have given you authority to tread on serpents and scorpions, and over **all the power of the enemy**, and nothing will injure you.
>
> —Luke 10:19 (NASB)

The serpents and scorpions are representative of demons (see also Mark 16:18; Acts 28:3–6). Since all Christians are His disciples, that same power and authority belongs to us as well. Note that He didn't give some power over the enemy but **all** power over the enemy. This means that not even Satan can stand against a Christian. All it takes is a little faith.

That position of being His sons and daughters should never be a point of pride. Pride is sin and will only lead to destruction. Remember Jesus, although He knew who He was while on this earth, humbled Himself and remained obedient and sinless, even to the point of death (Philippians 2:8). So too, we should follow this example of humility and obedience.

As children and joint heirs with Jesus, Christians are royalty. Matthew 28:18 states that Jesus has all power in heaven and on Earth. In 1 John 3:8 Jesus came to destroy the works of the devil. All the power in heaven and on Earth is shared by all Christians through Jesus. Heaven is the center of government for all creation. Although Christians are elevated to a high position through Jesus Christ, it comes with responsibilities to serve other people as Jesus did. He emptied Himself of His deity, and in like manner we are not to be prideful in our position in Him but to serve as

Jesus did, and to fulfill the great commission. Jesus was our example and He commissioned and empowered us to do the things He did. Because of the position as joint heirs through Jesus, we also have all power in heaven and on Earth at our disposal through His name. When someone says, "In Jesus name," in prayer, they are exercising a legal power of attorney and making a statement in the fullness of His character. We should expect the same results as Jesus did.

An example of this situation is the civil rights movement that started in the early 1960's. Slavery had been abolished at the end of the civil war but the wicked didn't want to loose their power and control over people. Nearly one hundred years later, people had enough and demanded their lawful rights and position in society. Through much effort, they were finally allowed to exercise their lawful status.

Similarly, we as Christians need to take back dominion of the world from the wicked. Not long ago the church had a solid position of dominion in the community and in the governing affairs of this nation. The primary method of regaining dominion is through repentance and prayer (2 Chronicles 7:14).

As a reminder:

> *It will invariably be more difficult and take more work and effort to recover from sin than it would to resist temptation in the first place.*

The church is responsible for following God's plan to regain the dominion. Regaining dominion will never happen through man's methods. The sooner this effort begins, the better. The more time that passes before the church rises up, the more difficult it will be to regain lost ground. Many Christians hear words spoken in sermons that they are children of the King and do nothing with this information except feel good about themselves. God's word must be put into action for results to be realized.

8.3 Rights, Privileges, Responsibilities

The pursuit of humanistic philosophies has become so prevalent in the church that it needs to be addressed. The primary purpose of life is not to attain fame, fortune, popularity, or to view God as a servant.

The prosperity the world has to offer are rights but they are not to be the primary goal. Therefore, we are not to pursue these things, but pursue Jesus. Matthew 6:33 says, "But seek ye first the kingdom of God, and his righteousness; and all these things shall be added unto you."

Bible Reading: Psalms 37:3–6; Matthew 6:33

The purpose of life is to:

- Know God. We are to know Him experientially and love Him from the depths of our soul and our entire being.
- Keep His commandments.
- Be conformed to the image of Christ (Romans 8:29).
- Fulfill the Great Commission.

We are to appropriate and enforce the victory that Jesus died to provide. Victory, first and foremost, is that position or level we attain in our relationship with Jesus that facilitates physical and spiritual dominion and the fulfillment of the Great Commission.

Jesus died on the cross for us. He did a complete and perfect job. We are new creatures in Christ. Therefore, we should not be focusing our time and energy on things that are already established but be focused on our responsibilities to minister to the people around us. How are we to go and do the things that Jesus did?

Bible Reading: Romans 12:2; 1 Corinthians 2:4–5

Part of the fulfillment of the Great Commission is to demonstrate the power of God through the Holy Spirit. Our witness to the world must be accompanied by the power of God and the demonstration of power through various miracles.

The carnal mind conforms to the world, thinks in worldly terms, is fleshy and not focused on heavenly things. For our minds to be renewed we must think the way God thinks. Christians are His children and have the mind of Christ (1 Corinthians 2:16). View things as though looking from heaven to earth, not the other way around. To have a renewed mind, develop the ability to distinguish thoughts, feelings, and emotions that are of the world or of God. Take every thought captive to the obedience of Christ (2 Corinthians 10:5).

The gateway to a renewed mind is repentance of sin. Matthew 3:2 says, "Repent, for the kingdom of heaven is at hand." Therefore, to experience the kingdom of heaven, repentance is required. The devil is a master of deception and lies. He has been around a lot, lot longer and any of us, and has gained a great deal of experience dealing with people. Sin is often extremely subtle. The Holy Spirit is our helper so we must always be watchful and attentive to Him. As such He is here to help us, guide us, empower us, and protect us. He gives us revelation into many things that we would otherwise miss, provided we are obedient. The process take education through learning His Word, repentance, and prayer to develop a relationship with Him.

As an example of the gravity and subtleness of sin, let's look at abortion. Most Christians understand that abortion is murder. When a woman becomes pregnant, the baby is a human being with human DNA. The baby is alive. Therefore, outside of a valid medical justification, aborting that baby is an act of murder. This country was established as a republic, and not a democracy. We the people are the government and we elect representatives to represent our will. When you vote for a representative that has a publicly stated position in that they are in favor of abortion and they get into office, what does this mean? When elected officials who publicly profess a pro abortion stance take office and sign or sponsor laws that legalize abortion, they become murderers by proxy. Since those who voted for that representative indicate by their vote they are in agreement with them, they too become co-conspirators and murderers by proxy. This is clearly sin and those who participate will be held accountable before God.

As of this writing, almost 60 million babies have been aborted in the U.S. since 1973[5] and almost 1.5 *billion* worldwide since 1980. The magnitude of this genocide is mind boggling. Understand that the mother to be is a co-conspirator with the person performing the abortion. Both parties are guilty of murder.

---

[5] Roe v. Wade, 410 U.S. 113 (1973). The website http://www.numberofabortions.com/ provides an abortion counter that gives estimates on the number of abortions in the U.S. and worldwide.

Do you think God will bless those who commit such grievous acts of murder of those so innocent? Do you think they will escape His judgment? Do you think God is deaf to the blood and cries of those who are so innocent? Indeed, His judgment is coming. This is one of the many examples and why we need to be vigilant about our relationship with Jesus and to apply it to every aspect of our lives.

Many people think miracles and demonstrations of power are reserved for people with a special anointing, or even that these things are not for today. People think that miracles were performed by Jesus in His position as God, rather than as man. Neither of these assumptions is true. Jesus could not heal the sick, raise the dead, cast out demons, or do any of the many other miracles in and of Himself. In John 5:9 we read, "...the Son can do nothing of Himself..." Jesus set His position as God aside to demonstrate what could be done by any Christian in right standing with God. We don't have to be anything more than humans saved by the grace of God and walking with Him to do the works of God. It is that simple and there is no excuse.

On the subject of faith, John 6:29 says, "Jesus answered and said to them, 'This is the work of God, that you believe in Him whom He has sent.'" Faith is gained by hearing and hearing by the word of God and by working it, for faith without works is dead. We gain faith by understanding who we are as Christians and putting the Word of God into action. This is like going to the gym to get our physical bodies in shape. If you wish to become strong you need to get exercise. Exercise takes effort. It takes working the muscles so they become strong. Similarly, faith must be exercised so it will grow.

> [20]But you did not learn Christ in this way, [21]if indeed you have heard Him and have been taught in Him, just as truth is in Jesus, [22]that, in reference to your former manner of life, you lay aside the old self, which is being corrupted in accordance with the lusts of deceit, [23]and that you be renewed in the spirit of your mind, [24]and put on the new self, which in the likeness of God has been created in righteousness and holiness of the truth.
>
> —Ephesians 4:20–24 (NASB)

Jesus lived in conflict with those around Him that were carnally minded. Is your life in contradiction with those in the world? Do you see the way God sees? One who thinks and operates with a renewed mind destroys the works of the devil. A renewed mind is one that is transformed through relationship with Jesus; a mind that dwells on righteousness and holiness having put away the old sinful self. A renewed mind causes earthly reality to match heavenly reality, proves the Word of God by deed and not just word, and experiences what it means to be a normal Christian.

Pastors and teachers need to understand that they will be in conflict with carnally minded people. Just as in Jesus' time, carnal people took offense to what Jesus said and did. The trend today has been to avoid offenses at all costs. Success in this endeavor is impossible, especially when people diligently search for something to be offended by. Don't be ashamed of the Gospel. Jesus didn't mince words, so lessons and sermons shouldn't either. Preach the truth and God will honor the effort.

8.4   Power of The Spoken Word

The power of the spoken word cannot be overstated. Words carry power and a lot more than most realize. Look in particular at Matthew 16:19 below. The true meaning of having the keys to the kingdom of heaven would likely be a real eye opener. As we grow in Jesus, we will gain more understanding and knowledge of the greatness of what it means to be a Christian. Our lack of knowledge should be a reminder of the need to treat words with careful consideration before speaking.

Bible Reading: Job 22:28; Matthew 12:37, 16:19; 2 Corinthians 10:3–5

James chapter three also has much to say about the dangers of the tongue.

As His sons and daughters, children of the King, a royal priesthood, the power of the spoken word must be taken seriously. Without recognizing the wiles of the devil, people often say things that allow the devil to interfere with and oppress us, and gain victory in situations where he would otherwise be a failure. We must allow the Holy Spirit and knowledge of His Word to assist in the process of self-discipline.

The process of disciplining one's self begins with the mind as is indicated in 2 Corinthians 10:5. In order to bring your thought life into the obedience of Christ, everything you receive with your senses or think must be filtered through the Word and through the Holy Spirit. The effectiveness of this effort, as always, is based on the level of your relationship with Jesus. The more you build that relationship, the more you will be empowered to build this discipline as well as accomplish the many other things you need to do. The Apostle Paul wrote in Philippians,

> I can do all things through Him who strengthens me.
>
> —Philippians 4:13 (NASB)

And in Philippians 4:6–8, Paul writes,

> [6]Be anxious for nothing, but in everything by prayer and supplication with thanksgiving let your requests be made known to God. [7]And the peace of God, which surpasses all comprehension, will guard your hearts and your minds in Christ Jesus. [8]Finally, brethren, whatever is true, whatever is honorable, whatever is right, whatever is pure, whatever is lovely, whatever is of good repute, if there is any excellence and if anything worthy of praise, dwell on these things.
>
> —Philippians 4:6–8 (NASB)

The power of the spoken word when spoken by someone in right standing with God was demonstrated by Jesus Himself as well as the apostles. When they spoke, demons were cast out, people were healed, and many signs, wonders, and miracles were manifest. The most dramatic demonstration of this power and authority given to a person can be found in Joshua 10:12–14 when Joshua spoke to the sun and it did not set for about a whole day.

When you come to the realization of who you are in Christ, build your relationship with Him, and put into practice the lessons written in His Word (faith without works is dead), you too will witness the hand of God move in miraculous ways!

CHAPTER 9

Spiritual Warfare

Christians are persecuted and murdered in many places around the world today. If the church fails to wake up then persecution and death will become common in the western world as well. The church has the responsibility to make sure this does not happen. Prayer is the key.

The spiritual warfare we engage in is real, and is just as real as any physical war. The struggle over life and death is also just as real. There are issues to deal with that the vast majority of Christians have never thought of much less had to face. Some people, out of fear, won't even consider the reality of spiritual warfare or others may think there is no such thing. Denial is clearly not biblical given what the Apostle Paul had to say in Ephesians 6.

> For our struggle is not against flesh and blood, but against the rulers, against the powers, against the world forces of this darkness, against the spiritual forces of wickedness in the heavenly places.
>
> —Ephesians 6:12 (NASB)

The importance of developing and maintaining a warrior mindset is necessary. Without such a mindset, defeat is more likely to be the norm. I have met Christians with the mindset that it is okay to just give up thinking they have a free ticket to heaven, or that no action is needed because God is in control. Their attitude is cowardly and dangerous in the light of what the Bible has to say. Revelation 21:8 and the book of Proverbs speak about the dangers of being a coward.

The material in this chapter will no doubt appear quite radical when compared to today's church culture and style of prayer, and particularly with most of the teachings in the church. The failure to wake up and take action now will make the job exponentially more difficult later. When the church does take its proper and rightful place in society, the persecution that has already started will be halted. It will become necessary for the average Christian to engage in spiritual warfare with the fervor and determination discussed in this chapter.

Persecution is not a measure of a higher level of spirituality as some have preached. It is a measure of failure. This needs to change. As the saying goes, "An ounce of prevention is worth a pound of cure." The church has failed to maintain its rightful position in society so gaining this back will take much more work than it would have to maintain it in the first place.

Nothing in the Bible says we can't go on the attack! The primary passage concerning spiritual warfare is Ephesians 6:10–17. Here, Paul outlines the nature of the warfare and touches on some important principles by using the Roman armor and weapons as an illustration. Paul does not however, go into the details of what is necessary from a mindset standpoint. Other places in scripture provide this information. The book of Joshua, in particular, sets the stage for what we need to do and how God will bless those efforts.

A war can never be won with passive resistance. Passive resistance, or just being passive in light of the knowledge given by God, is an act of laziness and cowardice. Spiritual war is a war that must be fought to win. When Israel entered the promised land, they fought to win and destroyed the inhabitants. Israel's success in conquest would not have been possible without God's great blessings. We must have the same fight-to-win attitude with the spiritual warfare set before us.

People who have no idea what spiritual warfare is and don't see a need for it have never experienced a frontal attack by the devil. The most likely reason is they have never demonstrated that they are a threat to the devil. If you desire to grow and enter into the promised land, expect a fight to get there. That said, there are some important aspects of war that need understanding. Not everyone will go through an intense battle.

With spiritual warfare, the battle is very asymmetric. To a great extent we are all on the front lines of battle. We therefore need to be that much more vigilant as a team to protect those who are weak or for whatever reason are not able to fight. Be aware of the tactics of the devil to divide and conquer.

Not everyone has a personality given to learn the mental toughness to be a warrior of the nature discussed in this chapter or in the books cited below, but it is very possible to learn. Laziness and cowardice are not excuses.

If the stage was set for anyone to be a total failure in life, it was me. I had no hope for success or even survival in the world. When I asked Jesus to be my Lord and Savior, everything changed. Since very early in my Christian life, I have dealt with spiritual warfare. Spiritual warfare is not something to be feared. Fear is of the devil. Faith is of God. Since I was a new Christian, I started experiencing demonic attacks. Looking back, it seems Satan knew God had some special plans for me that probably included spiritual warfare. Rather than leaving me alone, he acted out of instinct, which is completely devoid of wisdom, and went on a relentless attack. If he had left me alone, I would never have learned to fight and win!

Attacks didn't come because I was doing something wrong and thus gave the devil an open door. Rather, Jesus allowed attacks to happen so I would learn and eventually teach others. Often, I could see demons. They are ugly, evil creatures. One time I woke up in the middle of the night because a demon was trying to manipulate my dreams with evil thought patterns. What really woke me up was the fact that I could physically feel the demon pressing against my feet as it leaned over me.

In the early years I didn't know how to effectively fight these evil creatures because no one in the church had any clue whatsoever what spiritual warfare was. I was very much a babe in the woods and didn't understand what was going on or why. It took a long time to learn. Even as a new Christian and still in my spiritual diapers, God protected me. I learned early on to keep my mouth shut concerning the spiritual battles. Saying anything about them would cause people to run away in fear. I had absolutely no help or instruction from anyone in any church I had ever set foot in. Jesus was always with me teaching me and protecting me. It wasn't until more recent years when my wife and I attended a church that specialized in spiritual warfare and deliverance that we made a significant leap in the ability to win these battles. Today, and after all this time, I have many testimonies, some of which are quite amazing.

If I can grow under such adverse conditions to the point that I can teach others, then most anyone can learn too. If Jesus protected me through it all then He will do the same for you. This is His promise to us.

A couple of books worth reading on the subject of the warrior mindset are:

1. *Unleash the Warrior Within* by Richard J. Machowicz [13].
2. *Warrior Mindset, Mental Toughness Skills for a Nation's Defenders, Performance Psychology Applied to Combat* by Michael Asken, Ph.D., Lt. Col. Dave Grossman, and Loren Christensen [14].

Soldiers are trained and educated with fighting skills and knowledge necessary to win a battle. So far as the mental state is concerned, this education and training should also be taught for Christians, Spiritual warfare is far more asymmetric than conventional warfare. The church must go forward as a team! Keep in mind that many things a soldier learns from the physical wars are directly applicable to the spiritual wars we face.

> Jesus came up and said to them, "All authority (all power of absolute rule) in heaven and on earth has been given to Me.
>
> —Matthew 28:18 (AMP)

Realize that if you know Jesus as Lord and Savior, you have access to the same power and authority that was given to Jesus. It is up to you to grow in Him and use it.

Again, spiritual warfare is not to be feared. If you desire to grow in your relationship with Jesus to the point that you will be doing the things Jesus, the early apostles, and church did, expect to go through a number of battles to get there. The last thing the devil wants is a Christian who understands who they are in Jesus and exercises that power and authority. The devil has no power and authority over a Christian and he knows it. He knows that when Christians exercise such power and authority, it will be his destruction.

What most people don't realize is that victory and the promised land are there for the taking provided they are willing to do what it takes to get there. Getting there is a battle. Remember the nation of Israel. The experiences the entire nation went through to occupy the promised land are largely symbolic of the individual growth experienced by Christians. When Joshua led the nation into the promised land it wasn't a cake walk. They had many battles to engage in before their enemies were defeated and they could enjoy peace and safety. Even then, they never fully occupied the land God had given them. Similarly, we have not occupied the promised land God has for us to any appreciable degree.

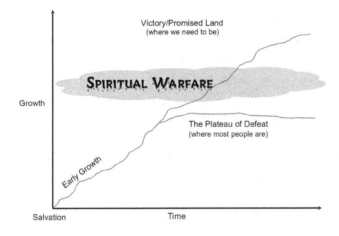

Figure 9-1: Spiritual Growth Throughout Life.

The typical spiritual growth process is illustrated in Figure 9-1. Predictably, people will grow to some level and plateau for the rest of their lives, but this is not good enough. Those who desire to grow beyond the plateau and on to victory and the promised land will likely find themselves in spiritual battles. Please don't misunderstand the issue of spiritual warfare. As soon as someone gets saved, they may be dealing with it in varying degrees. The real battle comes when someone starts to understand who they are in Jesus and starts using that power and authority against the devil and his works, and puts forth effort to live in a state of victory and enter the promised land. It may be beneficial to think of this battle as a Rite of Passage to the promised land and the victory Jesus has for each and every one of us.

An important and unfortunate point is that you should not expect any church to provide much in the way of support. It is a personal journey that you can expect to be just you and Jesus. Jesus is more than sufficient and He will be a constant companion, guide, and protector.

The process of becoming victorious and occupying the promised land can take years of learning, growing, and experience. Character building is accomplished through time and experience, which will inevitably be based on the individual. Anyone who becomes impatient or lax will simply delay the process. Jesus knows what He is doing and we would do well to keep focused on Him rather than the storms of life. Press forward with determination, persistence, and wisdom.

An important lesson to learn when dealing with spiritual warfare is understanding the subtleties of Satan's deceptions. Gaining the ability to see through deception comes with knowing the Bible and experience.

Bible Reading: 1 John 4:1–6

I found the above passage from 1 John to be very important during the process of learning and growing.

Bible Reading: Hebrews 6:11–12

Those in law enforcement and those who have been in battle in the military will tell you to "keep your head on a swivel." The mental attitude and practice of being aware of what is going on around you is called situational awareness and will serve you well for the rest of your life. Always be vigilant. Always be on the watch. Doing this should become an automatic, natural reaction.

Bible Reading: 1 Thessalonians 5:6; 1 Peter 5:8

We live in a wicked world, and the wicked are becoming more and more militant and vocal about their desire to kill believers. Don't forget that they view believers as sheep for the slaughter rather than the overwhelming conquerors we truly are (or should be). Circumstances are getting worse around the world.

Bible Reading: Romans 8:37; John 15:5

As long as Israel was obedient, God brought resounding success. In reading Joshua, you will find that God required the level of obedience to be very high. Failure meant defeat and death. Nothing has changed today. We cannot afford to be polluted by the world. It is absolutely essential to be holy and spotless. All of this requires prayer and surrender to the Holy Spirit.

As was stated earlier, the devil absolutely does not want any Christian to know who they are in Jesus and the power and authority they possess. If the church truly understood this fact, he would be profoundly diminished but not finished, since the majority of people are not Christians. Unfortunately, the church has been so deceived by the doctrines of demons that many run in fear when the words 'spiritual' and 'warfare' are spoken in the same sentence. Church leadership is primarily to blame for this situation. Far too many pastors are afraid of offending someone or preaching the importance of repentance of sins, the need for holiness, and so on. The result is that churches don't grow and pastors resign themselves to a life of complacency and the administration of religious social clubs.

Bible Reading: Psalms 105:15; Isaiah 54:17

Everyone needs to be very careful about what comes out of their mouths. Careless words give the devil permission to attack God's people. The best solution is to ask for wisdom. Ask and it will be given.

Bible Reading: James 1:5; Psalms 111:10; Proverbs 8:11; James 3:17

9.1 The Warrior Mindset

Knowledge of how to fight spiritual battles to gain and maintain a lasting victory is an absolute necessity if you intend to get to the promised land. Accomplishing such goals requires a warrior mindset. The doctrines of demons (1 Timothy 4:1) have so infiltrated the church that it has become perfectly acceptable to be overly passive and sound asleep.

For example, I've heard pastors go out of their way to avoid the slightest possibility of offending anyone. Jesus didn't mince words or hold back on speaking the truth so why should anyone today? The wicked and hypocrites are those who took offense to the things He spoke. Cowardice or being ashamed of the Gospel and its simplicity and power is not an option.

> For whoever is ashamed of Me and My words in this adulterous and sinful generation, the Son of Man will also be ashamed of him when He comes in the glory of His Father with the holy angels.

> —Mark 8:38 (NASB)

The parable of the talents (Section 5.2) makes it clear that without risk there is no reward. Those who were given talents and earned more had to take a risk in order to realize a gain. Risk must be taken to overcome any obstacles that may be encountered in order to become a winner.

I must emphasize again that this is a battle to be victorious and occupy the promised land. The devil does not want any Christian to know the power and authority they have through Jesus, much less use it. Victory is certain if and only if you fight to win. The approach of always being on the defense and never the offense is not the mark of a good soldier. A victory will never be won without a good offense.

> Some of us are already warriors in one form or another. Being a warrior means throwing your heart and soul into something you believe in and never looking back. Having a warrior mindset means you won't quit. It encompasses the Spartan philosophy of bringing back your shield or being carried back on it.

> Having a warrior mindset means doing whatever it takes to be prepared because warriors don't just survive, they overcome and win. At the end of the day, life is nothing but a mind game; it's important that you play to win. Your life depends on it.

> It's not always the biggest and strongest who make it, but those with the most heart; those who keep on going no matter what is thrown at them. It's a lesson you need to remember if you want to become a true warrior.

> —Amaury Murgado [15]

The quote from Amaury Murgado outlines the mental attitude you need to win. Don't give up. Refuse to allow your problem to survive. Pray through it until the job is done. If you become overwhelmed, get help.

Bible Reading: Psalm 18

In the days of Joshua, Israel had to spend time training their warriors. In the end, it was God who brought the victory but it would not have been possible if Israel had no idea how to engage in battle. The battles they engaged in before entering the promised land gave them the needed training, skills, tactics, and experience necessary to be overwhelming conquerors in preparation for the conquest of the promised land.

Many Christians are unaware of and even deny the fact that the devil is real and is a force to contend with. Doctrines of this nature are not scriptural, especially in view of Ephesians 6. People who have this attitude are already living in a state of defeat having believed the devil's lies, and are therefore not a threat to him. They think they are already in the promised land when they have no idea what it means to be there. The only way to get there is to fight for it as Israel did in the time of Joshua.

Like it or not, everyone is on the front lines of battle. The Apostle Paul outlines the tools and weapons of warfare at our disposal in his letter to the Ephesians.

Bible Reading: Ephesians 6:10–18

Ephesians 6 makes the reality of spiritual warfare and weapons clear. Verse 10 is the most important of the entire passage. There is no possible way to win without Jesus and His strength (John 15:5). Period. Paul uses the Roman soldier's armor and weapons as analogies of the spiritual armor and weapons we employ. Verses 13 through the first part of 17 discuss defenses to avoid being injured or killed. Paul presents the offensive weapons which are the sword of the Spirit (which is the word of God) and prayer. The primary battle is in the mind but also manifests in the physical. Physical battles are designed to degrade the mind. Through all of it we must practice what is provided in the Bible and not give up.

Truth God's truth is absolute and we are to stand on it and not listen to or be swayed by anything the devil may say, either directly or through other people. Knowledge of His Word is essential.

Righteousness The righteousness of Christ must not be allowed to fade. Sin is always knocking at the door. Sin gives the devil opportunities to bring defeat.

The gospel of peace Be prepared at all times to preach the gospel of peace. Being prepared with the gospel indicates the presence of mind to have in view of the world. Avoid giving the devil an opportunity. Use wisdom in all of your activities.

Faith This is the most important ingredient and is built by building your relationship with Jesus.

Salvation Through salvation we have all power and authority over the devil and anything he does. In the midst of a battle it can be easy to forget this. Don't ever let salvation and all it has to offer leave your mind.

Stand firm Having done all, we are to stand firm. This takes faith knowing our Lord will bring about a solution. After having done all according to His Word, stand firm and do not move off of it!

The sword of the Spirit The power of the Holy Spirit will operate through you to bring about a solution. The Holy Spirit will bring about action as you speak. In verse 17, Paul states the sword of the Spirit and the word of God are the same. The word of God may be words He provides from scripture and may also be the words the Holy Spirit gives you to speak since they come from Him. Because of the power and authority we have through Jesus, our words carry power and authority. By speaking we destroy the devil and his works. The sword of the Spirit and the word of God operate together to give two offensive weapons. Simplicity is a great advantage because there is less to learn and remember. The power and authority we have in the words we speak cannot be countered by anything the devil may have.

Prayer Prayer and its accompanying faith is the foundation upon which everything else is built. Through prayer your relationship with Jesus is built, and faith is increased so power and authority can be effectively exercised. Prayer is communication with God, and through prayer we petition Him to act on something that needs to be done.

The verses in Ephesians deal primarily with defensive measures with the sword of the Spirit being the only offensive weapon. Mentioning the sword of the Spirit as an offensive weapon is the primary theme discussed in this chapter. We are therefore directed to use the power and authority bestowed through the Holy Spirit as an offensive weapon in spiritual warfare.

In verse 13 we are to take up the full armor of God. What is this armor? Armor is a defensive protection from the attacks of the enemy. The full armor originates from a full and complete knowledge of the Word. Gaining knowledge is critical. As it says in Hosea 4:6,

> My people are destroyed for lack of knowledge. Because you have rejected knowledge, I also will reject you from being My priest. Since you have forgotten the law of your God, I also will forget your children.
>
> —Hosea 4:6 (NASB)

Clearly, Jesus takes gaining knowledge seriously. Knowledge of His Word is paramount. Knowledge of the world around us is secondary but also very important.

9.1.1   Doctrines of Demons

> But the Spirit explicitly says that in later times some will fall away
> from the faith, paying attention to deceitful spirits and doctrines
> of demons,

> —1 Timothy 4:1 (NASB)

The simplicity of God's provisions is unfortunately clouded by the traditions of man discussed in earlier chapters. These traditions are more often than not based on doctrines of demons. The doctrines of demons can be very subtle and are not doctrines or philosophies that are immediately recognizable as coming from demons and the devil. They may appear as godly and beneficial as can be. If it were readily apparent that a doctrine was of demonic origin, the church would recognize it and reject it. The key to recognition of these doctrines and deceptions is relationship with Jesus and knowledge of His Word. The church should take note of what those with the gift of discernment have to say as well. Once recognized, the church must be willing to accept and implement change to get rid of evil doctrines, regardless of how entrenched they may be in church culture. All doctrines of demons are designed to render the church as ineffective as possible when dealing with demonic activities in the church and throughout their communities, nation, and world.

An example of a demonic doctrine is the teaching that claims there are multiple ways to get to heaven. This is a clear violation of what Jesus said in John 14:6. Another example is the passive approach that says it's okay to just sit back and enjoy the ride to heaven. There are many scriptures throughout the Bible that make it clear we have responsibilities to fulfill.

Since many Christians are in a state of deception and don't want change, the warrior mindset for those who do see is essential. This is much like a David and Goliath situation. People may only be willing to change when they see the hand of God move in miraculous and powerful ways.

People are inherently resistant to change, especially when they don't see the need or want their religious social clubs or fiefdoms interfered with.

> "There is nothing more difficult to arrange, more doubtful of
> success, or more dangerous to carry through than initiating

changes. The innovator makes enemies of all those who prospered under the old order, and only lukewarm support is forthcoming from those who would prosper under the new. Their support is lukewarm partly from fear of their adversaries who have the existing order on their side and partly because men are generally incredulous, never really trusting new things unless they have tested them by experience."

—*The Prince*, ch. 6, Niccolo Machiavelli, 1514

As an example, most (but not all) pastors I have spoken to about the supernatural and spiritual warfare have felt threatened, even after I make it abundantly clear that I'm not interested in usurping their position or authority in any way.

Bible Reading: Romans 8:35–39

Christians are not the sheep for slaughter as the world views them. We are overwhelming conquerors through Christ. The time has come to press on toward the goal for the prize of the upward call of God in Christ Jesus (Philippians 3:14). The word conquer is a military term and means to overcome by force. Conquering is not just a state of mind but the pursuit of a goal through action. The devil will not willingly give up anything he thinks, however falsely, is of his domain. We need to fight for what is rightfully ours. Since Ephesians 6 makes it clear that the battle we face and its weapons are spiritual, this is where the focus should be.

9.1.2 The Warrior Ethos

Valuable lessons can be gleaned from the world around us, especially from the military, which has its own warrior ethos. The one most applicable and easy to remember is from the United States Army.

1. I will always place the mission first.
2. I will never accept defeat.
3. I will never quit.
4. I will never leave a fallen comrade.

The warrior ethos was written to be applied to physical warfare however it is just as applicable to spiritual warfare as it outlines the necessary mental attitude, and the subjects to keep in mind in the face of battle, and in every aspect of our Christian lives.

The church is supposed to be a team working toward the goal of fulfilling the Great Commission. Accomplishing this task cannot be done apart from the Holy Spirit. We are to do the things Jesus did, and more. Because of the distractions of the world and the spiritual warfare we deal with, maintaining focus is imperative. An army cannot be successful in battle if it is distracted and divided by things that detract from the mission at hand. Likewise, the church cannot afford to be distracted. Memorizing the Warrior Ethos will help just as it does with the Army.

Let's look at the Warrior Ethos again with some additional discussion.

I Will Always Place the Mission First

The Great Commission is the mission for each individual to fulfill. Each of us is to do their God-ordained part to fulfill it. Everyone has a specific function to fill and each requires focus and determination. Paul made this clear in his letters where he discussed the various spiritual gifts and offices. The mission is to be the primary focus in life. Focusing on the mission does not mean the daily responsibilities of income, family, and such are to be ignored or minimized. Rather, family and other activities can all be a platform from which to fulfill this mission. Accomplishing the mission more effectively may take some shifting of priorities and reorganization of how and when other responsibilities are fulfilled. Fulfilling the mission can take many forms. It may be a non-ministry profession God has directed someone to work in. It may be to fulfill some position within a ministry. Regardless of the function, the goal is the same and that is to fulfill the Great Commission.

For example, God called me to be an engineer. When He did so the message was loud and clear, and left no doubt in my mind what I was to do. In every job or position I have worked throughout my career there have always been opportunities to witness to others and to minister where it was needed. Outside of my career I have served as a deacon, taught and preached. The point is there are people in all walks of life that need to be witnessed and ministered to. God calls people in a variety of professions to be witnesses for Him. We all have ministry to accomplish, regardless of the profession. Wherever you are, whether you are working on a job or not, God has a job and purpose for you to fulfill.

I Will Never Accept Defeat

Defeat is not an option. We are overwhelming victors through Christ. Fight the good fight. Your own personal victories will increase as you grow. Remember, it is a learning and faith building process. If you reach the end of what you are able to deal with, ask your brothers and sisters in Christ for help. Use experiences as learning tools to apply them and be more effective in the future. Applying the lessons learned will make victories easier as time progresses.

> ²Consider it all joy, my brethren, when you encounter various trials, ⁴knowing that the testing of your faith produces endurance. ⁴And let endurance have its perfect result, so that you may be perfect and complete, lacking in nothing.
>
> —James 1:2–4 (NASB)

The battle may be hard and seem more than you can bear at times. It may appear easier to quit than to keep pushing forward. This is when you must rely entirely on Jesus' grace, strength, and endurance. In situations like this, you must learn to put all your trust and faith in a Savior who loves you more than you can possibly imagine. Ask for help and He will provide.

I Will Never Quit

Run the race to win. Jesus will strengthen you. You can never succeed with your own strength. Apart from Jesus you can do nothing so it is imperative to learn to rely on Him and trust Him (John 15:5). This too is a process that must be learned and built as faith increases. God will never allow you to be tempted beyond what you are able to bear. Battles and situations can and often will push the boundaries beyond what you thought you could bear.

> Fight the good fight of faith; take hold of the eternal life to which you were called, and you made the good confession in the presence of many witnesses.
>
> —1 Timothy 6:12 (NASB)

Rather than running from a battle, fight to win. If you fall on your face, get up! Dust yourself off, and get on with the battle. Fight to win and don't give up. As a team we should all be helping each other when circumstances get to the point it becomes necessary. Help may consist of prayer, fasting, and other spiritual and physical support. There is strength in numbers so fight as a team (Matthew 18:18–20; Acts 12:1–19).

I Will Never Leave a Fallen Comrade

Never ever shoot the wounded. This has been a serious problem and a subject of gossip in many churches. The wicked don't even do this. Rather they support each other regardless of how egregious the crime is. How much more so then should Christians be attentive to scripture when someone falls.

> Brethren, even if anyone is caught in any trespass, you who are spiritual, restore such a one in a spirit of gentleness; each one looking to yourself, so that you too will not be tempted.
>
> —Galatians 6:1 (NASB)

Lift up and help those who have stumbled knowing full well you are not immune to the deceptions of the devil, and that you too must deal with the weaknesses of the flesh. From the above verse in Galatians, Paul instructed his readers to be attentive to their own weaknesses and to avoid temptation. A temptation can be in any area. Everyone has weaknesses and the devil will attempt to exploit those weaknesses rather than their strengths. Bringing restoration is the most desirable outcome but there are times when someone falls and the situation warrants discipline (1 Corinthians 5:5; 2 Timothy 1:20). Realize too, that everyone shall stand before the judgment seat of Christ and give an account of what they have done in this life. Humility is a requirement for ALL Christians.

Be aware of the wiles of the devil. Gossiping, condemning, and ostracizing are some of the greatest sins that further wound those who have fallen. These sins are an abomination to God (Proverbs 6:16–19). Shooting the wounded is a tactic the devil uses to divide and conquer. This practice is a great evil and must be repented of.

Every Christian must watch out for each other and themselves. As long as people fall victim to this divide and conquer tactic, they will never have the blessings of God, only the fearful expectations of judgment.

9.2 Mercy

The majority of Christians have never had to deal with spiritual warfare to the degree discussed in this chapter, or deal with the subject of mercy within this context. Because lawlessness is increasing (see Matthew 24:3–14, and verse 12 in particular), addressing the balance between mercy and wrath has become more important.

> For judgment will be merciless to one who has shown no mercy; mercy triumphs over judgment.

> —James 2:13 (NASB)

Mercy is a Godly quality that is essential for all who know Jesus as their Lord and Savior. Most Christians I have known eagerly make this quality a part of who they are and look forward to being in a situation where they can put it into practice. This is all good. There are numerous other examples, particularly in the Old Testament where Israel displayed mercy toward their enemies with profoundly positive results. Ecclesiastes chapter three makes it clear that there is a time and a place for everything. When Christians fail to use wisdom and listen to the Holy Spirit, exercising mercy at the wrong time, or failing to do so when needed, can get them into trouble.

In view of the unfathomable mercy bestowed on us through our Lord Jesus it can be difficult to not show mercy. Balancing mercy and wrath have difficulties that become apparent when dealing with people. With demons this is simple. Don't show demons any mercy whatsoever. Period. They cannot repent and will only use any mercy you show them as permission to attack you and others. There are people who are into Satanism and witchcraft. These people are in Satan's camp. Through their witchcraft they can and do call up demons to do their bidding. They also use evil spiritual powers (Ephesians 6:12) to accomplish what they want done, which includes attacking Christians and other people. Being in the enemy's camp and doing what they do is their decision and they will suffer the consequences of that decision.

> You shall not allow a sorceress to live.
>
> —Exodus 22:18 (NASB)

> Now a man or a woman who is a medium or a spiritist shall surely be put to death. They shall be stoned with stones, their bloodguiltiness is upon them.
>
> —Leviticus 20:27 (NASB)

Dealing with the subject of mercy presents difficulties since God's desire is that no one perish but for all to come to the knowledge of the truth (1 Timothy 2:4). Every situation is different. Attentiveness and obedience to the Holy Spirit is therefore critical. If you are engaged in a battle with someone who is trying to kill you, then you can either give up or fight back so the enemy dies. This is the simple but harsh reality of war. We cannot afford to be naive about the evil that surrounds us. The world around us is far more wicked and violent than most realize, and is getting worse. Trying to hide, ignore, or deny this reality won't make it go away but rather, it will get worse if not dealt with. I don't want to belabor the point but I have met Christians who consider it easier and more noble to give up because they know Jesus, than to stand up and fight and be victorious. To give up is the act of a coward, and this has dire consequences. Realize that you have not just the right, but the responsibility to protect yourself, your family, and community against demonic and witchcraft attacks.

An example of the need to be attentive and obedient to the Holy

Spirit happened to me several years ago. I became aware that someone was practicing witchcraft in an effort to kill me. I commanded their witchcraft altars to be burned by the fire of God, as well as whoever was practicing the witchcraft (see 2 Kings 1). The Holy Spirit had me back off from completely destroying them. It was shortly afterward that I heard a story in church where someone had heard of a witch who had come to Jesus but only after being horribly burned while practicing her witchcraft. Although I have no way of knowing whether she was the one who had attacked me or not, the timing and circumstances couldn't be ignored. Regardless of the connection, this was an important lesson as to the care that must be exercised in these situations.

There are certainly those in Satanism and witchcraft that are so deep into it that they will never repent and have no desire to. Those who are Satanists have knowingly and willingly sold their souls to Satan. Most of these people view the mercy displayed by Christians as weakness. However unlikely, some of these people have asked Jesus to be their Lord and Savior. I sincerely hope as many as possible will come to Jesus.

Praying for their salvation and attacking the demons who are manipulating them is necessary. Intercession on behalf of the lost is but one of the responsibilities of a priest. The importance of praying for revival cannot be overstated.

Here are some simple rules to follow:

- Do not show any mercy whatsoever to Satan or any of his demons for any reason—*ever*. They will only use it against you.
- When dealing with people (Satanists, witches, warlocks), care must be taken. It cannot be emphasized enough that listening to and obeying the Holy Spirit is paramount. It may be difficult or impossible at times to know exactly what you are up against, but the Holy Spirit does know so listen to Him and be obedient.

From the last point above, learning and recognizing the voice of the Holy Spirit is critical. Distinguishing the voice of your Savior from others is something that can take some time and effort. Remember, even Satan can disguise himself as an angel of light. Pray at all times in the Spirit. Don't be naive about the wickedness in the world or what it takes to deal with it. Be sober and ready for action.

Bible Reading: 2 Corinthians 11:14; Ephesians 6:18

Keep the communication with the Holy Spirit going so you will learn and grow. The more you grow, the more of what is written in the Bible will become a living reality for you.

Bible Reading: 1 Thessalonians 5:6; 1 Peter 1:13, 5:8

9.3 Authority

Jesus tells us the level of authority we have through Him in the Gospels. Jesus provides instruction and gives authority to the seventy people He sent out in Luke 10. Acts 12:5–11 provides another example of His authority put into action—with miraculous results.

> [18]Truly I say to you, whatever you bind on earth shall have been bound in heaven; and whatever you loose on earth shall have been loosed in heaven. [19]I say to you, that if two of you agree on earth about <u>anything</u> that they may ask, it shall be done for them by My Father who is in heaven.
>
> —Matthew 18:18–19 (NASB)

In the verse nineteen above, the word *anything* is underlined. This is a powerful indication of that level of authority. Of course, there are qualifications that go with it. Everything must be within the scope of His will and word. The problem the church faces is that their view of the scope is far, far smaller than it really is.

Now let's look at a passage in Matthew:

> [21]And Jesus answered and said to them, "Truly I say to you, if you have faith and do not doubt, you will not only do what was done to the fig tree, but even if you say to this mountain, 'Be taken up and cast into the sea,' it will happen. [22]"And all things you ask in prayer, believing, you will receive."
>
> —Matthew 21:21–22 (NASB)

The above passage from Matthew is truly profound if only people would grasp the magnitude of it. Jesus' statement is not an analogy or metaphor. It is a straight forward and simple statement—if you have faith then this is the caliber of the results you can expect. If it were not possible for anyone to have this level of faith Jesus would not have made such a statement. Remember Jesus demonstrated what we as human beings can accomplish when in right standing with God.

> [19]Behold, I have given you authority to tread on serpents and scorpions, and over **all** the power of the enemy, and nothing will injure you. [20]Nevertheless do not rejoice in this, that the spirits are subject to you, but rejoice that your names are recorded in heaven.

> —Luke 10:19–20 (NASB)

Read these verses again and look at the scope of the authority. It is truly astonishing. Even Satan cannot stand against a Christian with faith.

> "And behold, I am sending forth the promise of My Father upon you; but you are to stay in the city until you are **clothed with power from on high**."

> —Luke 24:49 (NASB)

And then in Matthew 28:18–20 we see the Great Commission.

> [18]And Jesus came up and spoke to them, saying, "All authority has been given to Me in heaven and on earth. [19]Go therefore and make disciples of all the nations, baptizing them in the name of the Father and the Son and the Holy Spirit, [20]teaching them to observe all that I commanded you; and lo, I am with you always, even to the end of the age."

> —Matthew 28:18–20 (NASB)

All authority has been given to Jesus in heaven and on earth, and through the Holy Spirit we have that same authority. Growing in your relationship with Jesus is the only way to gain a greater comprehension of the scope of this authority. The conclusion is simple. All those who know

Jesus as Lord and Savior have power and authority over His creation, and over Satan and all his demons and weapons of warfare. Praise God!

> However, when the Son of Man comes, will He find faith on the earth?
>
> —Luke 18:8b (NASB)

9.3.1   Power, Love, and a Sound Mind

Power, love, and a sound mind are the key ingredients for a victorious life.

> For God hath not given us the spirit of fear; but of **power**, and of **love**, and of a **sound mind**.
>
> —2 Timothy 1:7 (KJV)

In order to have the power of God flow through you like it did with Jesus and the Apostles, you must have the love of God dwelling in you and have a sound mind. This sounds simple enough. Most will agree they have the love of God dwelling in them and have a relatively sound mind since they were saved. However, in order to attain the level written of in the New Testament, further investigation of the verse is necessary. Understanding the definition of each of the terms in the above verse and how our lives should be shaped to incorporate these values is important.

The best way to pursue the upward call of God is through prayer and education. The necessary education is lacking so the only, and perhaps the best, approach is through prayer and learning to allow the Holy Spirit to do the teaching (John 14:26). An education of this nature coupled with an earnest desire to grow, regardless of what trials are present, are what bring growth. Persistence and patience are also essential. The process is simple, but is seldom easy. Self dies hard.

> For whoever wishes to save his life will lose it, but whoever loses his life for My sake and the gospel's will save it.
>
> —Mark 8:35 (NASB)

Bible Reading: Matthew 16:25; Luke 9:24, 17:33; John 12:25; Philippians 3

Surrendering one's self to Jesus has eternal rewards that are immeasurable.

Bible Reading: 2 Corinthians 4:17–18

Jesus gave us power and authority. The state of possessing power and authority indicates ownership even though it all originates from the Holy Spirit for apart from Him we can do nothing. That power and authority is provided to fulfill the Great Commission in accordance with His will.

> I am the vine, you are the branches; he who abides in Me and I in him, he bears much fruit, for apart from Me you can do nothing.
>
> —John 15:5 (NASB)

With ownership comes some freedom of use and responsibility. That responsibility includes the use of His power and authority in a righteous and Godly manner. Without a sound mind and the love of God as the primary motivating factors and characteristics, the abuse of power will be inevitable. God's desire is that we do not harm others or ourselves. Harm can be in the physical, spiritual, or emotional. In a world that glorifies destruction, even for a righteous cause, it becomes more difficult to maintain the perspective of God's way of accomplishing a task.

> *The world brings death and destruction.*
> *Jesus brings life and restoration.*

The amount of power someone can be trusted with is based on the level of maturity. Developing a relationship with Him is absolutely necessary, and in the course of development, a mind freed from sin in thought and deed will result. Those who grow in Christ will see these characteristics develop more and more over time.

Power

Miracles can be manifest in many ways and each will depend on the need. In every case God gets all the glory since nothing can be done apart from Him (John 15:5).

Bringing life and restoration is an effective method of destroying the works of the devil (1 John 3:8). Bringing healing for physical ailments is one of the most profound of all the various miracles written about in the Bible. Healing is an enormous blessing to the one who gives and to the one who receives. These types of miracles are the most often applied area of where we are to use the power He has given us. Healing is effective for destroying the works of the devil but it is most effective for getting people saved. A miracle of healing and restoration that someone experiences personally or even witnesses is impossible to deny. Of course, there are many other miracles to be performed depending on the situation.

Some Christians and denominations believe God is quite selective about who is healed, if at all. They go through considerable effort to "listen to the Holy Spirit" in order to discern if a person is to be healed or not. This doctrine is heresy.

Bible Reading: Matthew 8:16, 12:15; Acts 5:16

Jesus healed and delivered *all* of the people, not some. It didn't matter who they were, what they had done, or what their spiritual state was. He healed all of them. Regardless of one's state, experiencing such a miracle is undeniable. God always gets the glory. Therefore, we should have this same goal and attitude when using the power and authority that has been given us!

The Love of God

The love of God is essential and those that possess it will have Godly love and compassion for people. Without His love as the primary motivating factor, the abuse of power will inevitably result. There is a time and a place for everything as Ecclesiastes 3:1 says. Preaching the gospel and bringing healing, restoration, and salvation to people are examples of when it is time for love and mercy. Battling Satan is not a time for love or mercy.

The love of God must dwell in one's heart to the extent that it is the primary motivation for every aspect of life. In a world that surrounds us with evil on every side it can be difficult to maintain the proper balance. It can only be accomplished through relationship with Jesus, for He and He alone provides that balance.

Bible Reading: 1 Corinthians 13

When addressing spiritual battles and issues, preachers often state *what* needs to be done without saying anything about the *how* and the work it takes to get there. The *how* is accomplished through prayer, experience, and trust in the Lord to provide an experiential education. Godly love will also be tested to see how deeply rooted it really is. Be careful to avoid closing your heart and allowing it to grow cold. Rather, be persistent and determined to grow and allow the Holy Spirit to work through every situation.

> [6]In this you greatly rejoice, even though now for a little while, if necessary, you have been distressed by various trials, [6]so that the proof of your faith, being more precious than gold which is perishable, even though tested by fire, may be found to result in praise and glory and honor at the revelation of Jesus Christ;
>
> —1 Peter 1:6–7 (NASB)

A Sound Mind

The definition of the word *sound* [1] as it is used in the King James Version is:

- Founded in truth; firm; strong; valid; solid; that cannot be overthrown or refuted; as sound reasoning; a sound argument; a sound objection; sound doctrine; sound principles.
- Right; correct; well founded; free from error; orthodox. 2 Timothy 1. Let my heart be sound in thy statutes. Psalms 119.

People with a sound mind will have God's word applied to every aspect of their lives. This goes beyond the four walls of the church. Every part of their lives, every philosophy they adhere to, and every aspect of life will hinge on His Word. The Apostle Paul speaks of this level of surrender in Philippians 3. We should all do likewise.

For example, I have encountered people who are well known and respected ministers, and although they present the appearance of godliness, they adhere to political or social principles that are completely contrary to Biblical morals and doctrine. This is not the indication of a sound mind, or of the level of maturity required for the position they hold. Someone who has a sound mind will demonstrate consistency across every aspect of their lives and the philosophies they adhere to. In spite of these short comings, God has blessed them and given them great success. One can only imagine what could be accomplished through someone in such a position if they had taken 2 Timothy 1:7 and Philippians 3 seriously and applied them to this degree.

9.4 Putting Jesus' Words into Practice

The best place to learn how to put spiritual warfare into practice is the Bible. The instructions provided in 1 Peter say it best.

Bible Reading: 1 Peter 1:13–25

Every verse in the above passage can have its associated lessons to teach and prayers to pray.

People often touch on powerful spiritual principles, barely scratch the surface, and then do nothing. I have heard numerous people, including preachers in churches and on television make statements similar to, "We take authority over the devil...," and then do nothing with that authority! The devil just sits back and laughs at people who do this. Fear and ignorance often hold people back from going further. Too many people are afraid of showing up on the devil's radar. If you know Jesus as Lord and Savior you are already on his radar. If you take that authority, *use it*! Don't be timid! Go on the offense and be aggressive about it. Start thinking outside the small box of church culture and learn to be an overwhelming conqueror! Never miss an opportunity to destroy the devil and his works!

If you come under a demonic attack then attack back. Of course, you may need to take defensive measures as well such as covering yourself or others with the protection that comes through the Holy Spirit, and through the knowledge of God's word. Go on the attack and don't stop with just the demons attacking you. Go after their support, replacements, command structure, their weapons and tools, and evil influences. Evil weapons, tools, and machines, do exist and have to be manufactured by some means. Destroy those facilities and the demons that manufacture them too. Be aggressive without hesitation. Destroy all of them! *Clear the field and don't back down until the job is done*! Do not give the devil or his demons any compassion or mercy whatsoever. They will use these Godly qualities against you. Remember, there is a time and place for everything (Ecclesiastes 3:1). Now is *not* the time for love, compassion, and mercy. This is war and you must set your mind to win.

When you maintain a warrior attitude and do these things you will be amazed at the results. As you become stronger you will not be afraid and you will win greater and greater battles. Demons will run from your presence. Satan himself will not be able to stand against you. You will have the attitude that says, "Okay Satan, bring it on! The more demons you send my way, the more will be utterly destroyed, and they will never bother me or anyone else again! And you are next!" I'm not suggesting you actually say this. It's the attitude and mental state that matters.

Satan and all his demons were once angels in heaven until they sinned and were thrown out. Many of them are quite intelligent and possess a considerable amount of knowledge. As we have the resources to manufacture a great number of things, they too possess resources to manufacture evil machines in the spiritual world. They then use these machines to perpetrate their evil on the earth.

Get in the practice of sending all these demons and all their garbage into the abyss (aka the deep, the bottomless pit) until judgment day in Jesus name. There is nothing in scripture that says you can't so don't let *anyone* convince you otherwise. Sending them there gets them off the earth and prevents them from doing any of their evil deeds. They are gone until the

Great White Throne Judgment and will never bother you or anyone else again.

As radical as this may sound, it works. I've been doing these things for decades and it is Jesus who taught me, and it is Jesus who has prepared me to teach others what I have learned. Keep in mind that "thinking outside the box" doesn't mean thinking or doing anything outside the boundaries of His Word or His will. Before I ever attempted to exercise my authority in this manner, I had read the Bible from cover to cover and spent time in prayer seeking the guidance of the Holy Spirit. Not getting a negative answer from either, I tried it and it worked. Since then, which was more than 40 years ago, I have experienced more victories and have more testimonies than I care to count, many of which are pretty amazing. I have even had demons come to me to tell me I can't do this. My response was simple. I said, "I just did. You go there too until Judgment Day in the name of Jesus," and they were gone.

Our Lord will never be inconsistent so it is perfectly acceptable for every Christian alive today to do the same things. Don't let anyone, even if it is the pastor of a church, convince you that you can't send demons to the abyss. They simply have no concept of the level of authority we have through Jesus. Others will hinder you simply because they don't want their lives or religious social clubs tampered with. Maintaining the status quo is easier for them than fulfilling their God-ordained responsibilities.

If the devil or any of his demons come to you and say they are going to do this or that to you or anything that concerns you, just say NO, then get rid of them! (Matthew 5:37). Do not get into a conversation with the devil. I'll say this again, do not get into a conversation with the devil! He is far craftier than you think. He has been deceiving people and using the words to his advantage for many thousands of years. Remember YOU have all power and authority over the devil and that it is YOUR word that stands. YOU have the final word, not the devil! Never *ever* compromise with the devil on anything. Destroy him!

Galatians 5:22–23 lists the fruits of the Spirit. The fruits of the Spirit are all wonderful Godly qualities that most Christians strive to experience and make a part of their lives. Demons do not and cannot have any Godly quality. They will attempt to get you to exercise any Godly quality on their behalf if it is to their advantage to do so. The only reason is to manipulate you into giving *permission* to continue with their evil deeds. Don't give it to them. Destroy them! We must address the fruit of the Spirit in this context. I have seen many instances of where Christians have been too eager to exercise Godly qualities in situations that don't warrant it. In the end, they become doormats for the devil and display themselves to the world as weak and as sheep for the slaughter. The phrase, "There is a time and place for everything," bears repeating here.

For example, let's say a man commits a heinous crime against a church by going into a Sunday service and murdering some people. The church later issues a press statement that it has forgiven the person for what he did. In the same press statement, the church should also say that even though it has forgiven him, he has a debt to pay to society for what he did and he should be prosecuted to the fullest extent of the law. If the crime warrants the death penalty, then so be it. The church will pray for the person and if possible, send people to the prison to witness to him in an attempt to get him saved. This balanced approach not only displays the fruit of the Spirit, but also strength and a sober attitude. People would respect the church more if it had not presented itself as a pushover by only offering forgiveness, but if in addition, it would have offered a firm follow through. People respect strength, but it must be balanced.

If the devil or any demon threatens to get back at you just say, "No!" Keep the answer simple. Don't let the devil manipulate you into making a statement anything more complicated. Just say, "No!".

> But let your statement be, 'Yes, yes' or 'No, no'; anything beyond these is of evil.

> —Matthew 5:37 (NASB)

I know a pastor who has an incredible deliverance ministry. I've been to his church and was amazed at the anointing in that place and how so many demons were driven out of people. The devil came to him one day and said he would destroy his ministry. The pastor's response was that the devil might have the power to do this or that and so on... It is subtle but what actually happened is that out of ignorance of what he said, he gave the devil permission to cause problems. As a result, he went through a divorce and problems abounded in his church.

I've said this before and it is worth repeating: *Do not give the devil any room whatsoever to deceive you into engaging in a conversation!*

Exercising your God given authority in ways like this inevitably falls outside the small box of church culture most are so familiar with. Many well-meaning Christians (and even pastors) will say you cannot exercise authority, but they won't be able to provide any solid Biblical evidence that you can't. As mentioned earlier, if you want victory, you must think outside the box and use the resources Jesus has provided. Don't let the nay-sayers stop you! History is full of nay-sayers but it was those enterprising individuals that saw beyond their negativism and resistance to change and brought about great accomplishments.

Sadly, the greatest resistance will often come from within the church. Those who provide the greatest resistance adhere to the doctrines of demons or have problems with demons themselves without realizing it. Understand too that Satanists infiltrate churches to cause divisions and any number of other problems, including practicing witchcraft against people.

The devil has deceived the church into thinking we don't have the power, authority, and position through our Lord Jesus that we in reality do have. The time has come to learn it and use it. Praise God for all He has given us!

The more you practice these tactics and maintain this attitude, the easier it will get and the sooner you will enjoy a sustaining victory. The result is you will enter the rest God has for you. Nevertheless, don't ever think this is an excuse to be lazy. We must always be vigilant.

As an illustration, there was a man working in the same building where I worked, whom I perceived to be a Satanist given the nature of the bumper stickers on his car. Every time I saw him it was clear that he had a mean, cold, hard, and angry spirit to the extent that he probably wouldn't bat an eye at murdering someone if it was to his advantage to do so. I noticed a considerable oppression in the building so on the way to work one day I took authority over all the demons, their devices and influences, and threw all of it all out and into the abyss. I did so for the benefit of all the people in the building, not just for myself. When I got to work, I noticed the oppression was completely gone.

The point is that Christians, as a priestly nation, must learn to intercede for others to get the job done, and get people saved. The spiritual warfare part of the job is necessary because it clears evil out of the way so people are more inclined to hear the Word and get saved. As much as we use the authority we have through Jesus to destroy the works of the devil, we must also pray for others to get saved, and that with as much fervency as for spiritual warfare.

The rest that God promises His people does not necessarily come at salvation, but through growth in relationship with Him. As growth advances, that rest will come.

Bible Reading: Joshua 22:4; Hebrews 4:8–11

The spiritual growth and development of your relationship with Jesus realized from gaining these victories is precious beyond measure.

Bible Reading: Matthew 6:19–21

9.5 Pressing Forward

Demons and satanic activities are not to be feared. Jesus won the victory on the cross and has overcome the world. All we need to do is tap into this victory. The path to victory is faith. Faith is like our physical muscles. When you want to get in shape you go to a gym and work out. It takes work, repetition, and sometimes some pain. After a while you become much stronger and physically fit than before. The same is true with faith. You need to exercise it, use it, and work at it (James 2:17). Faith will grow over time if you don't give up.

> I press on toward the goal for the prize of the upward call of God in Christ Jesus.
>
> —Philippians 3:14 (NASB)

Here Paul makes the statement that he *presses* forward. Pressing indicates an action in the presence of a resistance. Resistance is spiritual, physical, and personal. The spiritual part is the activities of the devil and his demons. The physical part is dealing with the world. The personal part is the quest for righteousness and to overcome sin. These forms of resistance can manifest in a variety of ways.

Romans 8:36–37 states that the world sees believers as sheep for the slaughter. Why? Because they hate us. Their minds are darkened by sin. Too many Christians focus on verse 36 to the point they welcome defeat and become willing to cave in to the pressures placed on them by the devil thinking this is a measure of their spirituality. Verse 37 ("But in all these things we overwhelmingly conquer through Him who loved us.") makes it clear that we are overwhelming conquerors through Jesus. Therefore, we need to claim and act on the blessings and promises that God has given us and what the devil has stolen because of our lack of knowledge and resolve. Understand that verse 36 shows how the devil wants Christians to be viewed. Verse 37 is truth and must be exercised to become reality.

Prayer is a very powerful tool! Not only is it profitable for our growth and building our relationship with Jesus, but it is critical for overcoming our enemies! When you exercise the power and authority granted through Jesus, gaining victory over the devil will become easier.

Bible Reading: Matthew 18:18–20

> *The church cannot fight and sleep at the same time.*

9.6 The Importance of Persistence

> He who watches the wind will not sow and he who looks at the clouds will not reap.
>
> —Ecclesiastes 11:4 (NASB)

Being persistent is a quality that is essential for getting results. Without persistence an army or even a single soldier cannot win a battle.

Webster [1] defines *persist* as:

> To continue steadily and firmly in the pursuit of any business or course commenced; to persevere.

One of the most notable examples in scripture is from Daniel 10. Here, Daniel prayed and fasted for three weeks before seeing the results. During this time Daniel was unaware of the spiritual battle taking place on his behalf. Similarly, we must be persistent in prayer.

Bible Reading: Hebrews 6:11–12; 1 Thessalonians 5:17

Everyone experiences adversity at various times and degrees throughout life. There are many examples throughout scripture of people (Daniel, Joseph, David, and Nehemiah to name but a few) who persisted while going through adverse circumstances. In every case, God honored their persistence and gave victory. Joshua 1:7–9 and Philippians 4:13 make it clear that it is our Lord who decrees and provides the strength and courage to press forward. We too must tap into God's provisions through prayer and building one's relationship with Jesus.

Bible Reading: James 5:16b; Ephesians 6:10, 13; 1 Corinthians 16:13

Adversity can come to build, refine, and test. It can also come as a result of demonic activities and attacks. In either case, persistence in prayer and standing on God's Word are the keys to victory. Memorize the warrior ethos in Section 9.1.

Bible Reading: Romans 8:28; James 1:2–4; 2 Corinthians 4:15–18

As long as you don't fall into a pattern of sin and suffer the consequences of it, trials have a purpose. Romans 8:28 is true. That purpose is to build your relationship with the Holy Spirit to the point that you are mature and lack nothing.

The more you learn to be effective in prayer the more you should expect the devil to attack. The last thing he wants is a Christian that knows their power, authority, and position through Jesus Christ. He realizes that once Christians gain this knowledge and faith he is done for because he has no power or authority against them. The more you grow, the less the devil will be able to pose a threat. Attacks will eventually diminish however don't expect them to disappear completely.

If you decide to go down the path toward victory and the promised land, realize it is a one-way path. If you persist, victory is certain and overwhelming because Jesus has promised this. If you go down the path to victory, then turn back, you place yourself in danger of vicious attacks by the devil.

9.7 To Conquer

I can say in all honesty that if God can bring such amazing victories for me, and bring me to the point of writing this book to teach others, He can and will do it with you if you let Him. You absolutely cannot rely on your own strength. You must rely on Jesus and the strength and courage He provides. You can do all things through Christ who strengthens you (Philippians 4:13).

> But in all these things we overwhelmingly conquer through Him who loved us.
>
> —Romans 8:37 (NASB)

Webster [1] defines *conquer* as:

> To gain by force; to win; to take possession by violent means; to gain dominion or sovereignty over, as the subduing of the power of an enemy generally implies possession of the person or thing subdued by the conqueror. Thus, a king or an army conquers a country, or a city, which is afterward restored.

Conquer is a military term and it implies a battle that is won through our Lord Jesus Christ and not of our own strength, knowledge, or ability. When we rely on Him, use His methods of warfare, the knowledge He provides in His Word, and by the Holy Spirit, the victory is not just certain, it is overwhelming! Praise God for His grace and mercy! Praise God for the victory we have through Him!

Bible Reading: Zechariah 4:6; Ephesians 6:10

Although ultimate victory is certain, the battle does not always come with ease or without work. Sometimes battles within the greater war are unfortunately lost. Adversity comes in countless forms and everyone has to deal with it. There are times when the battle becomes overwhelming and you need to ask for help from others. There is nothing wrong with this but you will find that with time and experience, faith will grow. When faith grows the victories will be easier and more certain.

Bible Reading: Psalms 37

Climbing a mountain takes work and persistence to get to the top. Once there, the glory of the scenery is spectacular. So too, when you climb this spiritual mountain and reach the top, the glories you see and experience will be beyond words. The rewards of persistence are far greater than you can imagine!

CHAPTER 10

Victory and the Promised Land

All Christians need to pursue a state of victory over the spiritual battles in life. The level of relationship with Jesus, and the faith and trust that go with it will make the troubles of life seem insignificant in comparison.

A vision of what lies ahead, however slight it may appear, provides a goal worth pursuing. In the course of this pursuit, many more discoveries will be realized.

> Where there is no vision [*no revelation of God and His word*], the people are unrestrained; But happy and blessed is he who keeps the law [*of God*].
>
> —Proverbs 29:18 (AMP)

The verse in Proverbs shows the importance of having a vision. When people lack a vision of their God-ordained destiny, they will flounder and never accomplish the mission in the way God intends.

Living in the victory Jesus has to offer opens the door to limitless possibilities in both the spiritual and the physical. The world is full of destruction and sin. Bringing life and restoration will bring more blessings than can be imagined. The advances that can be attained when done God's way will bring great benefits to all humanity.

Many of the experiences the nation of Israel went through from the exodus of Egypt through the occupation of the promised land are representative of the spiritual walk Christians experience today. To see that God can provide a demonstration with such accurate parallels worked through an entire nation is truly amazing and a miracle on grand scale. A demonstration at such a grand scale indicates the importance of learning these lessons and putting them into practice. One of the most notable observations is that Israel never fully occupied the land God gave them. Everyone therefore should strive to enter the promised land to the greatest extent possible.

Sadly, most people have never entered the promised land or occupied it to any degree. Some may get a glimpse and think it is sufficient. They have never truly crossed that Jordan River to enter into the promised land, much less fought the battles necessary to possess it.

The primary vision and goal Christians need to focus on is to fulfill the Great Commission.

Bible Reading: Matthew 28:18–20

An important point from the above passage in Matthew is that Jesus said ALL authority has been given to Him in heaven and on earth. All Christians have access to that same level of authority through Jesus. The goals set before us can *never* be accomplished without exercising the authority Jesus provides. Jesus made it clear that this is not an option. Fulfilling the Great Commission is a command and a clear and important responsibility all Christians have. To fulfill His commands, entering into the promised land and living in victory is necessary.

Victory and the promised land are set before every Christian and there for the taking. The keys to living in both are faith and trust in Jesus. The best places in scripture to learn the conquest are in the books of Exodus and Joshua. The objective of preparing for and entering the promised land was no different for Israel in the days of Moses and Joshua than for Christians in the present day.

Bible Reading: Joshua 1:1–3

10.1   Entering the Promised Land

Entering the promised land and living in victory takes action.

> *You can't enter the promised land by looking at it!*

God told Joshua and the people to arise, cross the Jordan to take the land, and to take dominion. Before Israel crossed the Jordan, God told them to bring provisions to sustain them when they crossed over (Joshua 1:11). Without provisions, Israel would have become weak and hungry, and would not have been able to fulfill their God ordained destiny. Similarly, we must go with the provision (power, love, sound mind, knowledge, understanding, wisdom, and the fruit of the Spirit) the Word of God and the Holy Spirit provides.

Bible Reading: Acts 1:8; Joshua 1:6–9; 1 Corinthians 2:9

Some people think they are in the promised land but are not. They have no concept of what it means to be there. Some think the above verse only pertains to what God has for His people in heaven. This assumption is false. God has so much more for us in this life than we can possibly imagine. For example, the nation of Israel had no idea what laid beneath the surface of the land God gave them. They had no knowledge or concept of the wealth of oil that would be discovered in the future. So too, we today have no idea what riches God has for us. Based on what happened with Israel in the days of Joshua, the treasures that God has are beyond our current level of understanding. Through revelation that come with developing a relationship with Him, these treasures can be revealed. These treasures are all for us and attainable if only people would pursue Him (Matthew 6:33).

In Joshua 3:13–17, the priests, as commanded by God, stepped into the Jordan, the river stopped flowing, and Israel crossed the Jordan. How many today stand on the bank of the Jordan afraid or unwilling to get their feet wet? The analogy of "getting their feet wet" means to step out in faith and obedience, and an act of surrender to His will and provision.

To "cross the Jordan River" requires knowledge of who we are in Jesus. Knowledge of His Word and the desire and determination that come with a warrior mentality are also necessities. God spoke to Joshua on several occasions and decreed strength and courage to him. Since this is written in the Bible for our benefit, God has decreed this for us as well. All that is required is to go after it!

For God hath not given us the spirit of fear; but of power, and of love, and of a sound mind.

—2 Timothy 1:7 (KJV)

Crossing the Jordan requires a step of faith, and that step also means being vulnerable and out of control. It is at this point the Holy Spirit] steps in and brings victories as He did with Israel. Obedience and faith allow the Holy Spirit to work and bring victory.

Simply put, Israel needed to mature in the wilderness before they were ready to cross into the promised land. Likewise, Christians also need to mature to the point they are ready to enter into the promised land.

The report of what God had done with Israel put fear in the people of Jericho. Their fear was expressed by Rahab's words to the two men Joshua sent into the land as spies.

Bible Reading: Joshua 2:8–11

So too, when Christians repent of their sins, pray for revival (Joshua 3:5), and start the journey to take dominion, the demons and the wicked will tremble in fear at the power and favor God places on His people. Everything needed for success in winning the battles necessary to enter the promised land and live in victory is already written in His Word for us to put into practice!

> The Israelites came to Jordan in faith, having been told that they should pass it. In the way of duty, let us proceed as far as we can, and depend on the Lord. Joshua led them. Particular notice is taken of his early rising, as afterwards upon other occasions, which shows how little he sought his own ease. Those who would bring great things to pass, must rise early. Love not sleep, lest thou come to poverty. All in public stations should always attend to the duty of their place. The people were to follow the ark. Thus must we walk after the rule of the word, and the direction of the Spirit, in everything; so shall peace be upon us as upon the Israel of God; but we must follow our ministers only as they follow Christ. All their way through the wilderness was an untrodden path, but most so this through Jordan. While we are here, we must expect and prepare to pass ways that we have not passed before; but in

the path of duty we may proceed with boldness and cheerfulness. Whether we are called to suffer poverty, pain, labour, persecution, reproach, or death, we are following the Author and Finisher of our faith; nor can we set our feet in any dangerous or difficult spot, through our whole journey, but faith will there see the prints of the Redeemer's feet, who trod that very path to glory above, and bids us follow him, that where he is, we may be also. They were to sanctify themselves. Would we experience the effects of God's love and power, we must put away sin, and be careful not to grieve the Holy Spirit of God.

—Matthew Henry's Concise Commentary [16] on Joshua 3:1–6

The Book of Acts coupled with Joshua present a picture of the promised land for us today. In Acts, the early church experienced miracles, signs and wonders, healing, and salvation coming to multitudes. In Joshua, many experiences, blessings, and dangers parallel those that everyone faces. Before going any further, it must be emphasized again that the promised land and all it means is based upon and dependent upon your relationship with Jesus. It really is this simple. As you grow in Jesus, Philippians 3:8–11 will become a living reality.

The church is supposed to think and operate in the supernatural. Doing so is supposed to be the norm for all Christians. A carnal mind can't comprehend the supernatural and tries to rationalize according to what is seen rather than act out of faith based on the Word of God. God said it, that settles it! If you examine yourself, you will find that you are drawn to the supernatural. We as Christians have an inherent desire to pursue the supernatural things of God. This is where we belong. The carnal mind learns unbelief and refuses to cross the Jordan. The carnal mind listens to the lies of the devil.

And do not be conformed to this world, but be transformed by the renewing of your mind, so that you may prove what the will of God is, that which is good and acceptable and perfect.

—Romans 12:2 (NASB)

Renewing the mind requires focus on God and His Word in addition to an active pursuit of holiness and righteousness. Such a pursuit requires consistent and effective prayer. Part of our responsibilities on this earth is to prove the good, and acceptable, perfect, will of God. Proving this is to do so by deed and not word only. We are to be ready in any circumstance to demonstrate God's power to people and thus fulfill the great commission.

> The Israelites came to Jordan in faith, having been told that they should pass it. In the way of duty, let us proceed as far as we can, and depend on the Lord.

—Matthew Henry's Complete Commentary on Joshua 3:1–6

The possibilities of what God can do with you are limitless. Rather than looking at your own frailties and weaknesses, look at the greatness of your Lord Jesus Christ. The time has come to get out of this very small environment of a comfort zone found in so much of our church culture! Be open to the Holy Spirit and willing to accept what He has for you. To "think outside the box" and accept the things God has for you is essential.

> *Limiting God limits what He can do through you.*

Keep in mind that the decision to think outside the box, and the accompanying mental attitude does not mean you open yourself to the deceptions of the devil. Although making such a decision is the first step, growing to the point you are able to accept what God has for you and reject the deceptions of the devil comes with time and experience. Your relationship with Jesus must come first. The act of putting your focus on Jesus means you are willing to allow the Holy Spirit to do anything and everything necessary to get you where you need to be.

The promised land for Christians is to live a life of faith and anointing as Jesus did. Jesus demonstrated what Christians can and should do when in right standing with God.

> Truly, truly, I say to you, he who believes in Me, the works that
> I do, he will do also; and greater works than these he will do;
> because I go to the Father.

> —John 14:12 (NASB)

Jesus made it clear in the above verse that we will do greater works than He did. Some people refuse to accept this out of a lack of faith and adequate relationship with Jesus. The reason we will do greater works than Jesus did is simple. Jesus lived life as an individual man while on the earth. It was not possible for Him in this capacity to encounter every possible situation that would require miraculous works.

10.2   Prayer

Prayer is the most effective and fundamental tool available to develop a relationship and realize these goals. Learning an effective method of prayer and applying it is imperative. Knowledge of God's Word is without exception another essential ingredient for building your relationship with Jesus. Relying on others to teach you has limited benefit. Learning to listen to the Holy Spirit and allowing Him to teach you is the only way to advance beyond the knowledge and experience of those around you.

The importance of prayer in the church is evidenced throughout the early church in the Book Acts of the Apostles. The advancement of the Gospel and the numerous miracles performed are clear evidence of answered prayer. If only the church would grab hold of the magnitude of this truth today and apply it!

Once the nation of Israel crossed the Jordan they engaged in many battles before they had peace and rest. This is true with us today.

Bible Reading: Hebrews 3:18–19; Hebrews 4:1

10.3   Faith and Rest

What is His rest? Rest is based on a level of growth where battles to occupy the promised land are won. If any more attacks by the devil manifest they are easily and swiftly dealt with. Rest is a level of relationship with Jesus, founded on faith, that gives the believer complete peace and rest regardless of circumstances and the condition of the world around them.

1. Faith comes by hearing and hearing by the word of Christ (Romans 10:17). This is the starting point. Read and study the Bible as a whole, and to do so on a consistent basis.
2. Faith comes only by working it. Everyone has a measure of faith and it each person's responsibility to work it and build it.
3. The working of faith throughout all of life's experiences is what makes it grow.
4. The avenue of building faith comes through the trust and willingness to allow the Holy Spirit to work in one's life regardless of where it may lead.
5. Fear and faith are completely incompatible. Listen to the Holy Spirit and not the spirit of fear.

Bible Reading: James 2:18–24; Hebrews 11:17–19

Abraham was a human being just like everyone else. He didn't arrive at a high level of faith overnight. It took years of building his relationship with God. So too, each of us must surrender to our Savior to be built and refined to such a level. The process of surrendering and working to build that faith and relationship doesn't come without its trials and tribulations. The blessings of pressing through it all are immeasurable and precious beyond comprehension.

Bible Reading: Matthew 16:19, 17:20; Joshua 10:12–14

Part of human nature is the desire to possess power and control. This fleshy nature has no place in the kingdom of heaven. Only as someone develops and grows in Jesus, is He is able to entrust them with more power and authority. The exercise of power and authority must be done in accordance with His will. With a little faith, incredible miracles can be accomplished through Him who loves us.

God has far more for us than we can possibly imagine!

Bible Reading: 1 Corinthians 2:9–16

10.4 Stepping Out

Even though all Christians have the mind of Christ through the Holy Spirit, few attempt to explore its depths. A relationship with Jesus must be built in order to realize it. This relationship is experiential and takes effort to build.

A small child does not possess the mental capacity to understand the details of how a satellite is placed into orbit and operated from the ground. So too, people who have not matured spiritually are not able to comprehend and operate in the things Jesus has for all of us.

To start on the path into the promised land, you must be willing to step outside the small box of the traditions of man. As a new Christian I made that decision without any knowledge of the consequences or of what I was really doing. I went to church one Sunday morning pondering over the carnality and cavalier attitude I had witnessed in the church over time. I wanted no part of this and told Jesus that He could do whatever He wanted with me. A few weeks later, Jesus presented me with a decision. I could have a nominal Christian life or I could take a different path that would lead me to a life with Him that would be much greater. Jesus made it clear that the path to a greater relationship with Him would be difficult. I chose this path but it wasn't without fear of the unknown and of the trials and tribulations I knew were to come. Since then, Jesus has shown me things and done things with me that many people have a difficult time accepting. That difficulty is present because God isn't constrained by church doctrines. You can't stuff God in a box!

> *The eternal benefits of surrendering to Jesus must be considered over the temporal comforts of this life.*

Today when I look back, I can only fall on my face before God and thank Him and praise Him for what He has done with me. That decision I made many years ago as a new Christian has been valuable beyond measure. Other than asking Jesus to be my Lord and Savior, this is perhaps the best decision I have ever made.

Entering the promised land is impossible by remaining in the comfort zone as defined by the church culture of today. You must make that choice and step of faith to cross the Jordan and subject yourself to the guidance and provision of the Holy Spirit.

In Joshua 1, God instructed and decreed that Joshua be strong and courageous. Keep in mind that God was not telling Joshua to rely on his own strength and courage. God decreed it and it was done in the same manner that He spoke and the universe was created. You cannot enter the promised land by being a faithless coward. Indeed, choosing to be faithless and a coward has grave consequences (Revelation 21:8). Unfortunately, many are in this state without realizing it.

Bible Reading: Matthew 7:21–27

Your divine destiny and responsibility are to live in victory and enter the promised land, and in so doing fulfill the Great Commission. Getting there as a "Lone Ranger" Christian is a difficult process but not impossible. Don't wait for someone to help. Learn to rely on the Holy Spirit and God's Word. Remember that Jesus is always present to provide the teaching and help you need to accomplish the tasks He has for you. Staying in the comfort zone of slumber will not go well for you. There are many scriptures that attest to this as well, including those above.

> *Do not allow those who are apostate to determine your walk with Jesus.*

Bible Reading: Hebrews 3, 4; Matthew 24, 25

So then, my beloved, just as you have always obeyed, not as in my presence only, but now much more in my absence, work out your salvation with fear and trembling;

—Philippians 2:12 (NASB)

10.5   The Victorious Life

The church's responsibility is to continue the work that Jesus started. That is, to preach the gospel and perform miracles and thus fulfill the great commission. Christians must develop their relationship with Jesus to the point the Holy Spirit is able to work through them to this degree which is one of the primary reasons why the Holy Spirit was given to those who accept Jesus as Lord and Savior. The work that Jesus did is impossible to do without the Holy Spirit for it is the work of the Holy Spirit, not the piety of man. None of us mere mortals have the ability to raise the dead, heal the sick, or do any of a myriad of miracles such as Jesus did.

As you develop your relationship with the Holy Spirit, Paul's words will become more of a reality. Understanding these scriptures with the mind is the beginning. To know and live it from the depths of your soul is the goal. The following is evidence of a relationship that is continually growing in Jesus. Each point demonstrates a general progression of this spiritual growth.

When you grow in your relationship with your Lord Jesus:

1. His Word will come alive. When you speak you will speak His Word. It will flow out of you like rivers of living water (John 7:38). It will be a priceless joy to you. The things of this world and your attachment to them will fade away and the glory of God will shine into and through you.
2. You will know what it means to be righteous and holy. Sin will be abhorrent to you. Righteousness and holiness are sweet and precious, as well as are the freedom, blessings, and fellowship with the Holy Spirit.
3. Your life will be blessed and you will be a blessing. The trials you experience will pass because you will learn the lessons much more easily than in the past. Your faith will grow and you will not be concerned about the things of the world, just as Jesus spoke of in Matthew 6:27–34. The calamities that those in the world tremble over will not concern you because of your faith in Jesus, and your knowledge of His Word. Others will see an anointing and peace on you and will want what you have.

4. Jesus will work through you in miraculous ways. Miracles, signs, and wonders will manifest through you. As a result, people will get saved, healed, delivered, raised from the dead, and experience many other miracles. You will not accept glory or credit for these things because you will be keenly aware of your humble state, and because you will know without a doubt that these miracles are from the Holy Spirit. This will be a lifestyle and a normal and natural experience, not a rare occurrence. You will consider the miracles, signs, and wonders worked through you to be of little consequence compared to the surpassing value of your relationship with Jesus. Knowing who you are as sons and daughters of the Most High through Jesus Christ will be cause to give Him praise and worship from the depths of your soul and every fiber of your being to a degree others cannot comprehend. The glory and fruit of the Spirit you experience and live in will be indescribable. The Word of God will come alive for you in ways you never dreamed possible.

The last point illustrates the victory we are to live in. Victory at this level of spiritual growth is that state where one lives in a consistent manner, and not just for brief moments. When the church in general grows to this point, it will become the focal point of society and civic affairs as it should be. Society will look to the church for guidance and support at all levels from personal to national.

Bible Reading: Philippians 3:8–14

10.6   Worldly Benefits of the Promised Land

Some of the content of this section may appear to be a diversion from the subject of building one's relationship with Jesus but this is not the case. It is very much related and dependent upon that relationship for reasons discussed earlier. The purpose is to provide a glimpse, however small, of the benefits of developing a relationship with Jesus, entering the promised land, and being a benefit to all mankind.

The extent of the information God has provided in His Word is truly amazing and a joy to discover. We have barely touched the surface. The spiritual aspects of what have been discussed in this chapter are without question the most important, however there is much more. This section presents a very small vision of what can be gained for the benefit of the whole world.

A word of warning: People are naturally curious about the unknown. The quest for knowledge has brought about countless scientific advances, and is why we continue to seek more. The spiritual world and the existence and nature of other realms also pique the curiosity of many. There is a danger in this, regardless of its perceived utility. This refers to witchcraft and Satanism, and its forbidden arts. The Bible is explicit about the danger of the dark arts. I am not saying that we should not pursue the advancement of our knowledge. Pursuing knowledge is good as long as that pursuit remains within the boundary of the Bible and God's will. So far as spiritual matters are concerned, the Holy Spirit is the leader. Trying to advance beyond where He leads or in areas that are not in accordance with His Word and will is sin.

God not only takes pleasure in us learning about His creation but He also makes it a *requirement*. The Bible contains a wealth of knowledge and guidance pertaining to mathematics and science. If math and science are done God's way [17] the boundaries are without limit. The scientific advances that could be realized would render much of our science fiction as laughable in comparison. God's way of doing things is much easier and more reasonable than we realize.

Bible Reading: Hosea 4:6; Psalms 111:2; Proverbs 19:2a

From Hosea 4:6 it is implicit that knowing God's Word is the highest priority followed by the knowledge of His creation. Both go together. From this foundation and by wisdom we gain knowledge and understanding of His works—the world around us and universe in which we live. When you build your relationship with Him you will find it a joy to learn about Him from what He has created. When viewed from the correct perspective you learn about God directly through relationship with Him as well as indirectly from what He has created. Note the priority here. Knowing Jesus is the primary goal. Everything else is secondary. Gaining knowledge of

His creation has a multitude of benefits for all humanity so this pursuit can be viewed as a form of ministry as well. A multitude of blessings and benefits that no one has yet envisioned wait to be discovered. The level of benefit to all should never be ignored or minimized. The other side of this issue is that there is a lot of knowledge that once gained could be used by the wicked to bring destruction. Therefore, care must be taken to avoid this problem. Realize that even though beneficial advances can be made, the vast majority will not be realized until after Jesus returns and the wicked are done away with.

Numerous verses throughout the Bible stress the wisdom of gaining knowledge.

Suggestion: Do a word study in the Bible on the word "knowledge".

God's works include science and mathematics since He is the creator of all things. I have known Christians that rejected gaining knowledge for various reasons. Based on the above verses alone, this is sin and a deception of the devil to keep Christians in ignorance, and therefore easier to manipulate and deceive. The first portion of Hosea 4:6 states, "My people are destroyed for lack of knowledge." One simply needs to look around to see that those who have knowledge will often lord themselves over those who don't. James Madison understood this well and wrote about it two hundred years ago.

> A popular Government, without popular information, or the means of acquiring it, is but a Prologue to a Farce or a Tragedy; or, perhaps both. Knowledge will forever govern ignorance: And a people who mean to be their own Governors, must arm themselves with the power which knowledge gives.

> —James Madison, letter to W. T. Barry, August 4, 1822

Human nature leads us to seek answers about the unknown and to attempt to be in control of every situation. The simple reality is we can't and shouldn't. If we had all knowledge and were in complete control of everything then there would be no perceived need to put our faith and trust in God. In all things, we must focus our attention on Jesus and trust

Him. There is therefore a need to approach the acquisition of knowledge from the point of view that doing so will reveal the glories of God and advance your relationship with Him. With this approach the pursuit of knowledge will be a joy and cause to worship and praise Him for all He has done.

Regardless of your aspirations, keep your focus on your primary mission on this earth, and that is to build your relationship with Jesus and fulfill the Great Commission.

> [5]Trust in the LORD with all your heart And do not lean on your own understanding. [6]In all your ways acknowledge Him, And He will make your paths straight.

> —Proverbs 3:5–6 (NASB)

The above verses from Proverbs have great relevance when viewed from the stand point of logic and mathematics. They provide guidance for working mathematical arguments of truth, and how to avoid falling into error. To solve a mathematical problem is to arrive at a solution that was previously unknown. There may appear to be multiple paths to take and each at the onset may appear to have viability. The wrong path will lead to incorrect conclusions. We are to rely on Jesus for his guidance in all things. Similarly, trusting in the foundational principles provided in His Word and applying them will lead to the correct conclusions. In addition, we are so accustomed to thinking by *logic processes* that the quantum nature (quantum physics, etc.) of reality [17] is so easily missed (Hebrews 11:3; Colossians 1:16–17). The quantum is not a process. It is the beginning and the end and is apart from a process—and much more. Through understanding the quantum nature of reality, a myriad of great discoveries will be revealed! Much, much more can be said concerning the quantum nature of reality.

Even though this is a very simple example, the Bible is full of guidance that has exceedingly more depth and detail. Throughout the Bible, passages address subjects that surpass our current level of understanding. If only we would recognize and acknowledge our errors and get in line with the truth!

> I do not know what I may appear to the world, but to myself I seem to have been only like a boy playing on the sea-shore, and diverting myself in now and then finding a smoother pebble or a prettier shell than ordinary, whilst the great ocean of truth lay all undiscovered before me.

—Sir Isaac Newton [18]

Isaac Newton's observation is just as true now as it was then. However advanced in science and mathematics we perceive ourselves to be compared to even half a century ago, we are still in the state that Sir Isaac Newton envisioned himself. The promised land that God has for us is vast and in more areas and of greater extent than we can possibly imagine! Again, the blessings and benefits that would come upon all of humanity as a result of entering the promised land are unfathomable!

The problem in exploring and learning God's ways is that the devil has infused error in even the most fundamental concepts of math and science. Understanding God's way is straightforward and simple. Reversing the error in our current way of thinking can take some effort because it goes against what we have learned from youth and used for generations, and especially with what is considered to be the absolute and undeniable truth. What we have learned and used has had its undeniable successes however it is nothing compared to what could be accomplished if we would do things correctly. God's ways make what we consider as untouchable and beyond our understanding to be well within our grasp. Knowing Jesus Christ as Lord and Savior is a requirement. Humility is also an important ingredient that will assist greatly in learning God's ways. You can't know His ways without knowing Him. Despite knowing Jesus, our sinful nature makes it all too easy to miss truth and venture into error, hence the need for guidance. Repeated efforts may be necessary to find the correct (true) path to a solution. The Holy Spirit and the Bible are our guides to ALL truth.

Bible Reading: 1 Corinthians 1:18–21

Gaining knowledge of God's ways and His creation will open the door to understand Him and to see His glories. The glory, magnificence, and perfection of all He has done will be the subject of praise and worship forever!

Bible Reading: Revelation 4:8–11

If Christians will attain the state of victory and enter into the promised land the benefits would surpass our current level of understanding. The nation of Israel had no comprehension of the wealth that lay beneath their feet (oil) and the benefit it would be for future generations and people all over the world when they entered into and fought for the promised land. We have no comprehension of what God has in store for those who love Him. The only way to find out is to go there. In so doing we will discover many things that will be a significant benefit for the present and for future generations. Those who fail to be obedient to our Savior and Lord will suffer in the present generation and subject future generations with difficulties that they would not otherwise have to deal with.

> The fear of the LORD is the beginning of wisdom, And the knowledge of the Holy One is understanding.
>
> —Proverbs 9:10 (NASB)

By wisdom we gain the knowledge of our understanding.

CHAPTER 11

Prayer

Israel crossing the Jordan, entering the promised land, and battles they engaged in to bring victory and rest are all physical representations of what we must accomplish in the spiritual. For the Christian, making a conscious decision to pray with this firm purpose in mind, without compromise, is analogous to crossing the Jordan.

An important observation is that Israel never went back. They went forward into the promised land and as long as they were obedient, victories were overwhelming. Had they collapsed in fear and retreated, their enemies would have pursued and destroyed them. Defeat is not an option, especially when Jesus has abundantly provided His people with all the resources necessary to be overwhelming conquerors (Romans 8:31–39).

Because of the battles Israel went through prior to crossing the Jordan, they had already learned how to fight and win. Similarly, we need to be prepared through learning an effective method of prayer to ensure victory against the devil and all he attempts to do.

11.1 Effective Prayer

> Therefore, confess your sins to one another, and pray for one another so that you may be healed. **The effective prayer of a righteous man can accomplish much.**
>
> —James 5:16 (NASB)

Effective prayer enables Christians to fulfill their God-ordained responsibilities. Prayer is communication with our Lord and Savior. Through prayer, or just normal conversation, we communicate with Him. Communication is the mechanism through which we build relationships with Jesus and with people.

The goal of prayer and relationship with Jesus is to grow to the point that faith will manifest as Jesus spoke of in Mark 11.

Bible Reading: Mark 11:22–24

An important point from the above passage from Mark is that if such a level of faith were not attainable, Jesus would not have said this. His statement is quite profound. Jesus was not speaking in a parable or using an analogy. He spoke of a literal mountain and sea. People have taken the words of Jesus and watered them down to excuse their lack of faith by claiming His words are just an analogy of the "mountains," or problems, we face in life. Moving something physical may *appear* to take more faith than it does to move problems, however this is not true. Rather than resigning to the lesser, push toward the higher goal! A little faith can go a long, long way.

To gain an understanding of the subject of prayer and faith, we need to look at some scriptures.

Bible Reading: Mark 11:24; John 14:13–15; Acts 4:31; Hebrews 4:16, 10:35–36; Ephesians 3:11–12

Ephesians 3:12 declares we are to have boldness and confidence coupled with faith. Without these qualities, access to Jesus will be limited. Some are of the opinion that prayer is to be spontaneous, Spirit-led, and generally of a "Caspar Milquetoast" [19] demeanor[6], or even ritualistic. One's spiritual level is often measured by such prayers. Although there is nothing wrong with spontaneous Spirit-led prayers, one's spiritual level should be judged by the *effectiveness* of their prayers, and not the style. Ritualistic prayers serve only to sound religious and are therefore useless (Matthew 6:5). The

---

[6] This refers to someone who exhibits a weak, timid, and unassertive character.

"Caspar Milquetoast" style of prayer so common today is not the prayer of a spiritual warrior nor is it the style we should adhere to.

To be blunt, most of the prayer meetings I have seen in churches are pathetic. There is no passion and people simply sit quietly and listen to someone else pray weak prayers. The end result is little or nothing happens. In the face of dire situations that require answered prayer, being meek and timid is not the answer. Persistence and aggression in prayer will bring results. It may seem easy to make such claims, however, I have seen countless answered prayers using this approach—it works!

The word *confidence* in verse 35 is important. Webster [1] defines *confidence* as:

> A trusting, or reliance; an assurance of mind or firm belief in the integrity, stability or veracity of another, or in the truth and reality of a fact.

John Gill's commentary [6] addresses the subject well and is worth repeating here:

> **Cast not away therefore your confidence,...** The same word is used here, as in Hebrews 10:19 where it is translated "boldness"; and may design here, as there, an holy boldness in prayer, free from a servile and bashful spirit; and which appears in a liberty of speaking to God, and in a confidence of being heard; prayer itself should not be left off, nor should freedom, boldness, and confidence in it be slackened, or laid aside: or else a profession of faith is intended, which ought to be free and open, bold and courageous, firm and constant; and which ought by no means to be let go and dropped...
>
> —John Gill's commentary on Hebrews 10:35

The foundation of confidence and boldness is faith. Therefore, let us not hesitate in pursuing faith. Without faith it is not possible to realize the victory and enter the promised land Jesus has for believers. Faith also speaks of the level of relationship with Jesus. Your relationship with Jesus is to be frank, open, bold, developed, and maintained with courage and faith. Confidence accompanied with works is the evidence of faith (James 2:26).

11.2   How to Pray

The style of prayer presented is aggressive, vocal, and animated. Each of these characteristics has a purpose, which is to build faith.

God has not given us a spirit of fear (or timidity). We are to approach the throne of grace *boldly* (Hebrews 4:16). I have known a number of people that with only a very little instruction in this style of prayer were amazed at how quickly and decisively their prayers were heard and answered.

- Stand up, walk around the room while praying. Don't be afraid to be animated about it. If you are in a prayer meeting with others, it may not be appropriate to walk around so it is okay to just stand.
- Speak out with authority. Do so aggressively and with passion, conviction, confidence, and boldness. If it helps to be loud then be loud.
- Pray to win and refuse to back down.
- Repeat each of the prayers as many times as needed. A tree doesn't always come down with one swing of the ax. Repetition helps to build faith. Try repeating each prayer several times.
- You have all power and authority in heaven and on Earth at your disposal through Jesus Christ—USE IT!
- Do not fear. Fear is the opposite of faith. The two cannot coexist. Keep your eyes and faith on Jesus. Fear is your worst enemy and will cause many problems. For example, in Genesis 20 you can see the problems that fear caused Abraham and Abimelech.

Expect results and you will get them. As faith increases you will find that a word spoken softly will have the same results as what previously took much longer, repetitive, and aggressive prayer. If a problem refuses to budge, there is nothing wrong with going back to the more aggressive style to get resolution. Do what needs to be done and keep pride out of it.

There is nothing wrong with repetition. Daniel spent three weeks praying without being aware of the spiritual warfare taking place on his behalf. Jesus spent hours praying in the Garden before His crucifixion. During this time, He probably did not engage in a single boring monologue.

Jesus most likely petitioned the Father over and over concerning what He was facing, and similarly with Daniel.

The only thing Jesus said negatively about repetition was against the meaningless repetition displayed by the Gentiles in Matthew 6:7. Here He rebuked them for their hypocrisy and vanity. They prayed to exalt themselves before people rather than God. When Jesus spoke against meaningless repetition it also implies repetition can also be meaningful provided it is used correctly as He outlines in that chapter.

A prayer session should follow the sequence listed below.

Preparation: A prayer meeting should be planned to address a specific subject. It may be for revival, health, issues within the church, and so on. Time may also be devoted to address specific issues people bring up. For the planned portion, have a list of prayers printed for all the attendees to make it easier for everyone to follow.

Repentance: Repent of any known sins, ask forgiveness, and ask the Holy Spirit to reveal any unknown sins. Be specific when asking forgiveness for sins. God knows them anyway but you should speak it out. If you are praying with other people and you don't want to disclose certain personal sins to others it would be best to deal with them prior to the prayer session.

Praise and worship: Sing a few praise songs before prayer. Worship Him, for God inhabits the praise of His people. Too many churches place praise and worship before repentance. When this is done the praise and worship tend to become more of an emotional experience because sin has not been dealt with first. Only after sin is forgiven and the worshiper is cleansed will the Holy Spirit be able to bring the experience of praise and worship in its fullness.

Pray: After praise and worship, pray against any spiritual matters that concern dealing with the devil and his activities. This will be followed with addressing specific issues. Repeat each prayer three or four times before going to the next. Even though it may seem time consuming to do the repetition, you will be surprised how quickly it is done. Rather than focusing on time, focus on getting the job done and seeing it through to victory. Keep in mind the repetition is a faith building exercise.

Thanksgiving: A short session of thanksgiving and praise for answered prayer at the end of the meeting will help seal the prayers.

Expect Results: Be confident as you leave the prayer meeting. Trust Jesus and He will answer.

11.2.1   Power, Love, and a Sound Mind

For God hath not given us the spirit of fear; but of power, and of love, and of a sound mind.

—2 Timothy 1:7 (KJV)

To have the power spoken of in 2 Timothy 1:7, the love of Christ must dwell in you. Developing and maintaining love is particularly difficult today because of the lawlessness that surrounds us (Matthew 24:12). Nevertheless, learning to allow the love of Jesus to become the primary motivating factor is essential.

A sound mind is free from sin, and is the characteristic of one who is righteous and holy. Webster [1] defines *sound* in this context as:

Founded in truth; firm; strong; valid; solid; that cannot be overthrown or refuted; as sound reasoning; a sound argument; a sound objection; sound doctrine; sound principles.

Without the love of Christ and a sound mind in their proper balance, power would be abused. God will give you power as you are able to use it in accordance with His Word and will.

11.2.2   Go Forth and Conquer

Bible Reading: Joshua 1:1–9; Romans 8:37; 1 Corinthians 15:57

An important concept to grasp in the above verse from Romans is that in order to conquer, action is required on our part. The word *conquer* is a military term that indicates a battle to be won. If we apply that action, victory will be attained through our Lord Jesus Christ. Victory simply cannot be attained by thinking you don't have to do anything because Jesus did it all on the cross. This mindset is a doctrine of demons designed to put the church in a state of defeat. Again, the devil does not want to relinquish what he thinks is his. It must be taken by force and is accomplished by aggression and fervor in our prayers. We are at war and victory is guaranteed only if Christians engage to win. Defeat is not an option. Remember, Jesus came to destroy the works of the devil (1 John 3:8) and He has passed that responsibility down to us.

The same victory can be experienced through the examples Jesus provided. Jesus destined His people to be over-comers and conquerors. The devil prowls about the earth seeking whom he may devour and has caused a significant hindrance in our lives and churches. The devil has lulled the church into a false sense of security with the resulting apathy. The mere fact that signs, wonders, and miracles are seldom seen today is ample evidence of this. God is the same yesterday, today, and forever.

God has called His people to be warriors, not cowards.

Prayer is powerful for warfare against the devil because of who we are in Jesus Christ, and because there is power in the spoken word (Proverbs 18:21).

Discipline is just as important (to whom much is given, much is required). See also James 3:1–12.

"You will also decree a thing, and it will be established for you;
And light will shine on your ways."

—Job 22:28 (NASB)

Care must be taken with what we speak. We must be careful not to curse or make negative confessions because they give the devil ground to cause even more problems.

Building your relationship with the Holy Spirit, as well as for solving problems and working your faith is an *upward* spiral. As you work toward this goal,

- You will grow closer and more intimate with the Holy Spirit,
- Your faith will grow.
- A greater and greater percentage of your prayers will be answered.
- Your worship will increase in quality.

11.3   Write Your Own Prayers

Many of the prayers in the chapters that follow are general enough to be used for multiple subjects and can be easily modified to suit other needs. Not every situation can be addressed in a single book so try writing your own prayers so there is no need to memorize them. Forgetting is too easy. Don't give the devil an opportunity to steal effective prayers the Holy Spirit gives you.

11.4   Be Mindful of the Enemy

The devil can and does set up evil networks in the spiritual realm against us. Such networks may be established by witchcraft or be purely demonic, or both (witchcraft is by definition demonic). Curses or demonic activities don't have to be done locally. They can be done from virtually anywhere in the world. Regardless, we as Christians have all power and authority over these things (Luke 10:19).

> *Rather than focusing on or being intimidated by the greatness*
> *of the problem, focus on the greatness of Jesus Christ!*

Remember when Jesus walked on the water (Matthew 14:28–31). Peter started sinking *after* he took his eyes off Jesus and saw the waves and storm around him.

> *Faith is not BELIEVING–it is KNOWING!*

Any Christian who wants to grow can expect to experience attacks by demons and witchcraft, sometimes viciously. Satanists often infiltrate churches to cause problems of many kinds. Be vigilant and close to the Holy Spirit so you are aware and can not only expose their evil, but also get rid of it. Ideally, the church should be so on fire for God and the presence of the Holy Spirit so powerful that no evil infiltrator would be able to enter into a church building. Those who have the gift of spiritual discernment must be allowed to do their job in the church. The church leadership has to follow up to deal with the problems. Although it would be ideal that the infiltrators get saved, remember they infiltrate the church for one purpose, and that is to destroy it. Such people are knowingly and willingly in the enemy's camp and need to be dealt with accordingly.

11.5 Fasting

Fasting is an important tool in growth and spiritual warfare. Its purpose is to weaken the fleshy nature and strengthen the spirit. Prayer and fasting must go together. One of the sins everyone has to deal with is pride that is of an arrogant nature. Fasting will help with becoming humble before our God. Pride and humility are opposites. Pride is rebellion against God, and humility enables the surrender of will and self to God.

Not everyone can fast, but it enables spiritual growth to take place quickly. If fasting is not possible, don't worry. God is not unreasonable and He will meet you where you are.

Bible Reading: Isaiah 58:5–9

Isaiah points out that the goals of fasting are to:

1. Humble yourself.
2. Loosen the bonds of wickedness.
3. Undo the bands of the yoke.
4. Take care of those who are less fortunate.

If you make fasting a practice, then God will fulfill His part:

1. The glory of the Lord will be your rear guard.
2. Your righteousness will go before you.
3. Your light will break out like the dawn.
4. Your prayers will be heard and answered.
5. The Lord will continually guide you.
6. You will be strengthened.
7. You will be like a watered garden, and a spring of water whose waters do not fail.
8. You will rebuild the ancient ruins;
9. You will raise up the age-old foundations;
10. And you will be called the repairer of the breach, the restorer of the streets in which to dwell.

Those who forsake the desires of the flesh and make their highest priority their relationship with Jesus will be greatly blessed. They will be blessed beyond their imagination. Praise be to our Lord Jesus Christ!

11.6 Praise, Worship, and Thanksgiving

Praise, worship, and thanksgiving are all part of the victory He has for every believer!

The book of Psalms is most notable for offering praise to God. The word *praise* occurs more times in Psalms than in all the other books of the Bible combined. David went through countless trials, tribulations, and life-threatening situations during his life. Rather than caving in to defeat, he always went before God and offered praise, worship, and rejoicing. God blessed him greatly in spite of his failures. Everyone should apply David's example regardless of what they may be going through. We should offer up the sacrifice of praise, worship and rejoicing in the good times and the bad. This will solidify our relationship with Him to a degree never dreamed possible. David experienced this and so can we.

Bible Reading: Psalms 50:14–15, 92:1–2; Hebrews 13:15; Psalms 18:3

If the angels in heaven worship and praise the Lord, how much more so should we whom He has redeemed with so great a price!

Bible Reading: Revelation 5:9–14

Thanksgiving, praise, worship, and rejoicing are essential ingredients for answered prayers. These activities will:

1. Give glory and credit where it is due. He is worthy!
2. Acknowledge the Lordship of Jesus Christ.
3. Help to build and solidify one's relationship with Jesus.
4. Provide a verbal confession and confirmation that prayers have been heard and answered.
5. Build faith.
6. Based on the power and authority we have through Jesus, provide a seal of finality on your prayers.
7. Move the hand of God in miraculous ways.

The above points are most visible throughout the book of Psalms. In many of the Psalms, David starts with a petition and ends it with statements of thanksgiving, praise, and worship for the answers to his prayers. David's actions are evidence of faith and confidence that his prayers were heard and answered. We would do well to follow his example!

Everyone goes through various trials. Often trials are for the purpose of refining us. Some trials are the result of demonic attacks, either directly or indirectly. Others may just be the result of dealing with a sinful world and sinful, wicked people. Some trials are self-imposed because of sin. Through these too, you must pick yourself up, repent, ask forgiveness, and go on. In any case, backing up your prayers and spiritual warfare with thanksgiving, praise, and worship will enable you to more easily endure and be victorious.

Don't let the devil steal your joy! Rejoice in the Lord always!

Bible Reading: Philippians 4:4–7

It can be difficult to do what Paul wrote in the above passage regardless of how beneficial it is when you are overwhelmed by problems, oppression, and attacks. When you are up to your ears in alligators it is easy to lose sight of the goal of the upward call of God in Christ Jesus (Philippians 3:14). Persistence and determination to press forward and put His Word into practice will be rewarded.

> *Thanksgiving, praise, worship, and rejoicing in our Lord are medicine for the soul and an avenue for the Holy Spirit to bring victory.*

²Consider it all joy, my brethren, when you encounter various trials, ³knowing that the testing of your faith produces endurance. ⁴And let endurance have its perfect result, so that you may be perfect and complete, lacking in nothing.

—James 1:2–4

In spite of the emotions we deal with, how painful the trials and tribulations are, or the difficulties involved, worship the Lord. Praising Him and rejoicing in Him opens the door to His provision. Praise, worship, and thanksgiving will open the door for Jesus to bring joy beyond description in the midst of any situation.

Praise, worship, and thanksgiving are an outward expression and confirmation of faith!

11.7   A Note on Prayers

The trials of life affect people in a variety of ways. Emotions or any number or other issues that pertain to one's mental state or health may need to be dealt with through a combination of spiritual, psychological, and medical means. Everyone is different and each situation is different, and therefore must be addressed on an individual basis. If a problem is of a nature that warrants professional help, then seek it. There is no shame in this.

The reader should use common sense and seek professional help if deemed necessary. Although prayer is certainly powerful and essential (James 5:16), it should not be viewed as the only means to solve a problem. There have been countless times when God has used the knowledge and skills of others to help bring about a solution.

CHAPTER 12

Prayers To Start With

The prayers here start with spiritual warfare to deal with demonic influences, witchcraft, and various types of oppression. Addressing these subjects first is important. Clear the field of these problems so you can focus on issues that need to be addressed. If this isn't done it will be more difficult to get through any of the other prayer subjects given in this book.

- Regardless of their perceived capabilities, every Christian has all power and authority over evil creatures and any and all of the resources they employ, including Satan himself.
- Jesus won the victory and through Him you can have that overwhelming victory too.

Having said these things, it is important to be aware of your limitations (level of faith). Don't go picking a fight with the devil just because you have come to realize the power and authority you have through Jesus. Let God pick your fights and He will be there with you and protect and teach you. It is best to not get yourself into a situation you are not prepared to deal with. I've been there and done that so I speak from experience.

Some people are of the opinion that the devil is a non-entity we don't need to be concerned about. This very mindset is a demonic deception designed to render Christians ineffective so the devil can go about his evil activities unhindered. Others will say Jesus won the victory so we don't need to do anything. This too is a demonic doctrine. Realize this philosophy takes a few verses out of context while ignoring the rest of the Bible.

These prayers are effective for defeating satanic networks. One of the prayers addresses evil machines. Many people have never considered the existence of these things, but they do exist. We should not be so naive as to underestimate the resourcefulness of demons or their ability to construct evil machines. Some of them are quite intelligent and having once been angels, so no doubt have a considerable amount of knowledge that they now use for evil. People in the ministry may deny these assertions but they do so in ignorance and without notable experience in these spiritual matters.

12.1   Scripture Reading

- Romans 9:33, 16:20
- Ephesians 5:11
- Colossians 1:13–15, 2:13–15
- Romans 8:31–35
- Acts 27:25
- Numbers 23:22
- Isaiah 8:8–10
- Ephesians 3:14–21

12.2   Confession

Speak out the following confessions, including the scriptures.

1. The Lord shall anoint me with the oil of joy above my fellows. (Psalms 45:7)
2. No weapon formed against me will prosper. (Isaiah 54:17)
3. My future is secure in Christ. He created me for a reason. I can never be thrown away or downgraded. (Romans 8:38–39)
4. I am the head and not the tail. (Deuteronomy 28:13–14)
5. I will trust in my Lord Jesus always for He can never fail. (Psalms 34:4–8)

6. There will be no poverty of body, soul, or spirit in my life. (Joel 2:26–27)
7. I have favor in the eyes of God and man all the days of my life. (Psalms 5:12; Proverbs 3:3–4)
8. I shall not labor in vain. (Isaiah 65:23)
9. I shall walk in victory and liberty of the Holy Spirit. (1 Corinthians 15:57; 1 John 5:4)

12.3 Prayers

1. Father Lord, I ask for forgiveness for all the sins [name them] I have committed against you in the name of Jesus.
2. Father Lord, cause my life, ministry and prayer life to be extremely dangerous to the kingdom of darkness in the name of Jesus.
3. By the authority I have in Jesus I stand against every distraction to prayer in the name of Jesus.
4. I command every distraction to leave my mind now in the name of Jesus.
5. Holy Spirit, cover my family, my job and career, my home, me, and everything that concerns me with Your anointing and protection in the name of Jesus.
6. Holy Spirit shield me against any power established to resist me in the name of Jesus.
7. I stand on the Word of God and declare myself unmovable in the name of Jesus.
8. I receive the anointing and power of the Holy Spirit in the name of Jesus.
9. I take the shield of faith and quench every fiery dart of the enemy in the name of Jesus.
10. My destiny is attached to God, therefore I decree that I shall never fail in the name of Jesus.
11. All plans of the devil concerning my life shall not stand in the name of Jesus.
12. I command every plan of the devil to be utterly destroyed in the name of Jesus.
13. No weapon formed against me shall prosper in the name of Jesus.

14. Father Lord, cause your purpose which no power can alter to be become operational in my life now in the name of Jesus.

15. Holy Ghost fire, destroy every strongman assigned against me in the name of Jesus (2 Kings 1).

16. Every generational curse operating in my life I render you null and void in the name of Jesus.

17. Every cycle causing repeated problems for me, break in the name of Jesus.

18. I destroy every evil device and machine established against me in the name of Jesus.

19. In Jesus name I ask you Father to help me get my eyes off the world and it cares and on You.

20. In Jesus name I ask you Father to draw me closer to You so I can know You better.

21. In Jesus name I ask you Father for revelation into the kind of relationship You want with me.

22. In Jesus name I ask you Father to move me into this relationship You want with me.

23. In Jesus name I ask you Father to bring me to the point of understanding the unfathomable riches of knowing You.

24. My Father, I give You all the praise, glory, and honor for answering my prayers in the name of Jesus.

25. **I believe and I receive** the answers to all my prayers in the name of Jesus.

26. Thank you, Lord, in Jesus name.

CHAPTER 13

Morning Prayers

Morning sets the stage for the rest of the day and starting it with prayer can have a positive effect. Morning is the best time of the day to clear the way for God's blessings to manifest throughout the day. This is the best time to clear the field of demonic powers and to decree blessings, prosperity, health, favor, and so on.

> ²Heed the sound of my cry for help, my King and my God, For to You I pray. ³In the morning, O LORD, You will hear my voice; In the morning I will order my prayer to You and eagerly watch.
>
> —Psalm 5:2–3 (NASB)

> But as for me, I shall sing of Your strength; Yes, I shall joyfully sing of Your lovingkindness in the morning, For You have been my stronghold And a refuge in the day of my distress.
>
> —Psalms 59:16 (NASB)

The nature of wickedness is to operate in the night because it operates in sin, is full of spiritual darkness, and doesn't want its activities exposed by the light.

> Consider the covenant; For the dark places of the land are full of the habitations of violence.
>
> —Psalms 74:20 (NASB)

Evil doesn't want light to be shed on its deeds, in either the spiritual or in the physical.

13.1 Scripture Reading and Confession

> [8]I have set the LORD continually before me; Because He is at my right hand, I will not be shaken. [9]Therefore my heart is glad and my glory rejoices; My flesh also will dwell securely. [10]For You will not abandon my soul to Sheol; Nor will You allow Your Holy One to undergo decay. [11]You will make known to me the path of life; In Your presence is fullness of joy; In Your right hand there are pleasures forever.
>
> —Psalm 16:8–11 (NASB)

1. I am seated with Jesus Christ in heavenly places above all principalities and powers. (Ephesians 2:4–7; Romans 8:38–39)
2. I am not the sheep for slaughter the world says I am. I am an overwhelming conqueror through Jesus Christ. (Romans 8:36–37)
3. I am a new creature in Christ and fashioned after Jehovah God. (Genesis 1:26; Ephesians 4:24)
4. I am justified by Jesus Christ and made to be the righteousness of God through Jesus Christ. (Romans 3:24; 2 Corinthians 5:21)
5. The Word of God says I am a royal priesthood, a holy nation. (Exodus 19:5–6)
6. I am a Christian and part of the church so the gates of hell cannot prevail against me. (Matthew 16:18)
7. I am empowered through the Holy Spirit to heal the sick and cast out demons. (Matthew 10:7–8; Luke 9:6)
8. I shall not fear the arrow that flies by day or the pestilence that stalks in darkness. (Psalms 91:5–8)
9. I am an overcomer because it is written that whosoever is born of God overcomes the world. (1 John 5:4–5)
10. By faith I overcome all the schemes of the devil for it is written that greater is the Holy Spirit that dwells in me than the devil who is in the world. (1 John 4:4; Luke 10:19)

11. No weapon formed against me shall prosper. (Isaiah 54:17)
12. I am the head and not the tail. (Deuteronomy 28:13)

13.2 Prayers

1. Lord, forgive me for the sins [name them] I have committed in the name of Jesus.
2. I command every evil power operating in the night to be destroyed in the name of Jesus.
3. I command all the elements of this creation to cooperate with me and refuse to cooperate with my enemies in the name of Jesus.
4. Oh Lord, establish me in every good work in the name of Jesus.
5. I command this day in the name of Jesus.
6. I decree that today is a day of blessing, favor, honor, and prosperity for me in the name of Jesus.
7. I decree that the devil shall fail at any attempt to cause me to stumble in the name of Jesus.
8. I destroy every evil network established to take dominion over this day in the name of Jesus.
9. Father Lord, raise me up to walk worthy of and pleasing to You in the name of Jesus.
10. Father Lord, deliver me from every temptation today in the name of Jesus.
11. Oh Lord, manifest the favor You have for me today in the name of Jesus.
12. I believe and I receive the answers to my prayers in the name of Jesus.
13. Thank you, Father, for hearing and answering my prayers in Jesus name.

CHAPTER 14

Evening Prayers

Evening is a special time in scripture and is a time to offer up the sacrifice of praise and thanksgiving to God. This is also a time to reflect on Jesus and a time to pray for God's protection and provision through the night. The wicked work their evil activities predominately during the night, such as establishing Satanic networks and performing witchcraft.

Evening is also a time of cleansing from the activities of the day. References to this are found in the book of Leviticus as well as situations and activities that make a person unclean until evening.

The night is when the devil attacks people in their sleep through evil dreams. A dream doesn't necessarily need to be full of demonic images and such. A dream might seem fairly benign, that is until you compare it with what is written in the Bible. The devil can be subtle and crafty at planting erroneous and evil thoughts through dreams. This is yet another example of why we must be well versed in Scripture and why the mental discipline to take every thought captive is so important.

14.1   Scripture Reading and Confession

- Psalms 141:2
- 1 Chronicles 23:30–31
- Deuteronomy 16:6

14.2 Prayers

1. In the name of the Lord Jesus Christ, Father God I give you all the praise and glory and honor and I thank you for seeing me through this day in the name of Jesus.

2. I take authority over all demons of the night, bad dreams, nightmares, and anyone or anything trying to get into my dreams, and I command them to die now in the name of Jesus.

3. Father send your warrior angels to protect my family, my property, me, and all that concerns me as I sleep in the name of Jesus.

4. I ask you Father for a fiery wall of protection around me in Jesus name

5. Father God, forgive me for the sins [name them] I have committed today in the name of Jesus.

6. I command every agent of the devil in the physical and in the spiritual working evil against my family this night to be destroyed in the name of Jesus.

7. I nullify every evil network established against me in the name of Jesus.

8. Father God, cover my family and I with Your anointing and protection tonight in the name of Jesus.

9. Father God, send your angels to stand guard around us tonight in the name of Jesus.

10. I command every plan of evil against my family and me to be sent into confusion and destroyed in the name of Jesus.

11. In the name of the Lord Jesus Christ, I subject my mind and dreams to the work of the Holy Spirit.

12. I ask you Lord to bind up all powers of darkness and forbid them to work in my dreams or any part of my subconscious while I sleep in Jesus name.

13. Father God, cleanse my mind of the evil I have witnessed today in the name of Jesus.

14. Father God, cause me to dwell on good in the name of Jesus (Philippians 4:8).

CHAPTER 15

Prayers for Spiritual Growth

Growing beyond the level of what is seen in most churches today can be difficult. You will likely be on a solo venture. Effort, determination, and a willingness to face the road ahead are needed. The Holy Spirit will guide you.

The road to victory is a one-way road. Don't expect an easy journey. If you quit and turn back you will be like the one written about in Proverbs 26:11. Realize that persistence will pay off and the rewards are of immeasurable value.

> ²Consider it all joy, my brethren, when you encounter various trials, ³knowing that the testing of your faith produces endurance. ⁴And let endurance have its perfect result, so that you may be perfect and complete, lacking in nothing. ⁵But if any of you lacks wisdom, let him ask of God, who gives to all generously and without reproach, and it will be given to him.
>
> —James 1:2–5 (NASB)

Pray your way through. Ask for wisdom. Learn everything you can along the way. Every trial, tribulation, and situation the Holy Spirit puts you in has something to be learned. Learning from these will help avoid going through the experience repeatedly.

By all means write your own prayers. Many of the prayers in this book can be used as a model and changed to suit a particular need.

You will never get where you need to be by your own strength, regardless of how strong you may see yourself. As Paul says in 2 Corinthians 12:9 and in Philippians 4:13:

> And He has said to me, "My grace is sufficient for you, for power is perfected in weakness." Most gladly, therefore, I will rather boast about my weaknesses, so that the power of Christ may dwell in me.

> —2 Corinthians 12:9 (NASB)

> I can do all things through Him who strengthens me.

> —Philippians 4:13 (NASB)

God will provide that strength and courage as He has promised. His power is perfected in our weakness. This gives no room for any of us to boast in our own strength and it gives God all the glory. Read how God spoke to Joshua in Joshua chapter 1. He wasn't telling Joshua to use his own strength but spoke an anointing for Joshua to be strong and courageous. Of course, Joshua had to work his faith to realize the results we see throughout this book.

15.1   Scripture Reading

- Hebrews 5:12–14
- Galatians 4:3
- Hebrews 6:1
- 1 Peter 2:1–3
- James 1:2–5
- Philippians 3:8–14

15.2   Confession

1. I am not what the world or the devil says I am. I am a child of God. I am a royal priesthood. As a child of God, I have been given power and authority through Jesus Christ.
2. By faith I overcome all the wiles of the devil.

3. By faith I apply the Word of God in my life.
4. By faith that I go down the road to spiritual maturity.
5. By faith I overcome the trials and tribulations the Lord uses to instruct me.
6. The Bible says that because I have received Jesus Christ as my Lord and Savior I have the power and authority to tread upon serpents and scorpions, and all the powers of the devil.
7. I will not fail. I am a success in the name of Jesus.
8. I shall live my life by the Word of God and not by the ways of the world.
9. I put my faith and trust in my Lord Jesus to see me through and bring me into His victory. It is through Jesus Christ that I have right standing with God. Through Jesus I have access to the throne of grace. God will not withhold any good thing from me.

> The LORD is the one who goes ahead of you; He will be with you. He will not fail you or forsake you. Do not fear or be dismayed.
>
> —Deuteronomy 31:8 (NASB)

> [20]Now the God of peace, who brought up from the dead the great Shepherd of the sheep through the blood of the eternal covenant, even Jesus our Lord, [21]equip you in every good thing to do His will, working in us that which is pleasing in His sight, through Jesus Christ, to whom be the glory forever and ever. Amen.
>
> —Hebrews 13:20–21 (NASB)

10. I am seated with Christ in heavenly places and am empowered to exercise dominion over His creation in accordance with His plan for me.
11. I am the head and not the tail as is written in Deuteronomy,

> [28]The LORD will make you the head and not the tail, and you only will be above, and you will not be underneath, if you listen to the commandments of the LORD your God, which I charge you today, to observe them carefully, [14]and do not turn aside from any of the words which I command

you today, to the right or to the left, to go after other gods to serve them.

—Deuteronomy 28:13–14 (NASB)

12. I am fashioned after the likeness of God through Jesus Christ.
13. I am redeemed by Jesus death on the cross.
14. I am the righteousness of God through Jesus Christ.
15. I am an overwhelming conqueror in Jesus name.

15.3 Prayers

1. Father God, forgive me of my sins [name them] in the name of Jesus.
2. Father God, cleanse me and make me holy and pure in Your sight in the name of Jesus.
3. Father God, show me my hidden sins in the name of Jesus.
4. Lord Jesus, empower me to be honest with myself and with You in the name of Jesus.
5. Father God, reveal to me sin as You see it in the name of Jesus.
6. Lord Jesus, put your strength and courage in me in the name of Jesus.
7. Father God, open my eyes to the areas of my life that need change in the name of Jesus.
8. Father God, give me the mindset of a warrior in the name of Jesus.
9. Father God, open my eyes to Your Word in the name of Jesus.
10. O Lord, give me revelation of the breadth, length, depth and height of the love of Christ in the name of Jesus.
11. O Lord, infuse in me the desire and drive to pursue holiness in the name of Jesus.
12. O Lord, increase and perfect what is lacking in my faith in the name of Jesus.
13. Father God, give me wisdom in the name of Jesus.
14. O Lord, make a way for me where there seems to be no way in the name of Jesus.
15. O Lord, give me the spirit of discipline in the name of Jesus.

16. O Lord, give me revelation into Your Word in the name of Jesus.

17. Teach me O Lord to listen to You in the name of Jesus.

18. Father God, give me wisdom, understanding, and knowledge of Your Word in the name of Jesus.

19. O Lord, empower me to put Your Word into practice in every area of my life in the name of Jesus.

20. The devil will not steal my divine destiny from me in the name of Jesus.

21. Every agent of the devil working against my divine destiny be scattered forever in the name of Jesus.

22. I am the head and not the tail and the devil will not steal from me in Jesus name.

23. I command every evil report concerning me to be erased now in the name of Jesus.

24. I command every evil plan established against me to be completely destroyed in the name of Jesus.

25. Every evil yoke upon my life, I break you now in the name of Jesus.

26. My Father, remove all physical and spiritual barrenness from my life in the name of Jesus.

27. My Father, revoke every generational curse operating in my life in the name of Jesus.

28. My Father, remove every oppression and fear in my life in the name of Jesus.

29. My Father, open every closed door of opportunity for me in the name of Jesus.

30. My Father, break asunder every hindrance to my breakthroughs in the name of Jesus.

31. Holy Ghost fire, destroy every demon affecting my life in the name of Jesus.

32. My Father, break asunder every obstacle to my divine destiny in the name of Jesus.

33. Thank you, Lord, for hearing and answering my prayers in the name of Jesus.

34. I believe and I receive the answers to my prayers in the name of Jesus.

CHAPTER 16

Prayers for Cleansing the Mind

The mind is the focal point of the battle for your soul. The devil is an expert at deception and has been deceiving for thousands of years. Situations we find ourselves in may appear on the surface to be normal, but in reality are the results of demonic activities that have occurred over a long period of time and with many people. The heretical teachings on part of some churches and denominations discussed earlier in this book are typical examples. The devil deceives Christians into thinking they have no power or authority, or that God is in control so there is no need to do anything. The list goes on and on.

Most people allow these ideas and thoughts to persist out of ignorance. Once enlightened, it becomes apparent how sinister the situation really is, and how crafty the devil is. Despite becoming enlightened, people may still adhere to ideas or philosophies that are not of God. This is a sign of immaturity on part of the Christian. We are supposed to know and act better.

Scripture makes it clear that things should not be this way. Our minds have become polluted with the world to the point that little in the life of a Christian distinguishes them from those of the world.

Be honest with Jesus and yourself. Repent and make changes so you can be transformed into the likeness of Jesus Christ. Honesty starts with repentance and cleansing the mind of worldly garbage. Spend time learning the Bible because it is truth, and truth sheds light on darkness. Learn from the Holy Spirit; learn to listen to Him.

Attacks from the devil and his demons can come in dreams, or in thoughts when you are awake. Regardless of how or when these attacks occur, they need to be dealt with.

> We are destroying speculations and every lofty thing raised up against the knowledge of God, and we are taking every thought captive to the obedience of Christ,
>
> —2 Corinthians 10:5 (NASB)

The above verse indicates the process of dealing with this issue involves both self-discipline and spiritual warfare. Dealing with dreams can be more difficult since it is common to forget the dream after waking up. Nevertheless, if you recognize dreams or thoughts that are of demonic origin, going on the attack is necessary.

16.1 Scripture Reading and Confession

- Romans 12:2
- 1 Peter 1:13–16
- Ephesians 4:20–24
- Titus 3:5–7
- Philippians 4:8–9
- Luke 11:24–26

16.2 Prayers

1. Father God, forgive me for allowing worldly influences in my mind in the name of Jesus.
2. Holy Spirit, cleanse me from every demonic pollutant in the name of Jesus.
3. In Jesus name Father God, remind me of Your Word whenever I entertain evil things in my mind.
4. In Jesus name Father God, convict me of my sins.
5. O Lord, transform me into Your likeness in the name of Jesus.

6. Father God empower me to think and do what is good and acceptable in Your sight in the name of Jesus.

7. Anointing for Godly thinking, come upon my life in the name of Jesus.

8. Every power using my thoughts against me be nullified in the name of Jesus.

9. Power of God arise and move me forward in the name of Jesus.

10. Power of God, arise and manifest in my life in the name of Jesus

11. Holy Spirit, breathe life into my destroyed virtues in the name of Jesus.

12. Father God arise and make a way for me where there seems to be no way in the name of Jesus.

13. I command every demonic influence on my mind and dreams to die in the name of Jesus.

14. Holy Ghost fire, as you came down on the day of Pentecost, come upon me now in the name of Jesus.

15. Father God, empower me to discipline myself to focus on You and Your Word instead of the world in Jesus name.

16. I command every unclean thought and image to get out of my mind now in the name of Jesus.

17. I destroy every agent of the devil assigned against me in the name of Jesus.

18. Father God, cover me with Your anointing and protection in the name Jesus.

19. Holy Ghost fire, destroy every evil power assigned against me in the name of Jesus.

20. No weapon formed against me will prosper in the name of Jesus.

21. I command every evil influence affecting my mind and thought life to be destroyed right now in the name of Jesus.

22. I command every demon, their support, command structure, replacements, devices, and influences over my mind and dreams in the name of Jesus.

23. I throw all of this evil garbage into the abyss until judgment day in the name of Jesus.

24. Thank you, Lord, for hearing and answering my prayers in the name of Jesus.
25. I give You Lord all the praise and glory and honor for answering my prayers in Jesus name.
26. I believe and I receive the answers to my prayers in the name of Jesus.

CHAPTER 17

Prayers for the Home

Cleansing and protecting your home spiritually are just as important as doing the same physically. The world is a filthy place and we often bring dirt into the house, both spiritually and physically. The physical dirt is easy to see and clean up. The spiritual filth is more difficult because it isn't always as visible. Diligence with spiritual cleansing is something that can't be overlooked. As with doing the physical house cleaning on a regular basis, doing the spiritual cleansing on a regular basis is necessary. To put this in perspective, "Deal with the dirt before it piles up."

In the home, demons and other spiritual filth can be attracted by inanimate objects such as pictures, statues, books, or religious objects. Some objects are obvious, like statues of other religious gods. You may need to go through your home and remove some things. What you have in your home is your decision and is between you and Jesus. When in doubt, pray. If He says get rid of the thing then get rid of it. Just be aware of the spiritual consequences given in Scripture (John 14:15).

Spiritual dirt can also be brought into the home through people. This happens through what we do and encounter throughout every day. It may not be intentional, or a result of committing a sin. Demons can do things that we are often not aware of, such as using an evil device or some form of an attachment placed on a person or an object that is brought into the home. They can also walk in and start causing problems simply because you are a Christian. If you are a Christian, you are a target. In any case, their sole purpose is to cause problems.

Sin allows demons to gain a foothold in people's lives so this too needs to be cleaned up.

The following may be done as a family or if you are not married you can complete these steps yourself.

The husband is the spiritual head of the family. His God given responsibility is to provide a spiritual covering for his family through prayer, Bible reading and education, spiritual protection, etc. Turn off the TV! Generally speaking, women are more sensitive to the world around them than men. Men tend to ignore many of the things their wives are aware of. The husband and wife are a team and as such need to listen to each other.

Both husband and wife should go around the house and sanctify and cover items such as furniture, etc., with an anointing regularly. The fact that you are a Christian doesn't prevent demons from getting in your home to cause problems. Pray over your pets and anoint them keeping in mind that demons can inhabit animals too (Matthew 8:32, Mark 5:13, Luke 8:33). Although demons don't care specifically about animals, they can and do use them as a vehicle to cause problems with people. I must stress that these points should be taken seriously. Both my wife and I have had several experiences where our pets were harassed by demons. And yes, we had to lay hands on them and deliver them. Animals tend to be more sensitive to spiritual things than people. Several times we have had our pets alert us to the presence of demons. Getting rid of the demons is a simple matter of using the power and authority you have through Jesus. If you endeavor to grow closer to Jesus and start using the power and authority you have through Him, expect demons to harass you. This isn't something to be alarmed about or fearful of. The devil and his demons are ones to be defeated and utterly destroyed. You have the power and authority through Jesus so use it and don't back down.

An unfortunate reality is that so much time is taken to provide an income. Work, eat, and sleep are common modes we all deal with on a daily basis. There is no question that finding the time to pray, grow, and deal with spiritual matters can be difficult, regardless of how important they may be. Maintaining a balance is difficult where there are conflicting priorities. Priorities need to change as much as possible. This could mean, among other things, to reduce the amount of time spent in front of the TV. There is a time and a place for everything.

The following are some starting points that should be done every morning by the husband, or yourself if you are a single. As a single you can lay hands on yourself and pray for God to do the same for you.

- Repent of your sins and ask forgiveness for them. Be specific. Ask God to reveal any sins you may not be aware of.
- Lay hands on your wife and children individually and pray for them.
- Cover yourself and your family corporately. "Father, surround us with walls of your angels, and the wall of your shadow in the name of Jesus."
- Cover each family member and decree blessings and prosperity over them. A good starting point is the Aaronic blessing found in Numbers,

> [24]The LORD bless you, and keep you; [25]The LORD make His face shine on you, And be gracious to you; [26]The LORD lift up His countenance on you, And give you peace.

> —Numbers 6:24–26 (NASB)

Keeping your home spiritually and physically clean will ensure that it will be a peaceful refuge from the world.

17.1 Scripture Reading and Confession

- Deuteronomy 7:25–26
- Joshua 7:11–12
- Deuteronomy 28:1–14
- 1 Chronicles 17:27

17.2 Prayers

Initial Prayers

1. My Father, forgive me for my sins [name them] in the name of Jesus.
2. O Lord, forgive me for being lukewarm in the name of Jesus.
3. O Lord, forgive me for my laziness in my walk with you in the name of Jesus.
4. O Lord, forgive me for failing to live up to the standards you established in your Word in the name of Jesus.
5. Lord, reveal all my unknown sins to me in the name of Jesus.
6. O Lord, cleanse me of all unrighteousness in the name of Jesus.
7. O Lord, remove anything from my life that is contrary to Your will in the name of Jesus.

Prayers for the Whole House

The following prayers should be repeated in each room of your home. Lay hands on furniture and other items. Lay hand on the walls too. Don't forget the garage and basement if you have them.

1. Holy Ghost fire, destroy every strongman established over my household in the name of Jesus.
2. I command every demon, their support, their replacements, their command structure, all evil devices and influences established against my home to be utterly and completely destroyed by the fire of God in the name of Jesus.
3. I cast all of this garbage into the abyss until judgment day in the name of Jesus.
4. Holy Spirit, cover everything in this room with Your anointing and protection in the name of Jesus.
5. I sanctify everything in this room in Jesus name.
6. I bind every demon and spiritual pollution in this room/object and cast it into the abyss until judgment day in the name of Jesus.

7. I dedicate, surrender, and consecrate this home/room and everything in it to my Lord Jesus Christ in Jesus name.

8. Father, send your angels to stand guard around this home in Jesus name.

9. Thank you, Lord, for hearing and answering my prayers in the name of Jesus.

10. I believe and I receive the answers to my prayers in the name of Jesus.

CHAPTER 18

Prayers Against Witchcraft

Witchcraft, or Satanism, has become much more prevalent in society. As of this writing, it is estimated that around one percent of the population in the United States practices witchcraft. There are many more around the world. This percentage will continue to increase as long as the church fails in its responsibilities.

> You shall not allow a sorceress to live.
>
> —Exodus 22:18 (NASB)

> Now a man or a woman who is a medium or a spiritist shall surely be put to death. They shall be stoned with stones, their bloodguiltiness is upon them.
>
> —Leviticus 20:27 (NASB)

> For rebellion is as the sin of witchcraft...
>
> —1 Samuel 15:23 (KJV)

Sadly, the subjects of witchcraft and Satanism are almost never addressed in churches. The most likely reason is fear. Many prefer to be in ignorance so they don't come under attack or have to deal with the subject. This logic is clearly flawed. The resulting ignorance leaves the door open for Satanists to infiltrate churches to cause problems. Problems can take forms such as sicknesses, personal problems within the church membership, and sexual sins, to mention just a few. More subtle problems may include being lulled into a false sense of security and turning a blind eye to their God-ordained responsibilities to be a nation of priests. The resistance to change may also be used as a tactic of the Satanists to keep the church in bondage, and thus ineffective.

Although there are people who are aware of the spiritual battles at hand, the majority don't know to deal with them. It is time for ignorance to end. The Bible has more to say on the subject of witchcraft.

Ezekiel 8 sheds light on some of the nature of these evil practices. One of the points is in verse 12. The Israelites practiced in secret and at night because they thought God would not see them. They didn't want the rest of society to see them either. The church has become so ineffective today that Satanists are now working openly.

> ¹Woe to the bloody city, completely full of lies and pillage; Her prey never departs. ²The noise of the whip, The noise of the rattling of the wheel, Galloping horses And bounding chariots! ³Horsemen charging, Swords flashing, spears gleaming, Many slain, a mass of corpses, And countless dead bodies—They stumble over the dead bodies! ⁴All because of the many harlotries of the harlot, The charming one, the mistress of sorceries, Who sells nations by her harlotries And families by her sorceries.
>
> —Nahum 3:1–4 (NASB)

The above passage from Nahum shows a number of connections between Satanism and death and sin. A few of the characteristics and goals of Satanism include:

1. Prostitution, perversion, and sexual sin.
2. Death and the shedding of blood including animal and human sacrifices.
3. Abortion is a form of human sacrifice for the Satanists.
4. The perversion of God's word.
5. The unbridled lust for power, control, and wealth.
6. Calling evil good, and good evil (see Isaiah 5:20).
7. Persecution against Christians and Jews.

8. Destroying Christianity and introducing a demonic religion to replace it. For example, the goal of communism is to abolish Christianity and force people to worship the government.

9. Lies to any extent to convince people to give up their rights and freedoms for the "collective good" and that a one world government is the only way to "save the world."

10. Establishment of a one world government and worship of the anti-Christ.

11. Employing any degree of violence necessary to subdue dissenters.

12. The death and eventual extinction of mankind to "save the planet."

13. Teaching children and young people that all of the above is good and righteous, and anyone who believes to the contrary is evil and must be exterminated.

All of the above items have been pushed on people by the wicked and displayed in numerous news sources for years.

18.1 Tattoos

Tattooing has its roots in witchcraft and invariably opens the door to demonic and witchcraft influences.

> You shall not make any cuts in your body for the dead nor make any tattoo marks on yourselves: I am the LORD.
>
> —Leviticus 19:28 (NASB)

The following article by Betty Miller [20] on tattooing is worth reading. The link to this article is:
https://bibleresources.org/tattoos/.

If you wish to have a tattoo removed you should first consult with a trained professional, such as a dermatologist, who can evaluate your situation and provide advice.

18.2   Scripture Reading

- Psalms 46:1–3, 50:15
- Matthew 28:18
- Luke 10:17–20

18.3   Confession

1. I am a Christian and part of the church so the gates of hell cannot prevail against me. (Matthew 16:18)
2. I shall not fear the arrow that flies by day or the pestilence that stalks in darkness. (Psalms 91:5–11)
3. I am an overcomer because it is written that whosoever is born of God overcomes the world. (1 John 5:4–5)
4. By faith I overcome all the schemes of the devil for it is written that greater is the Holy Spirit that dwells in me than the devil who is in the world. (1 John 4:4)
5. No weapon formed against me shall prosper. (Isaiah 54:17)
6. I am the head and not the tail. (Deuteronomy 28:13)
7. Because of what Jesus did on the cross, I have all power and authority over Satan, his demons, and all witchcraft. (Luke 10:17)

18.4   Prayers

1. Father, I ask you to forgive me for all the sins [name them] I have committed, in Jesus name.
2. I renounce and repent of any witchcraft that I may have performed, in Jesus name.
3. Every stronghold of witchcraft over my household and I, I break you now in the name of Jesus.
4. Holy Spirit cover my household and me and protect us from any onslaught of the enemy in the name of Jesus.
5. Every witchcraft act performed against my household and me, be destroyed by the fire of God in Jesus name.

6. I command every witchcraft altar established against my household and me to be destroyed by the fire of God in Jesus name.

7. I command every witchcraft spell sent against my household and me to go back to your sender in the name of Jesus.

8. Every strongman established over my household and me, be destroyed by the fire of God in Jesus name.

9. I take command over every demon and evil power established against my household and me in Jesus name. I command these demons and evil powers to be cast into the abyss until judgment day in the name of Jesus.

10. Every witchcraft curse holding my blessings, be destroyed now in the name of Jesus.

11. I command my blessings to find me now in the name of Jesus.

12. Every witchcraft curse hindering me from realizing God's plan for my life, be destroyed by the fire of God in the name of Jesus.

13. Every witchcraft curse keeping me from success, be destroyed by the fire of God in Jesus name.

14. (Lay your hand on your head.) Every witchcraft influence, pollution, or deposit in my body, be destroyed and flushed out by the Holy Spirit in the name of Jesus.

15. Every illness in my body (name them) cause by witchcraft, receive healing now in the name of Jesus.

16. Father I ask you to send your warring angels to encamp around us in the name of Jesus.

17. Goodness and mercies of God, overwhelm me now in the name of Jesus.

18. Thank you, Lord, for hearing and answering my prayers in the name of Jesus.

19. I believe and I receive the answers to my prayers in the name of Jesus.

CHAPTER 19

Health

Healing can be a very sensitive subject. Sometimes people don't get healed and sometimes others experience a dramatic healing miracle. I've witnessed peoples' legs grow, heart problems healed, experienced healing myself, and laid hands on people and seen them healed. Conversely, someone whom I felt well deserving of healing, failed to receive it and died from his illnesses, leaving a young family behind.

Health problems can have a number of sources such as genetic, demonic, diet and exercise related, sin related, or injuries, to name a few. Sins such as unforgiveness and bitterness are sometimes the mechanisms which inhibit the Holy Spirit from healing. You must be honest with yourself and evaluate the situation. The act of harboring unforgiveness and bitterness can and does give the devil a foothold to bring health problems. A situation early in life that brings about an illness may be totally forgotten. Openness to revelation from the Holy Spirit, either directly or through another person will help greatly in addressing a health problem.

Regardless of the cause, your case is not impossible for God. The Holy Spirit may tell you to do some things such as getting exercise and changing your diet and you will be healed this way. You may also experience a healing miracle.

Healing may not be realized for various reasons, some of which are listed here:

- Sin. This may also be generational.
- Demonic activities and the results of witchcraft.

- Lack of faith.
- Evil covenants.
- Generational curses or evil covenants made by ancestors.
- Wrong motives (such as tempting God).
- Unforgiveness or bitterness toward someone who has wronged you.

Many times, the reason for the lack of healing is unknown. Some people that don't get healed beat themselves up for a perceived lack of faith. Don't. Again, you may not know all the reasons. Because of the unknowns, it is necessary to pray and seek revelation. Regardless of the reason, pursue a closer relationship with Jesus. Some people in this situation did just this before they finally received their healing.

For anyone who needs to be healed, a first step is to make a good honest evaluation of yourself to see if there is anything in your life that has either caused the problem or will hinder you from receiving your healing. Generational issues are likely to be unknown but can be revealed through prayer and revelation.

Read the four Gospels. Jesus healed people without regard to their spiritual level or background, their physical or mental state, or what the cause was. He healed all who came to Him. Their act of coming to Him was an act of faith that was rewarded by their healing. For cases when those who needed healing were unable to come to Him, others either carried them or conveyed a message to Jesus. In either case, others interceded on their behalf and they were healed. Jesus never asked what church (or synagogue) they went to. He never asked what denomination they belonged to. He didn't pray for a half hour seeking to know whether God wanted a particular individual healed or not. He just healed them all. And so should we!

A key point is that healing is an undeniable miracle and it is personal. It presents the undeniable fact that the Holy Spirit is here and present with us today. Healing is a profound blessing. Sinners see and experience and get saved. God is always glorified through miraculous healing.

19.1 Scriptural Facts About Foods

The vast majority of illnesses today can be traced to poor diet, lack of exercise, and chemical contaminants in our food and water supplies. Diabetes and other problems have reached epidemic levels. Everyone should spend time to get educated in these subjects. In general, you should eat certified organic, non-GMO foods. Stay away from junk food, processed foods, and use only natural products.

> [19]Or do you not know that your body is a temple of the Holy Spirit who is in you, whom you have from God, and that you are not your own? [20]For you have been bought with a price: therefore glorify God in your body.
>
> —1 Corinthians 6:19–20 (NASB)

Obesity[7] has become a serious problem throughout many countries today and has a significant cost to society. Most of the time it is not due to disease or genetic problems but is caused by poor diet and the lack of exercise. The failure to take care of the temple of the Holy Spirit as reasonably as possible is sin. Obesity has many of its roots in the spirit of laziness.

Leviticus chapter 11 and Deuteronomy chapter 14 outline the foods that we are and are not to eat. Although not many adhere to a Kosher diet nowadays, dismissing what God has to say on the subject is disobedience and has its risks. There are reasons why He listed what we should and should not eat. Some of the practical reasons we know of today are that particular animals may be subject to certain nasty parasites. Some species are prone to carry certain diseases. Others we simply don't know. In any case, God knows best. A general, but incomplete, list of clean and unclean meats is listed here.

---

[7] See https://www.cdc.gov/obesity/data/adult.html for more information on of obesity.

General Categories of Clean Meats

1. Animals that part the hoof and chew the cud.
2. Fish that have scales and fins.
3. Birds that have clean characteristics (not birds of prey)
4. Insects of the locust family.

General Categories of Unclean Meats

1. Swine.
2. Animals that walk on paws—canine and feline, bears, etc.
3. Equine.
4. Reptiles and amphibians.
5. Birds of prey.
6. Rodents.

In reviewing the above lists, there is at least one common factor. Some of the animals listed as unclean have a greater potential, however slight, for eating recycled animal products. It was the man-made recycling of animal products that led to the mad-cow disease (Bovine spongiform encephalopathy) that spread primarily in England in 1986–1998. This disease was transmitted to people and by 2014 had killed over 200 people in Western Europe. Some 4.4 million cattle were slaughtered to eradicate this disease.

In general, our society consumes too much meat in proportion to the quantity of vegetables, nuts, and fruits.

You may wish to do further reading and research on healthy diets. There are a multitude of books and other materials available on the subject. A little research and common sense will go a long way.

19.2   Give Credit

No matter how your healing is done or who it is done through, the Holy Spirit is who does it. Give all glory, praise and honor to Him.

Bible Reading: Matthew 9:8, 15:31; Mark 2:12; Luke 5:25–26, 13:13, 18:43

The same Jesus who worked these miracles of healing, who never changes, who is perfect in all His ways, is here today. He can and does work the same miracles, and more, today. It doesn't matter what it is—a cold, cancer, an amputated limb, or any other issue. It can be healed. Period.

19.3   Scripture Reading and Confession

- 1 Peter 2:24
- Isaiah 53:5
- Psalms 103:2–3, 30:2, 107:20
- Exodus 15:26
- Proverbs 3:7–8
- Matthew 8:7, 16–17, 12:15, 15:30
- Luke 4:40—41, 17:15–16

Note that 1 Peter 2:24 and Isaiah 53:5 make it clear that the act of healing on part of our Lord is past tense. The work Jesus did on the cross to facilitate this has already be done.

The Gospel verses that concern healing are too numerous to list. Throughout the four gospels we see the demonstration of power and willingness of the Holy Spirit to heal. The Book of Acts also documents numerous cases after the Day of Pentecost and throughout the ministries of the Apostles.

19.4   Prayers

Because of the varied causes of health problems, prayers are categorized. The prayers for healing are general in nature. Feel free to adapt them to your specific needs. Also, many of the non-health related prayers can and should be used for any other applicable issue.

Forgiveness for Sins

1. Father God, reveal to me any sin I have committed that caused [name the medical issue] in the name of Jesus.
2. My Father, forgive me for committing these sins [name them] in the name of Jesus.
3. I forgive [name them] who have sinned against me in the name of Jesus.
4. Thank you, Father, for your grace and forgiveness in the name of Jesus.

Forgiveness for Generational Sins

1. My Father, forgive my mother and father for the sins they have passed down to me in the name of Jesus.
2. My Father, forgive my ancestors four generations back for the sins that have propagated down to me in the name of Jesus.
3. I break every evil hold these ancestral sins have on me in the name of Jesus.
4. I proclaim my freedom from all ancestral sins on both my father's and mother's side of my family in the name of Jesus.

Generational Curses

1. The earth is the Lord's and the fullness of it. I am a child of God in the name of Jesus.
2. I nullify any ancestral curse propagated to me in the name of Jesus.
3. I command every ancestral curse spoken against my family line to be nullified in the name of Jesus.
4. I command every curse spoken by my ancestors against my family line to be nullified in the name of Jesus.
5. I destroy the effects of every ancestral curse spoken against me in the name of Jesus.
6. I proclaim my freedom from the effects of every ancestral curse spoken against me in the name of Jesus.

Curses and Witchcraft

1. My Father, cover me from head to toe with Your protection in Jesus name.
2. My Father, send your angels to stand guard around me and protect me in the name of Jesus.
3. In Jesus name I command every witchcraft curse spoken against me to be nullified now.
4. In Jesus name I command every witchcraft altar established against me to be destroyed now.
5. In Jesus name I command every witch practicing against me to fall into their own traps now.
6. In Jesus name I command every witchcraft network established against me to be destroyed now.
7. In Jesus name I command every evil witchcraft device used against me to be destroyed now.

Evil Ancestral Covenants

1. Every evil ancestral covenant affecting my life and health, I nullify you in the name of Jesus.
2. I command every evil ancestral covenant to be erased in the name of Jesus.
3. I decree my freedom from every evil ancestral covenant in the name of Jesus.

Current Evil Covenants

1. Every evil covenant I may have agreed to, willingly or not, be erased in Jesus name.
2. I decree my freedom from every evil covenant I may have agreed to in the name of Jesus.

Demonic Influences

1. I command every demonic influence causing [name your medical issue] in Jesus name. I destroy you in the name of Jesus.
2. I command every demonic device established against me to cause [name your medical issue] in Jesus name. I destroy you in the name of Jesus.

General Prayers for Healing

1. Thank you, Lord, for your redemption in Jesus name.
2. Thank you, Lord, for healing me in the name of Jesus.
3. I lose myself from every infirmity in the name of Jesus.
4. My Father, heal every hidden illness in my body in the name of Jesus.
5. Holy Spirit, go through my body from head to toe and cleanse me in the name of Jesus.
6. Holy Spirit, go through my body from head to toe and heal me in the name of Jesus.
7. Holy Spirit, go through my body and restore [name your medical issue] so that it operates as it is supposed to in the name of Jesus.
8. I command my [name your medical issue] to be healed in the name of Jesus.
9. I command my [name the body part] to get in line with the Word of God and work properly in the name of Jesus.
10. My Father, cause every desire and expectation of the enemy to be nullified in the name of Jesus.
11. I decree my freedom from [name your medical issue] in the name of Jesus.
12. My Father, destroy every Satanic deposit in my body in the name of Jesus.
13. Lord Jesus, perform a creative healing miracle on me now in the name of Jesus.

14. Lord Jesus, I give you all the glory, all the praise, and all the honor for operating in my life today in the name of Jesus.
15. Thank you, Lord, for hearing and answering my prayers in the name of Jesus.
16. I believe and I receive the answers to my prayers in the name of Jesus.

CHAPTER 20

Salvation for Others

When people choose to reject the leading of the Holy Spirit they fall into the trap of Satan. For most, there is a distinct event where this occurs, usually at an early age. We have all done this, for all have sinned and fall short of the Glory of God (Romans 3:23). The devil then blinds people so they don't see the truth and deceives them to turn them away from the Gospel.

> ³And even if our gospel is veiled, it is veiled to those who are perishing, ⁴in whose case the god of this world has blinded the minds of the unbelieving so that they might not see the light of the gospel of the glory of Christ, who is the image of God.
>
> —2 Corinthians 4:3–4 (NASB)

> ⁴who desires all men to be saved and to come to the knowledge of the truth. ⁵For there is one God, and one mediator also between God and men, the man Christ Jesus, ⁶who gave Himself as a ransom for all, the testimony given at the proper time.
>
> —1 Timothy 2:4–6 (NASB)

The only way anyone will come to the truth is through the power of the Holy Spirit. And of course, the Holy Spirit will move on someone when others pray and intercede for them.

Influences from the world and from the devil distract and hide the truth from people. Intercession on behalf of these people is needed so they will be saved. This point of prayer is essential for the church to accomplish.

20.1 Scripture Reading and Confession

The following are but a few of the many scriptures throughout the Bible concerning the wonderful grace and salvation we have through our Lord Jesus Christ.

- John 3:16–17
- 2 Peter 3:9
- John 14:6
- Isaiah 49:25

20.2 Prayers

1. Father God, reveal to me any sin I have committed that caused [name the medical issue] in the name of Jesus.
2. My Father, forgive me for committing these sins [name them] in the name of Jesus.
3. I forgive those [name them] who have sinned against me in the name of Jesus.
4. I command every stronghold of the devil hindering [name] to be destroyed now in the name of Jesus.
5. Thank you, Father, that it is not your will that any perish but that all come to the knowledge of the truth in the name of Jesus.
6. My Father, open the eyes of [name] to your love and truth in the name of Jesus.
7. I claim [name] for the Kingdom of heaven in the name of Jesus.
8. I decree that every desire of the enemy upon [name] shall fail in the name of Jesus.
9. I break all curses upon [name] hindering them from coming to Jesus in the name of Jesus.
10. I destroy all evil powers of darkness hindering [name] from coming to Jesus in the name of Jesus.

11. Holy Spirit of God, move on [name] now to get them saved in the name of Jesus.
12. I bind the spirit of spiritual blindness in [name] in the name of Jesus.
13. I tear down and destroy every wall of rebellion toward God in [name] in the name of Jesus.
14. I tear down and destroy every wall of deception toward God in [name] in the name of Jesus.
15. My Father, cause your mercy and grace to overwhelm [name] in the name of Jesus.
16. Thank you, Father, for your grace and forgiveness in the name of Jesus.
17. Thank you, Lord, for hearing and answering my prayers in the name of Jesus.
18. I believe and I receive the answers to my prayers in the name of Jesus.

CHAPTER 21

Finances and Employment

Jesus has promised to take care of you. This fact is clear in scripture. There is a great deal of insecurity and instability in the world so standing on His Word for His providence is a must. It doesn't matter how bad things may appear, He has promised and He will keep His promises. This fact is emphatic throughout scripture. Place your faith and trust in Him. Faith without works is dead so at the same time you need to be active such as searching for a job, pursuing business deals, etc., and having done all, to stand firm on His Word (Ephesians 6:13).

All this sounds well and good but it is with direct experience with God's provision that I say these things. Over the years I have experienced miraculous provision on multiple occasions and had some truly profound experiences concerning God's provision. I have used the prayers in this chapter on multiple occasions and they work. It is often difficult to get one's eyes off the problem and on the solution, Jesus, when needs are pressing in. Remember what happened to Peter when he walked on the water and took his eyes off Jesus.

Although fairly long, the prayers in this chapter are a good model that can be modified to suit a wide range of needs.

21.1 Scripture Reading

- Deuteronomy 31:8
- Matthew 7:7–8
- Job 22:28

- Psalms 37:25, 28
- Matthew 6:25–34
- Hebrews 4:16
- Isaiah 41:10

21.2   Prayer and Confession

1. I confess that You Lord are the God of heaven and earth. You are all sufficient. You are the Alpha and Omega; the beginning and the end. You are the mighty God. Jesus Christ is the Son of God. Jesus is my Lord, my Savior, my King, my redeemer, my provider, and my victory in Jesus name.
2. Every generational curse of poverty over my family and I, I break you now in the name of Jesus.
3. I decree my freedom from the spirit of poverty in the name of Jesus.
4. I command every spirit of poverty affecting my family and me to be destroyed in the name of Jesus.
5. I command every evil garment placed on me to be destroyed by the fire of God in the name of Jesus.
6. My Father, put on me the garments of favor, honor, prosperity, priesthood, and kingship in the name of Jesus.
7. I decree prosperity for my family and me in the name of Jesus.
8. I command every spirit of distraction and hindrance to prayers to be destroyed right now in Jesus name.
9. Holy Spirit, shield my family and me in the name of Jesus.
10. I ask you Holy Spirit to move in my life right now and fulfill your promises to me in the name of Jesus.
11. I ask you Lord for the strength to press forward in the name of Jesus. I ask you Lord to renew my strength. The word of God says in Isaiah,

Yet those who wait for the LORD Will gain new strength;
They will mount up with wings like eagles, They will run
and not get tired, They will walk and not become weary.

—Isaiah 40:31 (NASB)

I ask you Lord to honor Your word that can never fail in the name
of Jesus Christ.

12. In the name of Jesus Christ I come against all obstacles and walls
the enemy has established against me. I command those walls to
fall down and to be crushed now in the name of Jesus. I command
all the agents of the devil in the physical and in the spiritual to be
bound in Jesus name. I command every demon assigned against
my progress to be destroyed now in Jesus name.

13. In Jesus name I come against all monitoring spirits that have been
keeping track of my movement and of the places I go for help. I
command them to be destroyed right now. I cast them to the abyss
until judgment day in Jesus name.

14. I cast out the spirit of ignorance and fear from my life in Jesus
name. I stand in the authority of the word of God. I stand in the
power of God. I command my situation to change for the best
right now in Jesus name. I will never beg. I am a lender and I am
not a borrower in Jesus name. God has blessed me. The word of
God says I am blessed and I am a blessing in Jesus name.

15. In Jesus name I cancel any negative confession I have ever made
against myself. I reject and I erase all of them. I cancel every negative
word said in times of worry or disappointment. I command all of
them to be destroyed right now in Jesus name. From today I speak
positive words for myself. I speak words of faith into my life in
Jesus name. I believe that everything I have spoken according to
God's will for me will come to pass now in Jesus name. I begin to
live as God has purposed that I live on this earth; in joy, peace,
prosperity, favor, and health in the name of Jesus.

16. In Jesus name, I cancel any spirit of confusion and indecision in
my life. I cancel any spirit of fear and oppression against me. I
have a sound mind in Jesus name. I reject any deceit or disgrace
against me and I refuse these things in Jesus name. Fire of the

Holy Spirit, consume any attempts of the devil to cause me to wander aimlessly because I seek a miracle for [jobs / businesses / finances] in Jesus name.

17. In Jesus name I reject and I destroy every spirit of tiredness, laziness, weakness, and defeat concerning this battle I am facing right now. Father I ask that You renew my strength and my mind in Jesus name. The Bible says in the book of Luke 1:37,

> "For nothing will be impossible with God."
>
> —Luke 1:37 (NASB)

18. I believe God's word is true. As it says in Isaiah 55:11,

> "So will My word be which goes forth from My mouth; It will not return to Me empty, Without accomplishing what I desire, And without succeeding in the matter for which I sent it."
>
> —Isaiah 55:11 (NASB)

19. My case is not impossible for God in Jesus name. In the name of Jesus, I ask for grace to trust God afresh in my situation. I ask for faith in God to arise in me. It is written in the word of God in Hebrews 11:6,

> And without faith it is impossible to please Him, for he who comes to God must believe that He is and that He is a rewarder of those who seek Him.
>
> —Hebrews 11:6 (NASB)

20. In Jesus name I destroy all attempts of the devil to cause people to keep disappointing me. I reject disappointments in Jesus name. Amen. I reject every plan of the devil to cause people to keep me giving and making me rely on promises that never materialize. I reject all these things. I command all of them to be bound and I cast them to the abyss until judgment day in Jesus name. Amen.

In Jesus name anything I do now shall be stable and fruitful. I will no longer go on fruitless ventures. I receive progress, promotion, success and prosperity in the name of Jesus Christ.

21. I command my spirit, soul, and body to be refreshed and renewed by the Spirit of God. I rise up in confidence and trust God for a miracle in my [job / business / finances] in Jesus name. In the name of Jesus Christ I command every plan of the devil to deceive me and to draw back my faith and trust in Jesus to be destroyed in Jesus name. It is written in the book of Hebrews 10:38,

> But my righteous one shall live by faith; and if he shrinks back, my soul has no pleasure in him.
>
> —Hebrews 10:38 (NASB)

In Jesus name I continue believing and standing in faith for my [job / business / finances] to manifest. The Bible says in Hebrews 6:12,

> so that you will not be sluggish, but imitators of those who through faith and patience inherit the promises.
>
> —Hebrews 6:12 (NASB)

22. I stand on God's promises to me as a child of God that I should live in abundance. God has spoken in His Word that the Lord is my provider and that I should lack nothing. Right now I seek God in confidence that He has already heard me and is still hearing my prayers in Jesus name. The word of God says in the book of Hebrews 10:23,

> Let us hold fast the confession of our hope without wavering, for He who promised is faithful;
>
> —Hebrews 10:23 (NASB)

The Bible says in the book of Romans 10:11,

> For the scripture says, Whoever believes in him shall not
> be disappointed.

> —Romans 10:11 (NASB)

in Jesus name.

23. Almighty God shall never fail for He is faithful and has promised
to see me through every tribulation. The Bible says He has
promised that He will never leave me nor forsake me in Jesus
name. Psalms 34:19 says,

> Many are the afflictions of the righteous, But the LORD
> delivers him out of them all.

> —Psalms 34:19 (NASB)

Deuteronomy 31:8 says,

> The LORD is the one who goes ahead of you; He will be
> with you. He will not fail you or forsake you. Do not fear
> or be dismayed.

> —Deuteronomy 31:8 (NASB)

Hebrews 13:5 says,

> "...I will never desert you, nor will I ever forsake you."

> —Hebrews 13:5 (NASB)

Lord lift me up in accordance to Your word and Your will for me
in Jesus name. Deuteronomy 28:13 says,

> The LORD will make you the head and not the tail, and
> you only will be above, and you will not be underneath,
> if you listen to the commandments of the LORD your
> God, which I charge you today, to observe them carefully,

> —Deuteronomy 28:13 (NASB)

Isaiah 41:10 says,

> "Do not fear, for I am with you; Do not anxiously look about you, for I am your God. I will strengthen you, surely I will help you, Surely I will uphold you with My righteous right hand."
>
> —Isaiah 41:10 (NASB)

Hebrews 4:16 says,

> Therefore let us draw near with confidence to the throne of grace, so that we may receive mercy and find grace to help in time of need.
>
> —Hebrews 4:16 (NASB)

The word of God says in the book of Psalms 23:1 that,

> The LORD is my shepherd, I shall not want.
>
> —Psalms 23:1 (NASB)

Numbers 23:19 says,

> God is not a man, that He should lie, Nor a son of man, that He should repent; Has He said, and will He not do it? Or has He spoken, and will He not make it good?
>
> —Numbers 23:19 (NASB)

Almighty Father, I ask you to honor your Word in my life today as I speak it. I remind you of your promises to me in Jesus name.

24. My Father, I ask you to manifest my [job / business / finances] for me in the name of Jesus Christ. You are my only helper. Your Word says I should not put my trust in man to help me so today Lord, I put my trust in you to arise to my help in Jesus name.

25. In Jesus name I ask you Lord to manifest Your favor for me in the sight of man. I ask you Lord to honor Your word to me that the

people I do not know will help me and that You will lead me, guide me, and direct my footsteps to the right places, [jobs / businesses / finances] in Jesus name. I decree that anywhere I go, I shall find favor and I will get exactly what I am requesting to be done for me, be it a job, contract, a business, or a financial miracle, in Jesus name. I will never be a loser. I am a winner in Christ. God has blessed me and I command those blessings to manifest in full now in Jesus name.

26. I ask you Lord for a good, stable, secure, and prosperous [job / business / finances] in Jesus name. I will have more than enough in Jesus name. Father, I receive Your blessings in the name of Jesus Christ.

27. In the name of Jesus Christ, I reject every suffering of any kind I am facing because of the lack of a [job / business / finances]. I command every spirit of hardship and difficulty to be bound in Jesus name. The Bible says in the book of Joel 2:26,

> You will have plenty to eat and be satisfied And praise the name of the LORD your God, Who has dealt wondrously with you; Then My people will never be put to shame.

> —Joel 2:26 (NASB)

It is written in the book of Isaiah 43:19,

> Behold, I will do something new, Now it will spring forth; Will you not be aware of it? I will even make a roadway in the wilderness, Rivers in the desert.

> —Isaiah 43:19 (NASB)

in Jesus name. Father, I believe that you will make a way for me. I ask for the way to be made now and I receive it by faith now in Jesus name.

28. It is written in the book of 1 Corinthians 10:13,

> No temptation has overtaken you but such as is common to man; and God is faithful, who will not allow you

to be tempted beyond what you are able, but with the temptation will provide the way of escape also, so that you will be able to endure it.

—1 Corinthians 10:13 (NASB)

In Jesus name I ask you Lord to provide me with an escape now. I ask you Lord to deliver me from my situation now in the name of Jesus Christ. I hold on tight to my escape. I hold on tight to my deliverance. I will make it in Jesus name. I have already made it in Jesus name.

29. I am a child of God. The earth is the Lord's and the fullness of it. I command everything God has purposed for my life to come to pass and manifest now for all eyes to see that I truly serve a living God in Jesus name. I decree a financial breakthrough. I decree [job / business / financial] openings to manifest now in the name of Jesus. I decree more than enough and I decree open heavens for myself in Jesus name.

30. I command all the doors to progress to open to me now in the name of Jesus Christ. The word of God says in the book of Revelation 3:7,

> ...He who is holy, who is true, who has the key of David, who opens and no one will shut, and who shuts and no one opens, says this:

—Revelation 3:7 (NASB)

I command the doors to financial breakthrough to open in Jesus name. I will never lack again. I will never suffer again. I will never be ashamed in Jesus name. I command my freedom from all these things in Jesus name.

31. Jesus Christ is the answer to all my needs. The word of God says in the book of Philippians 4:19,

> And my God will supply all your needs according to His riches in glory in Christ Jesus.
>
> —Philippians 4:19 (NASB)

in Jesus name. I receive my needs met in Jesus name. I confess that the needs of my husband/wife are met. I confess that my family is cared for and provided for in Jesus name.

32. Thank you, Lord, for your word says in the book of Matthew 7:7–8,

> ⁷Ask, and it will be given to you; seek, and you will find; knock, and it will be opened to you. ⁸For everyone who asks receives, and he who seeks finds, and to him who knocks it will be opened.
>
> —Matthew 7:7–8 (NASB)

in Jesus name.

33. God must be glorified in my life. I ask you Lord to use me as a testimony to bring glory to Your name. I ask that You use me to testify, to encourage, to show Your mercy, to show Your grace and faithfulness to the people of the world in Jesus name.

34. Lord, I have asked and I receive Your word. I believe and receive the answers to my prayers in the name of Jesus Christ. Lord, thank you for all the answers, and I give You all the praise and glory and honor in Jesus name. Amen.

CHAPTER 22

Family Relations

Family relations include relationships within and outside the immediate family such as relatives.

God created a hierarchy within the family with the husband as the head of the household followed by the wife and then the children. Of course, God is the head of the husband. The devil will attempt to upset this organization and cause division and unbalance through a variety of means. We need to be aware of these and recognize when attacks come. Each person in the family must be aware of and follow their God given roles and responsibilities. Each person in the family must understand that they are ultimately accountable to God for everything they say and do. We all make mistakes and when they occur, they must be dealt with in an appropriate and Godly manner. Everyone has weaknesses and it is a duty and responsibility to address them and become more Christ-like. It is also the duty and responsibility of others to help the one who falls in a positive and edifying manner according to scripture. Ephesians 5 and 6 outline some of the methods we are to use for situations within and outside the family.

There is a lot of truth to the saying that a family that prays together stays together. This becomes especially important in view of the ungodly and Satanic influences that are directed at children in the public schools. The family should be a team going forward to the common goal of building their individual relationships with Jesus to fulfill God's plan for their lives, and preparing for the future. Prayer is the key to maintaining peace and harmony, and to counter and destroy the attacks of the devil. Keep a watch out for the many 'divide and conquer' tactics the devil may attempt to employ.

22.1   Scripture Reading and Confession

- Ephesians 5:22–24
- Ephesians 6:2–4

22.2   Prayers

1. Father God, reveal to me any sin I have committed in the name of Jesus.
2. My Father, forgive me for committing these sins [name them] in the name of Jesus.
3. I forgive [name them] who have sinned against me in the name of Jesus.
4. Thank you, Father, for your grace and forgiveness in the name of Jesus.
5. I take authority over and destroy the demonic strongman established over my household in the name of Jesus.
6. I command every demon attempting to convince me that these prayers are nonsense to be completely destroyed now in the name of Jesus.
7. I command every spirit of contention and strife in my family to be destroyed by the fire of God in the name of Jesus.
8. I command all demons, their support, their replacements, their command structure, all evil devices, and influences established against my household to be utterly and completely destroyed by the fire of God in the name of Jesus. I cast all these into the abyss until Judgment Day in the name of Jesus.
9. I decree favor and blessing on every member of my family [name them] in the name of Jesus.
10. Holy Spirit, cover every member of my family [name them] with Your protection in Jesus name.

11. I command the devil to keep his hands off [name each family member] in the name of Jesus.

12. I command every evil plan [name it if you are aware of something] established against my family and I command it to backfire against the enemy in the name of Jesus.

13. I command every spirit of strife in my family to be destroyed by the fire of God in the name of Jesus.

14. I command every spirit of rebellion in my family to be destroyed by the fire of God in the name of Jesus.

15. Every generational family curse [name them if you know of any] on my mother's side of the family, be nullified in the name of Jesus.

16. Every generational family curse [name them if you know of any] on my father's side of the family, be nullified in the name of Jesus.

17. I decree the blessings of the Lord upon my family [name each family member] in the name of Jesus.

18. The husband should lay hands on each member of the family and proclaim the Aaronic blessing from Numbers 6:24–26 as follows:

> [24]The LORD bless you, and keep you; [25]The LORD make His face shine on you, And be gracious to you; [26]The LORD lift up His countenance on you, And give you peace.
>
> —Numbers 6:24–26 (NASB)

19. My Father, send your angels to stand guard around [name each family member] today in the name of Jesus.

20. My Father, give [name each family member] the strength and courage to stand in righteousness and to refuse sin in the name of Jesus.

21. Lord, I have asked and I receive Your word. I believe and receive the answers to my prayers in the name of Jesus Christ. Lord, thank you for all the answers. Amen.

CHAPTER 23

Ungodly Influences

Ungodly influences on an individual and family can come in many forms. Children are particularly vulnerable. I've heard many a parent justify sending their children to ungodly public schools with the thought that such an environment will provide balance and exposure to what they will face in the world when they grow and become more mature. This philosophy has a lot of problems with it, and is contrary to scripture. First, a child must be trained and raised in a godly manner and with knowledge of God's Word. These will provide a good moral foundation so when children are older and more mature, they will be better able to deal with the evils of this world successfully and not become a contributor to the social problems we have today. Being influenced by evil at an early and impressionable age does not provide the proper foundation for them to make qualified decisions.

Home schooling and private Christian schools are better than the public schools. If you are able to do this then it can be very rewarding for the entire family.

Similar statements can be made concerning individuals of all ages as well. Reading and studying the Bible is especially important as the world becomes more evil. Without the moral and spiritual foundation provided by the Bible we are doomed to failure.

The moral decay of society has made providing our children with a Godly foundation apart from the evils of this world very difficult. The devotion of an adequate amount of time to family prayer and instruction in the Bible is important for all.

In addition to the prayers and confessions that follow, repeat the prayers and confessions from Chapter 17.

23.1   Scripture Reading

- Matthew 7:13–14
- 1 Timothy 6:11
- Philippians 2:12–13
- Proverbs 22:5–6

23.2   Confession

1. I am not what the world says I am.
2. I am an overwhelming conqueror through Jesus Christ.
3. I am a redeemed child of God.
4. I am a royal priesthood through Jesus.
5. Because of the position I am placed in through my relationship with Jesus I have all power and authority over the devil and all that he does.
6. I am empowered through Jesus to exercise dominion over the devil and all his activities.
7. No weapon formed against me shall prosper. (Isaiah 54:17)
8. By faith I overcome all the tricks and deceptions of the devil.
9. Read Psalms 91.

23.3   Prayers

1. My Father, please forgive me for my sins [name them] in the name of Jesus.
2. Thank you, Lord, for your mercy and grace in the name of Jesus.
3. Holy Spirit, cover [name each family member] and me with Your anointing and protection in Jesus name.
4. Father God, give [name each family member] and me the strength and courage to resist the temptation to entertain ungodly influences in the name of Jesus.

5. Every evil plantation in [name each family member] and me, come out and be destroyed now in Jesus name.

6. I decree that evil influences and peer pressure will not touch [name each family member] or me in the name of Jesus.

7. I reject every evil influence over [name each family member] and me in the name of Jesus.

8. I command every evil influence over [name each family member] to be broken now in the name of Jesus.

9. I command every demon associated with influencing [name each family member] to be completely destroyed in the name of Jesus.

10. I command every demon, evil influence, evil network, all demonic replacements, support, command structure, and all evil devices targeting [name each family member] and me in the name of Jesus.

11. I cast all this garbage into the abyss until judgment day in the name of Jesus.

12. I proclaim my freedom from these things in the name of Jesus.

13. I proclaim freedom from these things for [name each family member] and me in the name of Jesus.

14. I proclaim blessings and godly influences and thoughts over [name each family member] and me in the name of Jesus.

15. My Father, send your angels to stand guard around [name each family member] and me day and night in the name of Jesus.

16. Thank you, Lord, for hearing my prayers in the name of Jesus.

17. I believe and I receive the answers to these prayers in the name of Jesus.

CHAPTER 24

Anger

Anger is a natural emotion that we all experience. Scripture warns that anger must be kept within certain boundaries. The devil uses anger as a tool to cause a myriad of problems both with an individual and with those around them. There are demons that specialize in anger and if someone has an inherent anger problem, they are more susceptible to demonic attacks. In any case, it is essential to work toward maintaining a healthy mental attitude and keep anger in check.

Anger can also be connected to the spirit of offense, insecurity, or lack of control. Other associations may include pride, or self-righteousness. Some have learned early in life to use anger as a defensive or coping mechanism. As such it is unhealthy and must be dealt with on several fronts. Even after all the spiritual aspects are dealt with, counseling may be necessary to break the cycle and retrain the mind to use more healthy means of coping with life's difficulties.

One of the primary sources of anger comes from offenses. John Bevere has an excellent book and DVD study titled *The Bait of Satan* [21] that deals with this subject.

24.1 Scripture Reading and Confession

- Proverbs 16:32, 19:11
- Ephesians 4:26—27, 31—32
- James 1:19—20

24.2 Prayers

1. My Father, please forgive me for my sins [name them] in the name of Jesus.
2. Thank you, Lord, for your mercy and grace in the name of Jesus.
3. Every inherited spirit of anger, die in the name of Jesus.
4. Every generational curse of anger in my life I nullify and cast you out in the name of Jesus.
5. I command every demon, evil influence, evil network, demonic replacements, demonic support, demonic command structure, and all evil devices of anger targeting me in the name of Jesus.
6. I bind all of this garbage and cast it into the abyss until judgment day in the name of Jesus.
7. I proclaim my freedom from these things in the name of Jesus.
8. Holy Spirit, put your strength in me to resist anger in the name of Jesus.
9. Holy Spirit, anoint me with the spirit of self-discipline in the name of Jesus.
10. Holy Spirit, heal my mind from the ravages of anger in the name of Jesus.
11. Holy Spirit fill me with your peace in the name of Jesus.
12. Holy Spirit, anoint me with the oil of gladness in the name of Jesus.
13. Holy Spirit, give me wisdom in all things in the name of Jesus.
14. I decree my freedom from unnatural anger in the name of Jesus.
15. Holy Spirit, I give you all the praise, glory, and honor for answering my prayers in the name of Jesus.
16. Thank you, Lord, for your mercies and grace in the name of Jesus.
17. I believe and receive the answers to my prayers in the name of Jesus.

CHAPTER 25

Anxiety, Fear, and Worry

Anxiety, fear, and worry can be the result of the lack of faith, or an inherent weakness, or they may be demonic in origin. Prayer is the key for building strength. It would be nice if faith built strong in one area would easily transfer to another area. Unfortunately, our minds don't always work in such a reasonable and logical manner. Our Lord has provided many scriptures that address these issues, too many to list here. Perhaps one of the more notable passages is found in the Sermon on the Mount in Matthew chapter six.

25.1   Scripture Reading and Confession

- Matthew 6:25–34
- Philippians 4:6–7
- Psalms 27:1–3, 46:1–3
- Proverbs 3:5–8, 25–26, 29:25
- Hebrews 4:16
- Romans 8:31–39
- Isaiah 54:17
- 2 Timothy 1:7
- 1 John 4:18

25.2 Prayers

1. My Father, please forgive me for my sins [name them] in the name of Jesus.
2. Thank you, Lord, for your forgiveness, mercy and grace in the name of Jesus.
3. I am a child of God therefore fear, anxiety, and worry have no place in me. Get out now in the name of Jesus.
4. My enemies shall stumble and fall in the name of Jesus.
5. I stand upon the Word of God and refuse to move off it no matter what I'm going through in the name of Jesus.
6. Every spirit of fear, anxiety, and worry I command you in the name of Jesus.
7. I cast all of these demons, their evil devices and influences, their support, replacements, and command structure into the abyss until judgment day in the name of Jesus.
8. I decree my freedom from these things in the name of Jesus.
9. My heavenly Father shall set me securely above my enemies in the name of Jesus.
10. My heavenly Father shall set a table before me in the presence of my enemies in the name of Jesus.
11. I put my faith and trust in Jesus in the name of Jesus.
12. No weapon formed against me shall prosper in the name of Jesus.
13. I am a child of God. I have the mind of Christ. I reject and cast out everything that has exalted itself above the Word of God in my life in the name of Jesus.
14. I refuse to live in fear, anxiety, and worry in the name of Jesus.
15. My enemies shall live in fear and dread in the name of Jesus.
16. I shall not be in the bondage of fear because the Lord is my shepherd in the name of Jesus.
17. God has not given me a spirit of fear. He has given power, love, and a sound mind in the name of Jesus.
18. All my enemies shall fall into their own traps in the name of Jesus.

19. My Father, I give you all the praise, glory, and honor for answering my prayers in the name of Jesus.
20. Thank you Lord for your mercies and grace in the name of Jesus.
21. I believe and receive the answers to my prayers in the name of Jesus.

CHAPTER 26

Depression and Suicide

A wide range of causes contribute to depression. Unfortunately, suicide is a common result of depression or the inability to cope with one or more situations. The scope of the problem throughout the world today is shocking.

Wikipedia [22] has a good discussion on suicide. Some excerpts are as follows:

> An estimated 1 million people worldwide take their lives by suicide every year. It is estimated that global annual suicide fatalities could rise to 1.5 million by 2020. Worldwide, suicide ranks among the three leading causes of death among those aged 15–44 years. Suicide attempts are up to 20 times more frequent than completed suicides.

> Incidence of suicide in a society depends on a range of factors. Clinical depression is an especially common cause. Substance abuse, severe physical disease or infirmity are also recognized causes. The countries of the Eastern Europe and East Asia have the highest suicide rate in the world. The region with the lowest suicide rate is Latin America. Gender difference plays a significant role: among all age groups in most of the world, females tend to show higher rates of reported nonfatal suicidal behavior, males have a much higher rate of completed suicide.

Depression and suicide are clearly major social problems in most places around the world. To an extent, hopelessness can lead to depression which can lead to suicide.

Ron Hutchcraft [23] has a good article on his website titled, *Too Close to the Edge*, concerning suicide.

Life is never easy, even for those who live in the lap of luxury. Every position in society has its own set of problems to deal with. People get close to the edge when they fail to put their faith, hope, trust, and eyes on Jesus. Remember Peter when he walked on the water:

> [28]Peter said to Him, "Lord, if it is You, command me to come to You on the water." [29]And He said, "Come!" And Peter got out of the boat, and walked on the water and came toward Jesus. [30]But seeing the wind, he became frightened, and beginning to sink, he cried out, "Lord, save me!" [31]Immediately Jesus stretched out His hand and took hold of him, and said to him, "You of little faith, why did you doubt?"

> —Matthew 14:28–31 (NASB)

In every situation, regardless of how long, hard, or painful it seems to be, it is essential that we stay focused on our Lord Jesus Christ. This is the only way. We must put our faith and trust in Him. No one can be a "Lone Ranger" Christian. If you are in a state of depression and have considered or even tried suicide it is essential to seek help. Of those societies cited in the Wikipedia article above, one of the detractors of depression and suicide is social cohesion. That is to say that people communicate with each other, seek each other out for help.

King David is a good example of someone who had to deal with numerous unpleasant and life-threatening situations throughout his life. Yet we read of the attitude and approach he used throughout the book of Psalms. The focus of his life and solution to all his problems was God. The praise, thanksgiving, and worship he offered up was medicine for his soul and as always, God not only delivered him but filled him with joy. It may not be easy to sing praises to God and to worship Him when it feels like the whole world just dumped on your face. It is nonetheless a pattern of behavior that must be built through discipline.

Someone who is struggling with difficult issues is a target of the devil since he wants to steal, kill, and destroy your life. Depression and suicide are often exacerbated by or are the direct result of demonic activities. The spiritual side must be dealt with as well as the physical and mental sides (counseling, medical help, etc. as needed).

26.1 Scripture Reading and Confession

- Psalms 118:17, 143:7–8
- Hebrews 1:9
- Luke 4:18–19
- Galatians 5:22–23
- Philippians 4:4
- 1 Thessalonians 5:16–18
- John 10:10

26.2 Prayers

1. My Father, please forgive me for my sins [name them] in the name of Jesus.
2. O Lord, forgive me for not putting my faith, hope, and trust in you in the name of Jesus.
3. Thank you, Lord, for your forgiveness, mercy and grace in the name of Jesus.
4. Every spirit of death and destruction in my life, die in the name of Jesus.
5. I refuse to accept a satanic destiny in the name of Jesus.
6. I nullify every curse against my life in the name of Jesus.
7. Every evil chain on my destiny, I break you in the name of Jesus.
8. Every spirit of depression and suicide I take command over you in the name of Jesus.
9. I cast all of these demons, their evil devices and influences, their support, replacements, and command structure into the abyss until judgment day in the name of Jesus.
10. I decree my freedom from these things in the name of Jesus.

11. Holy Spirit, fill me with your love in the name of Jesus.

12. Holy Spirit, fill me with all the fruit of your Spirit in the name of Jesus.

13. Holy Spirit, cover me with Your protection in Jesus name.

14. Holy Spirit, cause all my enemies to fall into their own traps in the name of Jesus.

15. I command any evil domination and control over my life to be destroyed now in the name of Jesus.

16. I nullify every conscious and unconscious covenant made against my divine destiny in the name of Jesus.

17. I command every evil power hindering my blessings from finding me to be destroyed now in the name of Jesus.

18. O Lord, revive and increase my prayer life in the name of Jesus.

19. O Lord, infuse me with your strength and courage in the name of Jesus.

20. O Lord, deliver me from my situation in the name of Jesus.

21. Holy Spirit, cause me to prosper to your glory in the name of Jesus.

22. Holy Spirit, put the gift of praise and worship in my mouth in the name of Jesus.

23. Holy Spirit, put your faith, hope, and love in my heart and mind in the name of Jesus.

24. Holy Spirit, raise me up to be an overwhelming conqueror in the name of Jesus.

25. Holy Spirit, I give you all the praise, glory, and honor for answering my prayers in the name of Jesus.

26. Thank you, Lord, for your mercies and grace in the name of Jesus.

27. I believe and receive the answers to my prayers in the name of Jesus.

CHAPTER 27

Failure at the Edge of Breakthroughs

Occasionally, when people are on the edge of receiving blessings from God such as a job, business, greater level of relationship with Him, finances, and many other things, the blessing is stolen. At a critical point, evil powers swoop in to steal the blessing. They do not attempt to hinder one from going down the path to receive a blessing, but steal it away at the last moment. That last moment is where these demons operate in order to provoke distrust in God, frustration, anger, and hopelessness. The goal is to bring defeat to God's people.

Often the greatest battles are at the edge of breakthroughs. Jesus experienced the same. We can see in Matthew 4:1–11 that the devil attempted to derail Jesus' ministry at the point it was about to take off.

We can see this same evil spirit in operation in many places throughout scripture. To name a couple, Israel was on the verge of entering the promised land (Numbers 13–14) but was prevented from doing so because the devil convinced them they couldn't, when they should have placed their trust in God. In the parable of the ten virgins (Matthew 25:1–13) with the lamps of oil, 50% of them failed to go with the bridegroom because of their failure.

The so called "Murphy's Law" we've become so accustomed to is more often than not the activity of demonic forces. This evil persists because most people are unaware of what is actually going on behind the scenes. Understanding the schemes of the devil will enable you overcome and destroy them.

27.1 Scripture Reading and Confession

- 1 Corinthians 16:9
- Joel 2:23–26

27.2 Prayers

1. My Father, forgive me for my sins [name them] in the name of Jesus.
2. O Lord, forgive me for being lukewarm in the name of Jesus.
3. Thank you, Lord, for your forgiveness, mercy and grace in the name of Jesus.
4. Every evil power attacking me at the edge of my breakthroughs, die in the name of Jesus.
5. Every generational spirit and curse causing failure at the edge of my breakthrough, I destroy you now in the name of Jesus.
6. I shall not die. My problem shall die in the name of Jesus.
7. Every satanic plan against my life be nullified in the name of Jesus.
8. I bind and cast out every spirit of bad luck in the name of Jesus.
9. I command every spirit of bad luck to be completely destroyed in the name of Jesus.
10. My blessings shall not be stolen from me in the name of Jesus.
11. Every spirit of disobedience operating in my life I destroy you now in the name of Jesus.
12. Every spirit of backwardness operating in my life I destroy you now in the name of Jesus.
13. Every spirit operating to cause failure at the edge of breakthroughs, I take command over you in the name of Jesus.
14. I cast all of these demons, their evil devices and influences, their support, replacements, and command structure into the abyss until judgment day in the name of Jesus.
15. I decree my freedom from these things in the name of Jesus.
16. My blessings will not be taken from me any more in the name of Jesus.
17. I command all my stolen blessings to be returned to me seven-fold over in the name of Jesus.

18. I decree that all the blessings God has for me will manifest for me in the name of Jesus.
19. My Father, cause me to prosper to your glory in the name of Jesus.
20. My Father, put the gift of praise and worship in my mouth in the name of Jesus.
21. My Father, put your faith, hope, and love in my heart and mind in the name of Jesus.
22. My Father, raise me up to be an overwhelming conqueror in the name of Jesus.
23. My Father, I give you all the praise, glory, and honor for answering my prayers in the name of Jesus.
24. Thank you, Lord, for your mercies and grace in the name of Jesus.
25. I believe and receive the answers to my prayers in the name of Jesus.

CHAPTER 28

Generational Problems

Many problems and personal issues are the result of the sins of one's forefathers as many as four generations back. Every Christian is in the unique situation as a new creature in Christ (2 Corinthians 5:17) and redeemed from the curse of the law (Galatians 3:13–14). 2 Timothy 4:18 says that the Lord will rescue us from **every** evil deed. Paul wrote this in the present tense. In order to avoid taking this verse out of context, other scriptures must be examined, Galatians 3:13 in particular, and all of the Bible in general.

Nowhere in scripture is the forgiveness of sins tied to time. Since Christ redeemed us from the curse of the Law and He rescued us from every evil deed, we no longer need to be in the bondage of the sins or curses of our ancestors. All that needs to be done is to use the authority through Jesus to break these bonds and be free. Praise God!

Once free of any generational problems or curses, there may still be behaviors that have been ingrained for many years. It can take more work to undo these patterns of behavior. As with any situation that deals with the mind, it may be necessary to seek counseling in addition to prayer.

28.1 Scripture Reading

- Exodus 34:6–7
- Galatians 3:13–14
- 2 Corinthians 5:17
- 2 Timothy 4:18

28.2 Confession

1. The Lord shall anoint me with the oil of joy above my fellows. (Psalms 45:7)
2. My future is secure in Christ. He did not create me for nothing. I can never be thrown away or downgraded. (Romans 8:38–39)
3. I am the head and not the tail. (Deuteronomy 28:13–14)
4. I will trust in my Lord Jesus always for He can never fail. (Psalms 34:4–8)
5. There will be no poverty of body, soul, or spirit in my life. (Joel 2:26–27)
6. I have favor in the eyes of God and man all the days of my life. (Psalms 5:12; Proverbs 3:3–4)
7. I shall not labor in vain. (Isaiah 65:23)
8. I shall walk in victory and liberty of the Holy Spirit. (1 Corinthians 15:57; 1 John 5:4)

28.3 Prayers

Forgiveness for Sins

1. Father God, reveal to me any sin I have committed that caused [name the problem] in the name of Jesus.
2. My Father, forgive me for committing these sins [name them] in the name of Jesus.
3. I reject every spirit of bitterness and anger against my ancestors in the name of Jesus.
4. I forgive my ancestors for their sins that have affected me in the name of Jesus.
5. I forgive [name them] who have sinned against me in the name of Jesus.
6. Thank you Father for your grace and forgiveness in the name of Jesus.

Generational Sins

1. My Father, forgive my ancestors for the sins [name them if you know them, especially those of evil powers] they have passed down to me in the name of Jesus.
2. My Father, forgive my ancestors four generations back for the sins that have propagated down to me in the name of Jesus.
3. I break every evil hold these ancestral sins have on me in the name of Jesus.
4. I proclaim my freedom from all ancestral sins on both my father's and mother's side of my family in the name of Jesus.

Generational Curses

1. I nullify any ancestral curse propagated to me in the name of Jesus.
2. I command every curse spoken by my ancestors against my family line to be nullified in the name of Jesus.
3. I destroy the effects of every ancestral curse spoken against my family in the name of Jesus.
4. I decree my freedom from the effects of every ancestral curse spoken against me in the name of Jesus.

Curses and Witchcraft

1. Holy Spirit, cover me with Your protection in Jesus name.
2. My Father, send your angels to stand guard around me and protect me in the name of Jesus.
3. I command every witchcraft curse spoken against me to be nullified in the name of Jesus.
4. I command every witchcraft altar established against me to be destroyed in the name of Jesus.
5. I command every witch practicing against me to fall into their own traps and be destroyed in the name of Jesus.

6. I command every witchcraft network established against me to be destroyed in the name of Jesus.
7. I command every evil witchcraft device and influence used against me to be destroyed in the name of Jesus.

Evil Ancestral Covenants

1. Every evil ancestral covenant affecting my life and health, I nullify you in the name of Jesus.
2. I command every evil ancestral covenant to be erased in the name of Jesus.
3. I decree my freedom from every evil ancestral covenant in the name of Jesus.

Current Evil Covenants

1. Every evil covenant I may have agreed to willingly or not, be null and void in Jesus name.
2. I decree my freedom from every evil covenant I may have agreed to in the name of Jesus.

Demonic Influences

Repeat the following prayers for every issue, medical or otherwise.

1. I command every demon causing [name the issue]. I command their support, command structure, evil devices, and influences in the name of Jesus.
2. I cast all of these into the abyss until judgment day in the name of Jesus.

Praise and Thanksgiving

1. Lord Jesus, I give you all the glory, all the praise, and all the honor for operating in my life today in the name of Jesus.
2. Thank you, Lord, for hearing and answering my prayers in the name of Jesus.
3. I believe and I receive the answers to my prayers in the name of Jesus.

CHAPTER 29

Power to Excel and Prosper

In the beginning before Adam and Eve sinned, God gave mankind dominion over the entire planet. After sin entered the scene, that dominion was passed on to the devil. He retained it until Jesus died on the cross. That dominion has now been passed back to its rightful owners—those who know Jesus Christ as Lord and Savior. The problem is, the devil doesn't want to relinquish what he thinks is his and it has to be taken from him by force. A similar situation is the civil rights movement of the early 1960's. Slavery had been abolished at the end of the Civil War, but the wicked didn't want to lose their power and control over people. It wasn't until nearly one hundred years later when people had enough and demanded their legal rights and position in society that they were finally given the freedom to exercise that status.

Through effective prayer, Christians need to take back dominion of this world from the wicked. Not that long ago the church had a solid position of dominion in the community and in the governing affairs of this nation. Unfortunately, it will take more work to take back that which was lost than it would have taken to keep it in the first place.

We have a God-ordained right to excel and prosper. This has nothing to do with the prosperity doctrines found in some churches today. Many have falling into this trap of humanism, and perhaps without realizing it, have viewed God as a means to gain wealth. This doctrine is sin and is contrary to Deuteronomy 28:1–14, Psalms 37:4, Matthew 6:33, and others.

The goal must never be of selfish motivation. Whatever He gives us should be used for His glory. We are to be good stewards of all He has given us, no matter how much or how little it may be.

Scripture makes it clear that prosperity is a conditional promise. If we are obedient to His Word then He will bless us.

In view of the spiritual battle set before us, there are many cases when the devil has used spiritual means in an effort to prevent Christians from enjoying the position they rightfully own. A spirit of poverty, spirit of failure at the edge of success, and filthy spiritual garments that cause people to view someone with disfavor are a few examples.

29.1 Scripture Reading and Confession

- Deuteronomy 28:1–14
- Psalms 37:4
- Matthew 6:33
- James 4:3–5

29.2 Prayers

1. My Father, forgive me for my sins [name them] in the name of Jesus.
2. O Lord, forgive me for failing to live up to the standards you established in your Word in the name of Jesus.
3. O Lord, cleanse me of all unrighteousness in the name of Jesus.
4. My Father, make me holy and pure in the name of Jesus.
5. Thank you, Lord, for your forgiveness, mercy and grace in the name of Jesus.
6. O Lord, remove anything from my life that is contrary to Your will in the name of Jesus.
7. Every garment of disfavor placed on me be destroyed by the fire of God in the name of Jesus.
8. My Father, give me an anointing of prosperity in the name of Jesus.
9. My Father, manifest Your favor for me in the name of Jesus.

10. My Father, give me an anointing to excel in the tasks you have given me in the name of Jesus.

11. I command every spirit of physical or spiritual poverty over me to die in the name of Jesus.

12. I release myself from the bondage of poverty in the name of Jesus.

13. O Lord, give me an anointing of excellence after the order of Daniel in the name of Jesus.

14. I am blessed in the name of Jesus.

15. I am prosperous in the name of Jesus.

16. I have favor from God and man in the name of Jesus.

17. My Father, I give you all the praise, glory, and honor for answering my prayers in the name of Jesus.

18. Thank you, Lord, for your mercies and grace in the name of Jesus.

19. I believe and receive the answers to my prayers in the name of Jesus.

CHAPTER 30

Sexual Sins

Sexual sins include pornography, fornication, adultery, homosexuality, and many other perversions. Those who are pro-homosexual, or are involved with other perversions, are becoming increasingly militant around the world. This subject must be addressed with what scripture has to say.

Bible Reading: Romans 1:26–32; Leviticus 18:22, 20:13; 1 Corinthians 6:9–10; Revelation 21:8

It doesn't matter whether anyone on this planet agrees with these scriptures or not. God said it and that settles it. His judgments are absolute and final. No amount of argument, rationalization, manipulation, justification, taking scripture out of context, or self-righteous posturing will in any way change God's truth. To reiterate a statement made earlier:

> *By rejecting the truth, you embrace a lie. In the end, truth will become an offense and object of hatred to you.*

Realize that scripture is for everyone's benefit. Because God loves us, He established boundaries of behavior for our benefit and provided the way of salvation. These were done to help us avoid falling into sin and eventually damnation, and to point us to the way of salvation.

God is neither male nor female. He is spirit and He created male and female for the purpose of procreation and continuance of the species. God created a hierarchy in which the man is the head of the household and

Jesus Christ is the head of everything. Because of this hierarchical order, God is referred to in the masculine sense.

I am not your judge and I do not judge you for your decisions. It is not my place to do so. God is the one who will judge you. All of us without exception will stand before Him on judgment day and give an account of what we have done in our lives. What you choose to do is your own personal choice and you will either suffer or enjoy the consequences of it.

> [11]For it is written, "As I live, says the Lord, every knee shall bow to me, and every tongue shall give praise to God." [12]So then each one of us will give an account of himself to God.
>
> —Romans 14:11–12 (NASB)

> [9]For this reason also, God highly exalted Him, and bestowed on Him the name which is above every name, [10]so that at the name of Jesus EVERY KNEE WILL BOW, of those who are in heaven and on earth and under the earth, [11]and that every tongue will confess that Jesus Christ is Lord, to the glory of God the Father.
>
> —Philippians 2:9–11 (NASB)

Sexual perversions are varied and are always the result of demonic influences. The devil perverts our natural instincts and sexual desires that God gave us which are to be enjoyed between a man and a woman within marriage. Sexual sins can be difficult to overcome. Overcoming requires prayer for discipline as well as defeating these demonic influences and activities. Before using the prayers in this section it would be good to use the prayers in Chapter 16, *Prayers for Cleansing the Mind*. It would be helpful to use both together on a regular basis.

Sinful patterns, sexual in particular, are often established at an early age, usually around puberty[8]. Such patterns of behavior become ingrained because of the physiological effects that take place in the brain. In other words, the brain becomes physically "wired" to a pattern of thought and behavior. Even after all has been said and done through prayer to deal with the spiritual, the problem or tendency may still persist. This requires

---

[8] It is estimated that around 30% of all traffic on the Internet worldwide pertains to pornographic materials.

exercising discipline on a regular basis. In addition, a physical healing that only Jesus can provide may be necessary. This is no different than any other type of physical healing and can be prayed for just as easily as any other problem. Don't look at the size of the problem. Look at the greatness of our Lord Jesus Christ.

30.1 Scripture Reading and Confession

- Romans 6:14
- Isaiah 49:25–26
- Leviticus 18

30.2 Prayers

1. My Father, forgive me for my sins [name them] in the name of Jesus.
2. O Lord, forgive me for failing to live up to the standards you established in your Word in the name of Jesus.
3. O Lord, cleanse me of all unrighteousness in the name of Jesus.
4. O Lord, remove anything from my life that is contrary to Your will in the name of Jesus.
5. I break every chain of sexual perversion in my life in the name of Jesus.
6. I break every ancestral curse of sexual perversion over my life in the name of Jesus.
7. I nullify the effects of any ancestral sin of sexual perversion in my life in the name of Jesus.
8. I break the spirit of lust over me in the name of Jesus.
9. I cast out every thought, image, and dream of sexual perversion in the name of Jesus.
10. Holy Spirit, take control of my eyes and my thoughts in the name of Jesus.
11. O Lord, fill my mind with your Word in the name of Jesus.
12. O Lord, cover my mind with Your protection in the name of Jesus.

13. I take command of every demon of sexual perversion, their evil devices and influences, their support, replacements, and command structure in the name of Jesus.

14. I cast all of this filth into the abyss until judgment day in the name of Jesus.

15. Every contamination brought into my life through dreams be wiped away by the fire of the Holy Spirit in the name of Jesus.

16. Holy Spirit, purge me of any food eaten in a dream in the name of Jesus.

17. I command destruction on all powers of darkness in my life in the name of Jesus.

18. I decree my freedom and deliverance from sexual perversions in the name of Jesus.

19. Holy Spirit plug all the holes in my life the enemy has used to attack me in the name of Jesus.

20. Holy Spirit fill me with You and Your righteousness in the name of Jesus.

21. My Father, I give you all the praise, glory, and honor for answering my prayers in the name of Jesus.

22. Thank you, Lord, for your mercies and grace in the name of Jesus.

23. I believe and receive the answers to my prayers in the name of Jesus.

CHAPTER 31

Finding the Right Spouse

You may be searching for the right God-ordained spouse. Or, you may have been searching and been through multiple relationships, none of which were suitable. God has a divine destiny for you. If the devil realizes that part of your destiny involves meeting the right spouse, he may attempt to hinder you from meeting the spouse God has for you.

In past generations, parents were generally more involved in the lives of their children. This included providing Biblical counsel and practical help with finding the right spouse. Times have changed a lot since then, and not for the better. Whether back in those days or today, with or without family involvement, the best course of action is to go to your heavenly Father in prayer. He is the one who will provide the proper spouse.

Put your faith and trust in God, especially in this age when the divorce rate is so high. Even if you think you have found the right person, it is wise to have marriage counseling before getting married. A good marriage counselor will be an objective observer, and should be able to identify issues that you may not be aware of and help arrive at a solution.

In addition to the prayers in this chapter, you may wish to use any of the prayers in any of the other chapters. Clear the field of as many known and unknown issues as possible. Ask the Holy Spirit to reveal anything that needs to be dealt with.

31.1 Scripture Reading and Confession

- Genesis 2:20–24

31.2 Prayers

1. My Father, forgive me for my sins [name them] in the name of Jesus.
2. O Lord, forgive me for failing to live up to the standards you established in your Word in the name of Jesus.
3. O Lord, cleanse me of all unrighteousness in the name of Jesus.
4. O Lord, remove anything from my life that is contrary to Your will in the name of Jesus.
5. I destroy all powers of darkness preventing me from finding the right spouse in the name of Jesus.
6. I destroy every generational anti-marriage curse spoken over me in the name of Jesus.
7. My Father, give me your wisdom in the name of Jesus.
8. I command every garment of disfavor on me to be burned by the fire of God in the name of Jesus.
9. My Father, put upon me the garments of favor and excellence in the name of Jesus.
10. O Lord, guide me to the right spouse in the name of Jesus.
11. I command all evil prospects to disappear now in the name of Jesus.
12. My Father, open my eyes to the one you have for me in the name of Jesus.
13. My Father, open the eyes of the one you have for me in the name of Jesus.
14. My Father, speak Your will clearly to each of us when we meet in the name of Jesus.
15. My Father, I give you all the praise, glory, and honor for answering my prayers in the name of Jesus.
16. Thank you, Lord, for your mercies and grace in the name of Jesus.
17. I believe and receive the answers to my prayers in the name of Jesus.

CHAPTER 32

Prayers Against Marriage Destroyers

The devil is doing all he can to destroy marriages and families. This destruction has long ranging effects on the family, and children in particular. All of us must be vigilant with protecting ourselves and our families from the destruction the devil wants to bring.

When there is a conflict between husband and wife, everyone is righteous in their own eyes, and humility and wisdom often take flight. Keep a proper Godly attitude, thus not allowing the devil an opportunity to cause disruptions and division.

> *Everyone is righteous in their own eyes.*

Humility, Godly wisdom, and the willingness to listen and communicate in a disciplined manner are essential for all parties. Resist pride and be willing to be wrong.

> "Catch the foxes for us, The little foxes that are ruining the vineyards, While our vineyards are in blossom."
>
> —Song of Solomon 2:15 (NASB)

As Song of Solomon 2:15 indicates, it is essential that the problems all marriages face are dealt with while they are little, and before they become larger issues. The devil uses the age-old tactic of divide and conquer. Learn to recognize this and combat it in prayer. You can take two people, not matter how well matched, and there will be disagreements and differences of opinion. The devil attempts to use these, no matter how innocuous they may seem, to cause division between husband and wife.

It might happen that these differences never disappear. Address them in prayer and set them aside if needed. Compromise on the part of both husband and wife is essential. The marriage relationship is vastly more important than squabbling over them. If the issues you are dealing with are of a nature where there is no clear way of resolution then counseling may be necessary.

You have the authority and power through Jesus Christ to deal with all the spiritual matters. Scripture makes it clear that agreement by multiple people on an issue will carry more weight.

32.1   Scripture Reading and Confession

- Hebrews 13:4
- Matthew 18:18–20, 19:4–6
- 1 Peter 5:8–9
- Ephesians 4:26–27
- Job 22:25–28
- John 10:10

32.2   Prayers

The following prayers should be prayed together if possible. Both husband and wife are a team and should be in agreement. Not every prayer is applicable to every situation so you may skip those that don't apply or add some that do.

1. Our Father, forgive us for our sins [name them] in the name of Jesus.
2. O Lord, forgive us for failing to live up to the standards you established in your Word in the name of Jesus.
3. My Father, forgive us for any evil things [name them] we have done to bring troubles into our marriage in the name of Jesus.
4. O Lord, cleanse us of all unrighteousness in the name of Jesus.

5. O Lord, remove anything from our lives that is contrary to Your will in the name of Jesus.

6. We destroy every vagabond spirit working in our lives in the name of Jesus.

7. We decree our marriage to be off limits to all evil powers in the name of Jesus.

8. We command every agent of the devil working in our lives to be destroyed in the name of Jesus.

9. We command every satanic plan established against our household to be destroyed completely in the name of Jesus.

10. We command every spirit of adultery operating in either of us to be destroyed in the name of Jesus.

11. We destroy every spirit of contention and conflict operating in our marriage to die now in the name of Jesus.

12. We command every spirit of misunderstanding between us to be destroyed now in the name of Jesus.

13. We command every thought, plan, or desire for divorce in our household to be destroyed now in the name of Jesus.

14. Our Father, protect and preserve our marriage in Jesus name.

15. Every curse spoken over our marriage; we break you now in the name of Jesus.

16. Every generational curse or sin that has caused problems in our marriage, we break you now in the name of Jesus.

17. Our Father, replace every curse spoken over our marriage with blessings in the name of Jesus.

18. We take command of every demon of marriage destruction, their replacements, support, evil devices and influences, plans, and command structure in the name of Jesus.

19. We cast all of this garbage into the abyss until judgment day in the name of Jesus.

20. We decree our marriage to be free of all the wiles of the devil in the name of Jesus.

21. Our Father, cause your peace to reign in our marriage in the name of Jesus.

22. Our Father, bring your divine healing to our marriage in the name of Jesus.

23. Our Father, we give you all the praise, glory, and honor for answering our prayers in the name of Jesus.
24. Thank you, Lord, for your mercies and grace in the name of Jesus.
25. We believe and receive the answers to our prayers in the name of Jesus.

CHAPTER 33

Epilogue

This book was written with the expectation that it would be read by people from a wide range of backgrounds and experiences. Many are so deeply entrenched in church or denominational doctrines that thinking or looking outside that small box is difficult or deemed unnecessary. The devil does everything he can to keep people in this small box so they will never be successful as Christians. For these reasons I addressed the traditions of man in Chapter 4 as well as throughout the book. Look past the traditions of man regardless of how truthful they may seem or how comfortable they may be and focus on Jesus and His Word. His Word is truth and not necessarily man's interpretation of it. Learn to rely on the Holy Spirit to teach you all things. This takes prayer and steps of faith. The result is that in time you will experience what the Apostle Paul wrote about in the third chapter of Philippians.

Scripture is clear that we will all stand before the judgment seat of Christ. Trying to excuse your actions by blaming someone else won't work. You will stand before that judgment seat and your Creator and Judge will ask, "What have you done with my Son?" What will you say? What will the cares and material things of this life matter then? Clearly, we all need to set our relationship with Jesus as the highest priority. We all have worldly responsibilities to attend to, and they can certainly be overwhelming at times. Apply discipline to make the time needed for building your relationship with Jesus. We are to be doing what He commanded us to do in this life. Jesus will be returning soon. Regardless of the signs of the times, no one knows exactly when.

⁴⁴"For this reason you also must be ready; for the Son of Man is coming at an hour when you do not think He will. ⁴⁵Who then is the faithful and sensible slave whom his master put in charge of his household to give them their food at the proper time? ⁴⁶Blessed is that slave whom his master finds so doing when he comes. ⁴⁷Truly I say to you that he will put him in charge of all his possessions.

—Matthew 24:44–47 (NASB)

¹⁸"Come now, and let us reason together," Says the LORD, "Though your sins are as scarlet, They will be as white as snow; Though they are red like crimson, They will be like wool. ¹⁹"If you consent and obey, You will eat the best of the land; ²⁰"But if you refuse and rebel, You will be devoured by the sword." Truly, the mouth of the LORD has spoken.

—Isaiah 1:18–20 (NASB)

The Apostle Paul wrote in 1 Corinthians 13:13:

But now faith, hope, love, abide these three; but the greatest of these is love.

—1 Corinthians 13:13 (NASB)

Faith, hope, and love are foundational characteristics upon which your relationship with Jesus is built and the Great Commission is fulfilled. The church, individually and corporately, must pursue these things.

Bible Reading: 2 Peter 1:2–11

In many respects, the book of Joshua presents a picture of the spiritual walk we have with Jesus. When Israel entered into the promised land, they had many battles to engage in and win. As long as they were obedient to God, their victories were overwhelming. It wasn't until the land had been conquered that God gave them peace and rest. Today we enter the promised land through relationship with Jesus, and gain the power and authority to do His will in this world.

Bible Reading: Hebrews 4:1–16

The importance of pursuing victory and entering into the promised land cannot be over emphasized. The above passage from Hebrews, as well as Joshua and many others, make it clear that Jesus expects us to pursue this end.

The more you grow in Jesus, the more you will see the importance and benefits of this pursuit. God's blessings and plans for His people are not simply "icing on the cake of salvation," or to be considered optional. These blessings and plans are a responsibility for each and every Christian to pursue and gain.

Countless generations to come could be heirs of God's blessings and plans, bringing immeasurable benefits to all. The magnitude of this is beyond words. Please understand that I do not make such a statement lightly or for any sensationalistic purposes. It is only when people grow in their relationship with Jesus that they will be prepared to receive what He has. Growth and the guidance of the Holy Spirit are imperative because one who is immature will not be able to bear the blessings He wants to provide.

> [12]"I have many more things to say to you, but you cannot bear them now. [13]"But when He, the Spirit of truth, comes, He will guide you into all the truth; for He will not speak on His own initiative, but whatever He hears, He will speak; and He will disclose to you what is to come.
>
> —John 16:12–13 (NASB)

> But prove yourselves doers of the word, and not merely hearers who delude themselves.
>
> —James 1:22 (NASB)

Those who are hearers only delude themselves into thinking there are no worries and are just fine where they are in Jesus. Those who are doers are those who accomplish great things.

> *The doers of the God's word are those who attain victory and enter the promised land.*

Appendix A

The Plan of Salvation

If you don't already know Jesus as Lord and Savior, I urge you to ask Him into your life. Being a Christian is not a religion. It is a relationship. In order to have a relationship, all parties must be real. A relationship must be tangible. It must have substance. You can't have a relationship with a fantasy or a philosophy. God is real. He is alive. God loves you more than you can imagine regardless of what you may think or know.

Learn about God. Give Him a chance. If you take a few minutes and read these pages, you will discover God's greatest gift and miracle for mankind. It doesn't matter who you are or what you have done. God will always love you and receive you with open arms.

Step 1

Understand that God's desire for you is life, abundant, and eternal. The Bible says:

> The thief comes only to steal and kill and destroy; I came that they may have life, and have it abundantly.

> —John 10:10 (NASB)

Giving you abundant life required the supreme sacrifice:

> For God so loved the world, that He gave His only begotten Son, that whoever believes in Him shall not perish, but have eternal life.
>
> —John 3:16 (NASB)

God desires fellowship and companionship with you. What a wonderful gift the Father has given, yet if God gave His own Son to provide an abundant and everlasting life, why don't more people have what He has designed for us to receive? It is a question answered by this sobering realization.

Step 2

Realize that you are separated from God. There is a gap between God and mankind. He has provided a way for us to receive an abundant and eternal life, but people throughout the ages have made selfish choices to disobey God Almighty. These choices continue to cause separation from the Father. God is holy and that nothing unholy can enter heaven. How do we deal with this? God provided Jesus to be sin for us, to take away our sins thereby making us holy.

God's Word shows us that the result of sin is death. He says in His Word:

> There is a way which seems right to a man, But its end is the way of death.
>
> —Proverbs 14:12 (NASB)

And God also said,

> But your iniquities have made a separation between you and your God, And your sins have hidden His face from you so that He does not hear.
>
> —Isaiah 59:2 (NASB)

Paul the apostle states in Romans,

for all have sinned and fall short of the glory of God,

—Romans 3:23 (NASB)

And in Romans 6:23 we read:

For the wages of sin is death, but the free gift of God is eternal life in Christ Jesus our Lord.

—Romans 6:23 (NASB)

Every human was created with the ability and need to know God and fellowship with Him. Augustine, a minister who lived during the fourth and fifth centuries, called this longing in each of us "that God-shaped vacuum."

Every day we hear of all kinds of people who are self-righteous, who are always good to others. Many think that all they achieved in their lives was with their own wisdom and strength. They don't realize that God was there with them, helping them. People don't realize there is a creator who created all and He is holding all things together. If not for Him, there would be no order in the universe. Evidence seen in the microscopic components of a single cell to discoveries in the galaxy clearly points to intelligent design.

Even though people may have accolades for various achievements, or have risen to prominent positions in society, they still try to fill that empty void in their lives with "things." They even try good works, morality, and religion. Yet they remain empty, for only God, through His Son, can fill that emptiness.

Step 3

Accept the fact that God has provided only one solution to sin and separation from Himself. Jesus Christ, His Son, is the only way to God. Only He can reconcile us to God the Father. Mankind may seek other solutions and worship other gods, but Jesus Christ, alone, died on the Cross for our sins and rose in triumph over the grave and eternal death. He paid the penalty for our sin and bridged the gap between God and mankind.

The Bible explains:

But God demonstrates His own love toward us, in that while we were yet sinners, Christ died for us.

—Romans 5:8 (NASB)

We are also told,

For Christ also died for sins once for all, the just for the unjust, so that He might bring us to God, having been put to death in the flesh, but made alive in the spirit;

—1 Peter 3:18 (NASB)

There is only one way provided:

For there is one God, and one mediator also between God and men, the man Christ Jesus,

—1 Timothy 2:5 (NASB)

For in John 14:6 we read,

Jesus said to him, "I am the way, and the truth, and the life; no one comes to the Father but through Me."

—John 14:6 (NASB)

God Almighty has provided the only way. Jesus Christ paid the penalty for our sin and rebellion against God by dying on the cross, shedding His blood, and rising from the dead to justify and reconcile you back to God the Father.

Step 4

Pray to receive Jesus Christ into your life. You can be brought back to God, and your relationship with Him can be restored by trusting in Christ alone to save your life from destruction. What an incredible exchange: Your worst for God's best! This step happens by asking Jesus Christ to take away your sin and to come into your heart to be your Lord and Savior.

God's Word is very clear:

> Behold, I stand at the door and knock; if anyone hears My voice
> and opens the door, I will come in to him and will dine with him,
> and he with Me.

> —Revelation 3:20 (NASB)

And the Bible tells us,

> that if you confess with your mouth Jesus as Lord, and believe in
> your heart that God raised Him from the dead, you will be saved;

> —Romans 10:9 (NASB)

- Are you willing to let go of your burdens and sins?
- Are you willing to turn away and repent from your sins?
- Are you willing to receive Jesus Christ as your Lord and Savior now?

Step 5

Pray to Receive Jesus Christ into your life. At this moment you can
pray the most important prayer of your life by simply saying:

> Lord Jesus,
>
> I believe You are the Son of God. I believe You came to earth 2,000
> years ago. I believe you died for me on the cross and shed Your blood
> for my salvation. I believe you rose from the dead and ascended on
> high. I believe You are coming back again to earth. Dear Jesus, I
> am a sinner. Forgive my sins. Holy Spirit cleanse me now and come
> into my heart. Save me now. I am giving you my life. I am receiving
> You now as my Savior, my Lord, and my God. I am Yours forever,
> and I will serve You and follow You the rest of my days. From this
> moment on, I belong to You only. I no longer belong to this world,
> nor to the enemy of my soul. I belong to You, and I am born again.
>
> Amen!

By praying this prayer and meaning it with all your heart, confessing your sins, and receiving Jesus Christ into your heart, God has given you the right to become His forgiven child. The Bible gives you this assurance:

> But as many as received Him, to them He gave the right to become children of God, even to those who believe in His name,
>
> —John 1:12 (NASB)

REFERENCES

1. N. Webster, Webster's Dictionary of the English Language, (public domain), 1828.
2. A. a. D. Berkowitz, Torah Rediscovered: 5ᵗʰ Edition, Revised 2012, 2011.
3. I. Productions, The Passion of the Christ, Icon Productions, 2004.
4. A. Barnes, Albert Barnes' Notes on the Bible, public domain, 1847–1885.
5. A. Clark, Adam Clark's Commentary on the Bible, public domain, 1810–1826.
6. J. Gill, John Gill's Exposition of the Entire Bible, public domain, 1748–1763, 1809.
7. Conservapedia, Separation of Church and State, 2017.
8. H. A. Long, The American Ideal of 1776, The Twelve Basic American Principles, Your Heritage Books, Inc., 1976.
9. C. H. Spurgeon, The Treasury of David, (public domain), 1869–1855.
10. G. W. Seevers, Revelational Ministry, (possibly a seminary paper), early 1970's (?).
11. M. G. Easton, Eason's Bible Dictionary, (public domain), 1897.
12. J. H. S. a. D. B. Towner, Trust And Obey, (public domain), 1887.
13. R. J. Machowicz, Unleash the Warrior Within, Da Capo Press, 2008.
14. M. A. P. a. L. C. D. G. a. L. Christensen, Warrior Mindset, Mental Toughness Skills for a Nation's Defenders, Performance Psychology Applied to Combat, Human Factors Research Group, Inc., 2012.

15. A. Murgado, Developing a Warrior Mindset, www.policemag.com, May 2012.

16. M. Henry, Matthew Henry's Concise Commentary, public domain, 1708–1714.

17. J. P. Colvis, The First Generation Book I, Quantum Mathematics, (unpublished), 1979.

18. S. D. Brewster, Memoirs of the Life, Writings, and Discoveries of Sir Isaac Newton, Vols. II, Chapter 27, N/A, 1855.

19. Wikipedia, Caspar Milquetoast, Wikipedia, 2015.

20. B. Miller, What the Bible Says about Tattoos, BibleResources.org, January 28, 2012.

21. J. Bevere, The Bait of Satan, Charisma Media, 2004.

22. Wikipedia, Epidemiology of Suicide, Wikipedia, 2017.

23. R. Hutchcraft, "Too Close To The Edge," August 2005.

24. H. Hurnard, Hinds' Feet on High Places, Tyndale House Publishers, 1979.

CPSIA information can be obtained
at www.ICGtesting.com
Printed in the USA
LVHW011922020422
714977LV00006B/142